TACKLING TEXT
[AND SUBTEXT]

Barbara Houseman is a well-known and highly respected voice, text and acting coach and a director. She has thirty years' experience in theatre. She initially trained as a teacher at the Central School of Speech and Drama and then as a director at the Bristol Old Vic Theatre School. She won an Arts Council Director's Bursary, after which she directed in repertory theatres and drama schools as well as teaching voice, text and acting.

In 1991 she joined the voice department at the Royal Shakespeare Company. During her six years there she worked with over two hundred and fifty actors and thirty directors on more than sixty classical and modern plays. On leaving the Royal Shakespeare Company she became Associate Director at the Young Vic, where she worked on *The Comedy of Errors* and *More Grimm Tales*.

Freelance, she has conducted voice and text work on productions as diverse as *Doctor Dolittle* by Leslie Bricusse, *Cleansed* by Sarah Kane, *Art* by Yasmina Reza, Complicite's *Mnemonic*, *Further Than the Furthest Thing* by Zinnie Harris, *The Play What I Wrote* by Sean Foley and Hamish McColl, *Treats* by Christopher Hampton and *Equus* by Peter Shaffer. She has also worked in film and television and held workshops in Australia, China, Columbia, New Zealand, Sri Lanka and the United States.

Tackling Text [and Subtext] is the second in a trilogy of books. The first – *Finding Your Voice* [published by Nick Hern Books in 2002] covers all aspects of voice work. The third – *Enabling Actors* – will look at ways in which directors and others who work with actors can help them to produce their best work.

Barbara Houseman

TACKLING TEXT [AND SUBTEXT]

A Step-by-Step Guide for Actors

Foreword by Daniel Radcliffe
Preface by Kenneth Branagh

NICK HERN BOOKS

London

www.nickhernbooks.co.uk

A Nick Hern Book

Tackling Text [*and Subtext*]
first published in Great Britain in 2008
as a paperback original by Nick Hern Books Limited,
14 Larden Road, London W3 7ST

Cover designed by Ned Hoste, 2H
Typeset by Country Setting, Kingsdown, Kent CT14 8ES
Printed and bound in Great Britain by Cromwell Press, Trowbridge

A CIP catalogue record for this book
is available from the British Library

ISBN 978 1 85459 799 1

Mixed Sources
Product group from well-managed
forests and other controlled sources
www.fsc.org Cert no. TT-COC-2082
© 1996 Forest Stewardship Council
FSC

To my parents

*who have wholeheartedly supported me
throughout my career*

Contents

Foreword

When I was offered the role of Alan Strang in *Equus*, one of the biggest hurdles I knew I would face was being able to cope vocally with eight emotionally charged perfomances a week, and it was suggested that I work with Barbara Houseman.

We started working together eighteen months before I set foot in the rehearsal room, and working with her was a complete joy! It was an intense, exciting and challenging time for me, developing a technique that would help me, not just with *Equus*, but in my long-term career.

Barbara is a passionate teacher and, as an actor new to the stage, there was no better person to be working with on this first venture in the theatre. She is an inspiring teacher, and I left every session stimulated with the new discoveries we had made, marrying vocal technique with the text we had been working on. Vocal skill is an ongoing process, and I continue to work with her, as I find her a hugely motivating force in my work.

Daniel Radcliffe

Preface

If you want to improve as an actor, read this book. Do what it tells you. Simple as that. I have worked as an actor for twenty-seven years and here are some observations.

Actors need to stay sharp. When working or not working. Inside or outside the rehearsal room. On stage, screen, on radio, and especially when unemployed.

When we are employed, we don't always have the help of a Great Director.

Thankfully, we now have the help of this book. It articulates the advice I was given many years ago by a wise old actor, and which I have happily passed on ever since. When in trouble with a role or, more fundamentally, with the very process of acting, go back to the text – or find a text – and look at it anew. The way to refresh your imagination will be in the text and in the way you tackle it.

Easier said than done? Not any more. You have a friend in these pages.

I have worked with Barbara Houseman and know that her techniques and suggestions all come from long-term practical experience at the highest level. They will show you how to release your imagination, and make genuine improvements. The book also heads off that sometimes fierce and deeply unhelpful inner critic which can sabotage the best efforts. You can say farewell to that kind of useless negativity, particularly at auditions and castings, where the advice set down here should have a remarkable effect.

Best of all, this book helps restore the hard work of the actor as fresh, playful and fun, and puts the ownership of that process firmly in the best hands – the artists themselves. I consult it frequently myself and happily recommend it to you. Have fun!

Kenneth Branagh

Acknowledgements

I would like to thank all the actors I have worked with over the years. It was looking for ways to enable them that led to the development of the exercises in this book.

My husband, Mark Bauwens, made excellent suggestions regarding the order, which enabled the book to flow far more smoothly.

Tom Lewis patiently read through the manuscript twice and gave me a great deal of valuable feedback about how the book related to his experience of my work.

Nick Hern edited the book with a care, precision, sensitivity and patience which brought the manuscript together into a coherent whole.

Matt Applewhite offered invaluable assistance in pulling the book together so that it was clear and uncluttered.

Robin Booth, Jodi Gray and Tamara von Werthern were a fount of enthusiastic suggestions regarding possible pieces for inclusion in the modern text chapter.

Daniel Radcliffe and Kenneth Branagh both took the time out of their busy schedules to write the Foreward and Preface. I am grateful for their generosity in doing so. I have found them both, in their own ways, a great inspiration to work with.

Mike Alfreds was one of my earliest professional influences. I assisted him on Gogol's *Marriage* in the 1980s and he was an inspiration in many ways. From him I learnt to be specific, that every moment mattered. I also learnt about the importance of keeping the work fresh and spontaneous by discovering moment by moment on stage. Finally, I learnt that specificity and spontaneity require a great deal of detailed preparation in rehearsal – in other words, the freer you wanted to be, the more carefully you needed to prepare. Mike has always been very generous in his support – willing to take the time to talk about what he is doing and why; and to offer advice when it's asked for. His generosity and his ability to talk eloquently and lucidly about his work continue to be something I value on those rare occasions when we meet. His book *Different Every Night* takes you through his rehearsal process and is well worth reading.

Cicely Berry was a later influence. I had the good fortune to work with her for six years at the RSC in the 1990s and again she was a great inspiration. She has had an immense influence on the way in which directors and actors approach text: making the work, on classical text especially, less reverent and more robust and alive. Watching her and working alongside her answered so many questions and provoked many new ones. If you have not read her books *Voice and the Actor*, *The Actor and the Text*, *Text in Action* and *From Word to Play*, then seek them out; they are well worth the effort.

From watching Cicely and hearing about her work with Peter Brook, during his time as a director at the RSC, I came to understand how the detail and complexity of both text and subtext – words and internal dynamics – could be explored physically and so be brought to life for an actor in a simple and effective way. Every aspect of the play – language, thought, feeling, character, relationship and situation – can be explored tangibly and so lead to work that is simple and clear and yet contains all the complexity and subtlety of life.

Sonia Moriceau and Marshall Rosenberg have both had a profound influence on my work and yet neither of them is involved in the theatre. Sonia is a Shiatsu and meditation teacher[1] and Marshall is a clinical psychologist who has developed what he calls *non-violent communication*:[2] that is, speaking to oneself and others in a way that is non-judgemental and which is more proactive than reactive. From them I have learnt a great deal about ways of working that are more positive: how to work without judgement and fear and yet with rigour and detail.

Barbara Houseman

The author and publisher gratefully acknowledge permission to quote from the following:

Reunion by David Mamet, published by Methuen Drama, an imprint of A&C Black Publishers Ltd.

All My Sons by Arthur Miller, copyright © 1947, Arthur Miller; reproduced by kind permission of the Wylie Agency; all rights reserved.

The Caretaker by Harold Pinter, and 'The Horses' by Ted Hughes, both published by Faber and Faber Ltd.

The Way Home by Chloë Moss, *Orestes: Blood and Light* by Helen Edmundson, *Notes on Falling Leaves* by Ayub Khan-Din, *Shimmer* by Linda McLean, *Mojo* by Jez Butterworth, *A Mouthful of Birds* by Caryl Churchill and David Lan, and *The Cherry Orchard* by Anton Chekhov, translated by Stephen Mulrine, all published by Nick Hern Books Ltd.

Every effort has been made to trace all copyright holders, but if any has been inadvertently overlooked, the publishers will be pleased to receive information and make the necessary arrangements at the first opportunity.

PART ONE

Introduction and Basics

Why Read This Book?

HOW THIS BOOK CAN HELP YOU

Why read this book? Firstly, because it is full of practical exercises to help you explore text, character and situation. These exercises have been developed through working with actors of all ages and experiences over many years.

Secondly, because you can use the exercises in this book outside the rehearsal room to support and deepen your work with a director. You can also use them when preparing for auditions and castings – whether for stage, television or film. They will enable you to become more self-sufficient and more certain of accessing your best work, whatever the situation and however great the pressure you're under.

Thirdly, this book also explores issues such as building confidence; dealing with criticism; handling auditions and castings; moving from rehearsal space to performance space; and offers simple yet effective tools for overcoming any problems that may arise in these areas.

Tangible Exploration

At the heart of this book is the idea of discovering by doing: getting on your feet and exploring text, character and situation physically. No specific physical skill is necessary for any of the exercises; however, you will find that by working in this way you will gain a great deal of physical confidence and freedom. You will also find that it is a much easier and more concrete way of working, which enables a far more detailed and subtle connection with both the text and subtext. The exercises allow you to have a much more direct relationship with whatever play, scene or speech you are working on and, as a result, to feel far more in charge of what you are doing and more able to solve issues for yourself.

Layering

Another important aspect of this work is the idea of *layering*: in other words, focusing on one element of text, character or situation at a time, then letting go of that element and trusting that you will remember what you have learnt and will be able to put it together with everything else you have discovered. This allows you to go more deeply into each element; and the resulting mix, because it is achieved unconsciously, is richer and more exciting than any conscious mixing would be. It is also far easier to achieve and much more fun!

Noticing

Every exercise in this book is designed to raise your awareness, to enable you to notice what is there. This awareness has three benefits. Firstly, it allows you to be far more self-sufficient, because you don't need to wait for others to point things out to you. Secondly, it allows you to connect more deeply because you are making discoveries for yourself and so they have a much greater significance for you. Thirdly, it allows you to be far more specific and detailed, which in turn allows you to produce work that is more truthful and original both for you and the audience.

Essential Information

Two essential sets of rules allow you to navigate your way through any situation in life: *situational rules* and *personal rules*. *Situational rules* deal with what is acceptable in any given situation: it is not acceptable to walk down the street without any clothes on – unless you are in a nudist camp; or to drive on whichever side of the road you feel like; or to visit someone's home and help yourself to their possessions. Your *personal rules* deal with what you feel is acceptable and unacceptable behaviour for yourself: whether it is alright, or not, to shout or cry in public, or even at all; how much personal information you share with people on first meeting; whether or not it's alright to be physically affectionate in public and so on.

Since you are expert at improvising your way through life based on these two sets of rules it makes sense that if you can identify the *personal rules* of any character, and the *rules of each situation* in which that character finds him/herself, you will have the essential information you need to navigate your way through any play. All the work in this book is designed to help you identify these rules – especially where they are different from your own and from the rules of the situations you are used to. Throughout, you will be encouraged to ask the *essential question*, described below, as a way of shifting away from yourself and your own situations, whilst at the same time making use of all the experience you have as a human being.

Essential Question

It was Stanislavsky who pointed out the power of an actor behaving *as if* they were a certain person in a certain situation. He argued, as an example, that if you asked someone to 'be a tree' he/she may well go ahead and attempt to do this, but his/her brain would be saying: '*But I'm not a tree.*' On the other hand, if you asked someone to behave *as if* he/she were a tree, then his/her brain would have no problem with this. The *as if* makes all the difference.

The essential question linked to *as if* is '*What if . . . ?*': '*What if these were my words? What if this were my rhythm? What if this was what was important to me? What if this was the situation I found myself in?*' '*What if . . . ?*' kick-starts your imagination and sends it searching for the crucial information needed to connect with any role – whether in terms of text or subtext.

Text and Subtext

Text is what is said. Subtext is what lies under and between what is said; it is expressed by body language, tone of voice and moments of silence. Text and subtext each inform the other and it is vital that both are equally explored. I always start with text work because it is the most tangible and because it is what the writer principally gives us – the subtext is implied by the text. By starting with the text you can be sure that you honour the voice of the author: that you tune in to his/her style. As John Gielgud said: 'Style is knowing what play you're in.' Text is rather like the framework around which everything else is built and it is much easier to access the subtext once that frame is in place.

It is sometimes said that there is no subtext in Shakespeare and other classical text: that the action happens on the lines rather than between them. While it is true that much more of what characters are thinking and feeling is expressed in words in classical text, this does not mean that subtext disappears altogether; it is still there, underneath, informing the text and needs to be explored. Equally, it is sometimes said that text is less important in modern plays: that what happens in between and under the text is more important. Again, it is true that there is often a shift in balance so that more of what the characters are thinking and feeling may be expressed non-verbally; however, the text is still there and, with any good writer, it will have been well crafted – in terms of sound and rhythm as well as sense. It is not a question of any old words will do. So it is important to explore both text and subtext fully, whatever play you are working on.

Technique versus Instinct – Leonardo's noses!

Technique and instinct often seem to sit very uneasily together for actors. For some, technique is the enemy: they fear that it will make them less spontaneous and truthful, more showy and set. For others, technique is their cornerstone, giving them shape and structure: they see relying on instinct alone as messy and even dangerous. However, when technique and instinct work together well, they give the actor the best of both worlds. It is a question of timing. When an actor is on stage performing, the audience need him or her to be moving through the play moment by moment, responding instinctively to what is happening around them. Only in this way can the audience truly be taken on a journey themselves. In order, however, for the actor to let go and trust his/her instinct on stage, technique does need to be applied in the preparation period. Now each actor's technique may be very different – it may not even look like a technique from the outside – but it involves some kind of detailed exploration of the components – internal and external – that contribute to the whole: whether that be in terms of exploring text, character, situation or journey within the play, or preparing the body and voice.

A story about the artist Leonardo da Vinci may help to illustrate what I mean. Apparently, as part of his practice, he drew all the different noses, mouths and eyes he came across – he even numbered them! However, when he came to draw or paint a portrait he didn't consciously think: 'Ah, nose number 5, mouth number 3, eyes number 6.' He responded in the moment to what he saw in front of him. However, the fact that he had spent time noticing and exploring individual parts meant that he had a vast store of detail that could support him as he worked instinctively on the whole.

In this way, technique, which could also be called exploratory preparation, becomes a *framework for freedom* within which your instinct can flourish securely. This is the core intention of this book: to give you a way of preparing that frees you in performance to be utterly present and respond instinctively to what is happening around you.

On the subject of frameworks, the next chapter sets out the basics, which can provide a firm foundation for all work on text and subtext, whilst this chapter ends with suggestions on the different ways in which this book can be used and hints as to the most enjoyable and effective way to work with the exercises.

A Note About Learning

Did you know that there are four stages of learning?[3]

1. Unconscious incompetence

2. Conscious incompetence

3. Conscious competence

4. Unconscious competence

Stage One is to a degree a blissful state of ignorance, although it may be frustrating in that we have a sense that things are not as we want them.

Stage Two can be very uncomfortable: now we know what we don't know and this is often the stage where people give up, especially if they are lacking in confidence. Yet it is a necessary part of the learning process and not a sign that we lack the ability to acquire whatever skill is involved.

Stage Three requires all our attention: in other words, in order to achieve whatever it is we are focusing on we have to concentrate on that to the exclusion of everything else. This is often the point at which an actor will cry: '*I can't do this on stage!*' The answer to this is: '*Of course you can't.*' However, by taking the time offstage, in order to focus consciously on whatever behaviour or habit you want to establish, you will, in time, be able do it unconsciously on stage – and you will have reached Stage Four: unconscious competence. So be prepared to spend time in Stages Two and Three, knowing that this is where the learning takes place.

Using this Book

You can use this book in various ways depending on what you wish to achieve. You can work through it from beginning to end if you want an overview of the whole process before customising it to fit your own way of working. You can consult individual chapters to fill in gaps in your knowledge and experience. You can go straight to the troubleshooting section if there are specific issues that you want to address. The Index will also help you to find exercises and information on particular areas of work. However you choose to use this book, trust your instincts and I'm sure you will find what you need.

Some Helpful Hints

○ *Do the exercises rather than just reading them through – this is the only way they will work! Knowledge is only rumour until it's in the muscle.*

○ *Work with curiosity and a sense of humour; play and enjoy yourself. You'll learn more that way.*

○ *If it's difficult, that's fine: it means you're learning something new, so celebrate. There's no point practising what you can do already!*

○ *Let go of striving to achieve and certainly forget about perfection. Just do the work and the results will come by themselves.*

○ *Pay attention and avoid mindless repetition.*

○ *Focus only on one exercise at a time, trusting that what you learn will be remembered.*

○ *Use your common sense, and trust that if you have explored the exercises thoroughly with commitment and openness you will learn what you need to learn.*

Where Do I Start?

THE BASICS

What are the underlying essentials that enable your individual talent to flourish? Firstly, the ability to produce your best work whatever the circumstances: to establish what I call your 'Creative Bubble'. Secondly, the ability to empathise deeply with character and situation: to develop and use your imagination to step away from yourself and your world into the character and their world. Thirdly, the ability to communicate your thoughts and feelings to the audience effectively: to develop your body and voice so they can easily and powerfully express text and subtext.

ESTABLISHING YOUR 'CREATIVE BUBBLE'

Your 'Creative Bubble' allows you to work well under pressure, whether this pressure is coming from yourself or others. It removes the fear and judgement that may close you down and so enables you to remain open and responsive to your own instincts and to the input of the director.

The exercises below all contribute to establishing the 'Creative Bubble'. They are about learning how to access the natural ease, confidence and poise you have when you feel good about yourself and your work, so that you can click into that state at any time, no matter how stressful the situation.

Centring

To enable you to feel secure and relaxed

I am sure you know only too well what happens to you in stressful situations: muscles tense up – especially around the stomach, shoulders and jaw – and your breath becomes shallow or even held. Your body is in defence mode, and as you seize up physically you also tend to seize up mentally. So what can you do about it? By learning how to centre yourself you can undo the physical tensions and release your breath and so release your mind. You may still feel somewhat nervous or uncomfortable about the situation, but because you have relaxed your body and released your breath you will be able to operate more effectively.

Exploring Your Un-centred State

It's useful to explore what specifically happens to you in stressful situations. Often there is a particular part of the body that is at the core of your tension. If you can work out which part that is and learn to release it you will be able to relax and centre yourself more rapidly.

○ *Recall a time when you felt stressed. See what you saw, hear what you heard and feel what you felt.*

○ *Notice where in your body you hold your tension in that situation – feet, knees, buttocks, belly, back, chest, shoulders, neck, jaw, arms, hands – maybe all of the above!*

○ *What happens to your breath? Is it higher in the body and faster? Or are you holding your breath completely?*

○ *Is there anything else you notice?*

○ *Shake out or stretch to let go of the stressful situation.*

Below are two ways of centring. In the first you simply imagine each part of the body relaxing. In the second you use an image to help the body relax. Some people prefer one; some the other; some like to use a combination of the two. Try both for yourself and then make up your mind what works for you.

Stage One

○ *Stand with your feet directly under your hips and allow the soles of your feet to relax and your toes to spread.*

○ *Relax your legs: checking that your ankle, knee and hip joints are loose.*

○ *Relax your buttocks and belly.*

○ *Focus on your spine, which runs through your body from your tail bone to the top of your neck.*

○ *Imagine it lengthening – down towards the floor and up towards the ceiling – so that it can support you as the muscles in your back and neck relax.*

○ *Imagine your head balancing freely on top of your spine.*

○ Let your chest and shoulders relax as your shoulder blades drop down your back.

○ Let your arms and hands hang heavy.

○ Again, imagine the spine lengthening and the head balancing freely on it.

○ Let your face relax – especially your eyes, lips, tongue and jaw.

○ Rest in this position for a minute or two, deepening the relaxation in each part of your body.

○ Notice how you feel – physically and mentally.

You may feel heavier in your lower body, more stable and more aware of your legs and feet. You may also feel calmer, more at ease and notice that your breathing is slower and deeper.

Stage Two

○ Stand as above.

○ Imagine that you have an hourglass inside you. Imagine that the top of the hourglass is level with the top of your head and the bottom is resting deep in your pelvis.

○ Imagine that the sand in the hourglass is gently pouring down and settling into and spreading across the base, which rests in your pelvis.

○ Once you have imagined the sand settling, then imagine it pouring down your legs into your feet and turning into roots that enter the ground.

○ Imagine the roots going deep into the ground – 3, 6, 9 metres [10, 20, 30 feet].

○ Rest in this position for a minute or two, continuing to imagine the roots going deep.

○ Notice how you feel physically and mentally.

Again, you may notice that the lower body feels more stable and that the breath is deeper.

Once you have established which method or combination of methods is most effective for you, it is simply a matter of practising regularly so that when you are next in a stressful situation it is easy to access your centred state. It is useful to practise when travelling on public transport and standing in queues: firstly, because it doesn't take up any extra time; and secondly, because travelling and queuing are often frustrating and, therefore, stressful situations and so good opportunities to practise dispelling tension.

What you are aiming for is to be centred for as much of the time as possible. To get to this point it is important that you notice as soon as you are un-centred and that you stop and take the time to re-centre, rather than just carrying on regardless. The more you do this, the quicker being centred will be your habitual state and the easier you will find it to access that state in times of stress.

Note: Obviously, not all the characters you play will be centred. However, if you have built up a habit of being centred, you will be able to keep that sense of inner stability and security underneath any ungrounded character you are playing without having to think about it. The advantage to you is that you will be able to play the character with greater flexibility, subtlety and control.

Backward Circle

To be able to stay centred in action

You may find that you can centre before you start a pressured rehearsal or performance but that it is hard to stay centred during it. This next exercise – which is based on a Tai Chi movement – is superb for dealing with this problem and also for reconnecting you emotionally and vocally. If you practise it regularly you will find that you will be able to come back to centre much more easily, however frenzied things around you become. Also, you will be able to perform with much greater ease, which will be less tiring for you and more engaging for the audience.

Ideally you practise this exercise with a speech or scene you want to work on, but we are going to start with the physical movement alone so you can feel the difference it makes to your body, breath and mind.

Practising the Backward Circle

○ *Stand or sit, as you prefer, with your feet hip-width apart and resting on the floor.*

○ *Start with your hands resting on your thighs near your hips. Move your hands out in front of you as far as they will go, then, bring them up to shoulder level, and then in towards your shoulders and down the front of your body until they are back where you started.*

○ *Repeat this Backward Circle several times, noticing what happens to your body, breath and mind.*

How did you find that? Not everyone notices a difference immediately.

However, once the exercise starts to work you will notice that your body becomes more relaxed, that your breath is deeper and slower and that you feel less rushed.

○ *Circle several times in the other direction, i.e. a Forward Circle, to feel the difference.*

You may feel the energy rising higher in the body, taking tension up into the shoulders and breath into the chest. You may also have a feeling of rushing, of almost toppling forward. This energy is to be avoided, since it will destabilise you and is tiring both for you and the audience.

○ *Now return to the Backward Circle again and notice how the body relaxes, the breath settles and the sense of rush disappears.*

Note: Just as many characters are un-centred, there are many characters who seem to 'forward circle'. Again, however, if you have developed a habit of backward circling this will stay in place, underneath the forward circling of the character, and will keep you vocally connected and prevent strain. It will also allow your performance to remain unforced and therefore more engaging for the audience.

If this part of the exercise is making a big difference for you, it is worth practising it – *Backward Circle* only – gently for a minute or two each day. If you are not sure whether it's making any difference, go on to the next stage, where you use the *Backward Circle* with text, and see if that makes a difference.

The Backward Circle with Text

○ *Do the Backward Circle slowly and smoothly while speaking some lines of text, either from the play you are currently working on or from a piece you have worked on previously. Let the circle flow continuously without pause.*

○ *Notice how your voice feels. Notice what your connection with the text is like.*

You may well find that your voice feels easier and more connected and that speaking the text feels more truthful.

○ *Again, circle in the other direction – Forward Circle – while speaking the text to feel the difference.*

You may well find that your breath rises and that you feel less connected vocally and textually.

○ *Then, finish by backward circling again, slowly and smoothly, with text.*

If you practise the *Backward Circle* regularly with speeches and scenes you will learn how to stay centred however great the pressure. It is an excellent way to stay grounded when playing high-energy characters or scenes.

○ *Regularly practise your text at the energy you wish to play it whilst making the Backward Circle movement. At this point it's fine to speed up the movement as long as you keep it on the Backward Circle.*

○ *Once you feel you can play the scene at high energy and stay centred when making the Backward Circle movement, alternate between making the movement and not making it so that you know you can retain the centred state without the actual Backward Circle movement.*

Having practised you may find that even the smallest backward circle movement, made with one hand, clicks you back into a centred state if you lose it. The more you practise going about your daily life with *Backward Circle* energy the easier you will find it to stay with that energy in rehearsals and performance. In addition you will find a greater ease and relaxation in all you do.

Spine Roll

To increase energy, stamina and confidence

When your spine is working well it supports your whole body so that your muscles can work efficiently, without tension. This gives you more energy and stamina. It also helps your confidence. When we feel confident we naturally tend to stand tall, whereas when we feel less confident our spine often sags a little. By learning to keep your spine supporting you fully whatever the circumstances, you can maintain at least some degree of confidence in a difficult situation rather than feeling it all drain away. So, whether you want more confidence, more stamina or more energy, this is the exercise to do, and it only needs to take a few minutes each day.

Note: As with the Centring and Backward Circle, not all characters stand tall. However, once you have established a supportive spine it is possible to adapt your posture as necessary, without collapsing or tensing. Spine Rolls before and after rehearsals will help to keep your body, breath and mind flexible and at ease.

○ *Stand with your back against a wall, so that your feet are about a foot's length away from the wall and your legs are slightly bent.*

○ *Let the bony base of your spine rest against the wall and also the insides of your shoulder blades.*

○ Keeping the insides of your shoulder blades touching the wall and breathing out gently, let your head drop forward, rolling down through your neck, vertebra by vertebra, until your chin is as near to your chest as possible.

○ Rest in this position and breathe in.

○ Then, breathing out gently and keeping your arms relaxed, let your shoulder blades slowly come away from the wall as you roll down through your back, vertebra by vertebra, until your upper body is hanging over.

○ Rest in this position and breathe in gently.

○ Then, breathing out gently, keeping your arms and shoulders relaxed and your head hanging down, roll up through your back, vertebra by vertebra, until your body is upright and your shoulder blades in contact with the wall again, but with your head still hanging down.

○ Rest in this position and breathe in gently.

○ Then, roll up through the neck, vertebra by vertebra, until your head is upright.

○ Repeat twice more.

At first you may find you seem to be rolling down or up in blocks of vertebra rather than one by one. Or you may feel that there are certain parts of the roll where you lose any sense of your spine. This is normal at first. However, if you persevere, working slowly and gently and imagining each vertebra peeling away from the wall as you roll down, and then building back up, one on top of the other, as you roll up, you will find that you become more in touch with your spine and that it becomes more flexible. Three *Spine Rolls* a day will make a huge difference, especially if you also, throughout the day, imagine your spine lengthening in both directions: the base of your spine dropping down and the crown of your head floating up.

The more energised your spine, the more confidence and dynamism you can retain whatever the external stresses and strains.

360-Degree Vision

To allow your mind and body to work freely

Do you find that you lose a sense of perspective when you are under pressure? That you get stuck in tunnel vision, unable to see beyond the present issue? This next exercise is an excellent way of regaining perspective and so freeing your breath, body and mind. It is a very quick exercise that you can do anywhere. In order to fully appreciate its effect it is best to start by exploring what happens to your sense of space under pressure and then move on to regaining a sense of perspective and therefore space.

○ *Recall a situation in which you felt stressed. See what you saw, hear what you heard and feel what you felt.*

○ *Notice what happens to your sense of space.*

Does it seem to get smaller – even tunnel-like?

○ *Notice how the reduction in your sense of space affects your body, breath and mind.*

Now let's shift to 360-Degree Vision and see what difference that makes.

○ *Look across the room at the wall in front of you. Keep your eyes relaxed.*

○ *Imagine that you can see through the wall and out across the buildings or countryside beyond.*

○ *Still looking forward, become aware of the walls on either side of you and imagine that you can see through them and out across the buildings or countryside either side of you.*

○ *Still looking forward, imagine that you can see behind you, through that wall and out across the buildings or countryside behind you.*

○ *Notice how you feel.*

Do you have more sense of space around you? Does your body feel more relaxed? Has your breathing become slower and deeper? Does your mind feel clearer?

Note: If you feel spaced out having done this exercise, simply reduce the distance somewhat in all directions until you come back into focus.

This exercise is an excellent way of settling yourself quickly and giving you room to manoeuvre. You can do it at any point in rehearsal if you feel under pressure and your breath will deepen immediately.

Purposeful Walk

To bring confidence and energy to your work

Have you noticed what happens when you trust yourself to do something? You just get on with it. Whereas when you lose trust you either become tentative and hold back or you become overeffortful and push. The tentativeness de-energises your work, making it dull and predictable. The overeffortfulness overenergises your work, making it forced, busy and unsubtle. When you trust, your work has a natural energy: you can be playful, inventive and original.

Note: Trust is not about thinking you are wonderful or fooling yourself about your ability. It is about working in a way that allows you to access the best you are capable of at the time. In this way you will have a much more accurate sense of your strengths and of what you need to improve.

Again, it is useful to explore the behaviours you *don't* want before you go on to explore the one you do want, since this gives you a good contrast.

Walking Tentatively

○ Walk around the room tentatively, as if you don't trust yourself to do it well.

○ Notice what happens to your body and breath.

○ Notice what happens to your energy physically and mentally.

○ Continue to walk around in this way while speaking some text.

○ Notice what happens to your voice.

Did you notice that you had less energy and felt less confident? Did you notice that the voice was less expressive and dynamic?

Walking Overeffortfully

○ Now walk around the room using a lot of effort to compensate for the fact that you don't trust yourself to do it well. Try hard!

○ Notice what happens to your body and breath now.

○ Notice what happens to your energy physically and mentally now.

○ Continue to walk around in this way while speaking some text.

○ Notice what happens to your voice.

Did you notice that you had tensed up and that the voice was more strident?

Walking with Purpose and Ease

○ Now walk around the room with a sense of focus and purpose, trusting yourself completely, so that you walk with absolute ease and certainty.

○ Keep increasing both the sense of purpose and the sense of ease and certainty.

○ Notice what happens to your body and breath now.

○ Notice what happens to your energy physically and mentally now.

○ *Now continue to walk in the same way, maintaining the level of purpose, ease and confidence, and speak the same text.*

○ *Notice what happens to your voice now and ask yourself how you feel about speaking the text when you walk in this way.*

How was that? Did you have more energy and feel more confident? As you commit to this purposeful walk, your attention and energy can all flow in one direction, without effort or strain. And the effect goes beyond the physical and vocal. Walking in this way brings a feeling of trust in yourself and your work.

This exercise is useful at any time and can be a good way to warm up before rehearsal or performance. It is also very useful when you are first speaking a text aloud since it allows you to really commit without having to make an interpretive choice.

Purposeful Walk Warm-up

○ *Firstly, walk without speaking, focusing on the sense of purpose, ease and certainty.*

○ *As you walk, keep increasing the sense of purpose, ease and certainty.*

○ *Then, continuing to walk in this way, speak some text.*

Whenever you feel tentative about your work, or you are aware that you are pushing and have lost all sense of ease, work with this exercise to regain your trust. Focus on increasing your sense of purpose and certainty, if you are feeling tentative, and on increasing your sense of ease, if you are feeling overeffortful. Spend time walking without speaking until you know you have really achieved the sense of purpose and certainty or of ease that you need to shift your state. Only then add in the text.

Note: Of course, the character you are playing may be tentative or overeffortful to a greater or lesser extent and, obviously, that needs to be played. But that is entirely different from you as an actor being tentative or overeffortful. The question to always ask yourself is: 'How can I play this character/this moment/this scene with trust and ease?'

Cameras Out

To remove any sense of self-consciousness

Where is your attention when you are confident about what you are doing and comfortable with the people around you? Would it be fair to say that your attention is on what you are doing and the people you are with and that you leave yourself alone? What about when you are in a stressful situation where you are less confident about what you are doing and less comfortable with the people around you? Would it be fair to say that your attention turns in on yourself and you become self-conscious? You may find that your inner critic starts up: giving a running commentary on everything you're doing wrong. And if things get really bad you might find that you start assuming that everyone else thinks the same as your critic! So what can you do about this? Well, it is possible to choose where you focus your attention and in this way remove self-consciousness and shut the inner critic up.

Note: It is true that the inner critic is often trying to improve what you are doing, but it is not helpful to listen to it during rehearsal, performance or indeed an audition. In the chapter on dealing with the inner critic I will look at the question of when it is useful to listen to your inner critic and how to turn it into an effective adviser that can help you improve, but for now I want you to learn to put it on one side so that you are free to work.

Using the Metaphor of Cameras

It is useful to think of your attention as a pair of cameras. When all is going well and you feel good about yourself, your cameras point out on to the world leaving you free and unself-conscious. When all is going less well and you are feeling less comfortable, your cameras may turn in, leaving you extremely self-conscious and judgemental. All you need to learn to do, therefore, is to be able to turn your cameras out at will, which is completely possible.

It is useful to do this exercise with other people, but it can be done alone by imagining that the objects in your room are people. As in previous exercises you are going to practise the behaviour you *don't* want – *cameras in* – before you go on to practise what you *do* want – *cameras out*.

Cameras In

○ *Stand or sit, as you prefer.*

○ *Look around at the other people or at the objects in the room that you have chosen to represent people.*

○ *Ask yourself a question like: 'What do they think of me?' This is a sure-fire way to turn your cameras in!*

○ *Notice what happens to your body and breath, notice how you feel, notice if your inner critic starts up.*

Did you feel less comfortable physically? Did the breath tighten up? Did your critic start listing a whole load of things you might be doing wrong or had done wrong in the past?

Cameras Out

○ *Now put your attention on the other people or the objects in the room.*

○ *Start to notice the colour and style of the clothes the people are wearing, or the colours, shapes and textures of the objects you are looking at. Make sure that you are looking with curiosity rather than judgement.*

○ *By noticing what you are seeing you anchor your attention away from yourself and prevent it from turning back on you.*

Did you feel more comfortable and relaxed and less self-conscious?

You may find at first that your cameras swing back and forth. That's fine: as soon as you notice, simply turn them out again. This is an excellent exercise to practise as you go about your daily life and especially as you enter a space where there are other people. Apart from the fact that you will feel far less self-conscious, you will also notice more, and other people will perceive you as being open and interested as well as confident.

Note: It is of course vital that you look at others with curiosity and interest not judgement. No one else wants to be judged any more than you do!

Whilst rehearsing or performing a scene, keep your focus on the other actors, on what they are saying and doing. If your cameras turn in, swing them straight out again if necessary by repeating in your head the words people are saying or by focusing on their movements or the colour of the clothes they are wearing – anything that anchors your focus back on them.

If you feel the director is criticising you, rather than taking it personally and letting your cameras turn in, repeat to yourself: *'What is it he/she is wanting?'* In this way you will keep your focus on the director and off yourself and have a much better chance of staying open and hearing them and being able to give them what they want without feeling destroyed.

Daily Workout for Establishing Your 'Creative Bubble'

○ *Complete three Spine Rolls as part of your morning routine.*

○ *Follow these with one minute of Backward Circling.*

○ Whilst travelling anywhere, and whilst queuing, practise Centring, Lengthening Spine and 360-Degree Vision.

○ As you walk down the street and whenever you enter a room or get onto a bus or a train, practise having your Cameras Out.

○ Each day practise the Purposeful Walk and Backward Circle with text for at least a minute each.

In total this will only add *five minutes* to your day!

DEVELOPING AND USING YOUR IMAGINATION

Have you ever stopped to think what it is you are actually doing when you imagine something? When you imagine a person or place or situation you take information from your memory and put it together in new ways. I am pretty sure that you have never seen a pink seagull. If I ask you to imagine one, though, you can do it. You have a memory of the colour pink and of a seagull and so you can put the two together.

So, one of the important aspects of developing your imagination is having a rich memory to draw on. This is not about having had an exciting life, it is about acute observation: about seeing, hearing, feeling, tasting and smelling in greater detail. Whether you are observing people, places or situations, the richer the detail you take in, the richer and more original your imagination.

Sharpening Your Senses

To increase the quality and quantity of information you take in through your senses

○ Each day choose a sense to focus on as you go about your daily life and allow yourself to experience the world through that sense.

○ When you choose sight, focus on everything you see. Notice colour, shape, texture and size. Notice also movement and stillness and whether the movement is flowing or staccato. See the world as if you were a painter or photographer.

○ When you choose sound, focus on sounds of machines, of people and of nature. Notice pitch, pace, tone and rhythm. Hear the world as if you were a sound recordist or a musician.

○ When you choose touch, focus on the feel of your clothes and of the weather on your skin, of anything you pick up or brush against whether natural or man-made. Notice changes in texture and temperature. Touch the world as if you were a sculptor.

○ *When you choose taste, focus on everything you eat and drink. Notice temperature, texture, sweetness or sourness, moistness or dryness. Taste the world as if you were a wine or food connoisseur.*

○ *When you choose smell, focus on everything you smell. Notice the strength or delicacy of the smell, whether it is fragrant or pungent, bitter or sweet. Smell the world as if you were a perfumer.*

By doing this you will not only increase the richness of your memories but also your general level of awareness.

Noticing the Detail

To practise taking in people's behaviour in more detail

The last exercise will have sharpened up your observation of detail so let's take that further now and focus on the minutiae of what people say and do.

○ *Start by observing what people do physically. How do they stand? How do they walk? What gestures do they make? Notice the different rhythms they have. Can you recreate these?*

○ *Then, listen to people's voices. Listen for the pitch and tone of voices. Notice the rhythm – is it more staccato or flowing or does the rhythm change a great deal? Is the volume and speed regular or fluctuating? Focus on the tune in their voice: is it monotonous or is there great variation? Can you recreate these?*

○ *Then, focus on the feelings people express – where is there hardly any emotional shift and where is there great emotional shift in a short space of time? Notice how many different ways the same emotion can be expressed.*

By noticing this level of detail you will deepen your powers of observation and also increase your store of information about how people react, which will naturally feed into your character work, without you consciously having to think about it.

Stepping Into Others' Shoes

To see the world from other people's perspective

This is an essential skill for an actor. The ability to put yourself in someone else's shoes; to see the world through their eyes; to understand their behaviour, however different it might be from your own and from your own experiences and values. There can be no judgement of a character as good or bad, interesting or boring, clever or stupid. You need to get under his/her skin, so you understand what he/she is thinking and feeling and present that to the audience for them to make up their own minds. This is the greatest task and privilege of the actor: to extend beyond yourself, beyond your views and beliefs, without judgement, to understand and accurately portray others.

How do you develop this skill?

○ *Read stories – novels, biographies, newspaper articles, interviews, etc. – about people's lives.*

○ *Pay attention to how they experience the world. Ask yourself: 'What if I thought as they think, felt as they feel?'*

○ *Watch and listen to people without judging them and wonder: 'What would it be like to be them, to live their life, to feel their feelings, think their thoughts, be in their body?'*

Wondering encourages your imagination to expand beyond the limits of your own experience. Wondering is at the heart of acting: '*What if I were that person, in that situation, what would I think and feel and do then?*' Wondering opens you up; it makes you curious to find out more. Whereas judging closes you down: it encourages you to label someone and confine him/her to a box. Nothing is explored and so nothing is learnt.

Daily Workout for Developing and Using Your Imagination

○ *Each day Sharpen Your Senses by focusing on one sense and allowing yourself to experience the world through that.*

○ *Notice the Detail of people's behaviour: how they move and speak; their different rhythms and emotions.*

○ *Step Into Others' Shoes, seeing the world through others' eyes, imagining what is important to them and understanding why they do what they do.*

All these exercises can be done as you go about your daily activities and therefore do not require any extra time!

COMMUNICATING YOUR THOUGHTS AND FEELINGS EFFECTIVELY

It is your body and voice that enable you to communicate the thoughts and feelings of your character to the other actors and the audience. If you lack physical and vocal stamina, strength and flexibility, it is unlikely that you will have the energy or sensitivity to express yourself fully or accurately. So work in this area is vital.

To give specific physical and vocal exercises would take up the entire book, and there are already plenty of books covering these subjects. What I want to give you here is an overview of what kind of physical and vocal work needs to be done and why, so that you have a framework for approaching exercises in books or classes with a greater understanding and confidence.

Serious Play

It is useful to regard this work as a way of reclaiming the power and freedom you had physically and vocally as a child. Unless a child has suffered emotional or physical trauma, their movement and sound is free and easy, with a natural strength. Children constantly stretch and bend, accompanying their movements with sound. They experiment with and enjoy their bodies and voices. It is important as an adult to recapture this curiosity and joy, rather than seeing physical and vocal work as a chore. So find the pleasure and ease in any exercise. If you are mentally forcing, you are likely to physically force, which will help neither your body nor your voice. Whereas if you are at ease; interested and enjoying what you are doing; your body and voice will, in time, regain their natural energy and freedom.

Physical Work

As I mentioned in the introduction to this section, there are three areas that need to be focused on: stamina, strength and flexibility. The key is to find enjoyable and effective ways of working on each so that they are all equally developed. Use the descriptions below to work out what it would be best for you to do to extend your abilities in each area and obtain a good balance between them.

Stamina

Why is stamina important? Whether during rehearsals, performing on stage or a day's film shoot, you need to sustain your energy – mentally and physically. The physically fitter you are, the easier this is. Not only does this help you to access your own best work but also to be more responsive to the director and the other actors.

The best exercise for stamina is cardio-vascular exercise – it could be walking, running, roller-blading, cycling, swimming, rowing, dancing and so on. What did you enjoy as a child? What would you enjoy now? Once you have chosen an activity, it is important to do it three to four times a week at a level that safely raises your heart rate and keeps it raised for twenty to forty minutes. If you are in any doubt as to what is safe for you, consult your doctor and then an exercise specialist. When exercising, your breath should not be forced and you should not feel dizzy, faint or sick. If you do feel any of these you should stop immediately.

Strength

Physical strength also allows you to sustain energy and work with ease, and it is vital for healthy and subtle vocal work.

Strength is not about being able to lift heavy weights. It is about having toned muscles, especially core muscles, which support you so that you can move with ease. Pilates[4] is excellent for developing this kind of strength, as is Yoga[5] and also Callanetics.[6] The Alexander and Feldenkrais Techniques[7] are good for dealing with postural imbalances and enabling you to regain good body use. If you want to work at the gym make sure that all your movements are done without strain and that your breath is free and practically silent. Also, make sure that you exercise all the main sets of muscles so you keep them in balance with each other and stretch before and after to keep your flexibility. Whatever you choose, always make sure that it is safe and something you enjoy: something that reconnects you with your body and allows you to revel in its aliveness.

Flexibility

In order that your body can reflect all your nuances of intention, thought and feeling, it needs to be flexible. Flexibility allows you to respond sensitively and spontaneously not only physically but also mentally. Any gentle stretching is helpful: Pilates, Yoga and Feldenkrais are effective ways of increasing flexibility. Always stretch on the out-breath. Stretch fully but without force and avoid bouncing when you are at full stretch since this simply strains the ligaments. It is important to work towards stretching both sides equally since this will give you greater balance and less likelihood of strain. As with the stamina and strength work, stretch in a way that is safe and also enjoyable. Think of the way a cat stretches on waking.

And then, Connection . . .

The work above is about tuning your instrument in order that you can play whatever music you want with it. To play wonderful music you need to connect – with what your character is saying, *text*, and with the situation they are in and what they want to do to the other characters, *subtext*. The exercises in the following chapters will help you to do that.

Vocal Work

Stamina, strength and flexibility are as important vocally as physically, and good voice work develops all three. However, different terms are used to describe the various areas of voice work, so I have used those terms here to make it easier to connect this overview with exercises you might find in other books or classes. In each area I simply describe the work that needs to be covered and a good order for covering it. For specific exercises please look at my voice book, *Finding Your Voice*, or at another voice book that you are familiar with and find helpful, or ask your voice teacher if you are working with one. As with the physical work, use the descriptions below to work out what you need to focus on to extend your abilities in each area.

Note: It is not possible to have healthy vocal energy if your muscles are sluggish or tense. Only toned muscles produce easy and balanced vocal energy. That is part of the reason why the physical work above is so important.

Working with an attitude of trust, as you explored earlier in the chapter, is also vital. If you are mentally tentative, your muscles are likely to respond sluggishly, and if you mentally push, your muscles are likely to tense up. Always approach your voice work with the attitude that you will be able to do whatever you are attempting given patience and practice.

Free Centred Breath

For your voice to be free, your breath needs to be free and centred. In other words, you need to use your diaphragm and lower ribs when you are breathing in and your abdominal muscles when you are breathing out, rather than heaving your chest up on the in-breath and dropping it on the out-breath.

The first step is to focus on exercises that develop good posture: relaxed yet alert, with a lengthening spine. Good posture prevents the body from collapsing and therefore allows the correct breathing muscles to move freely.

Then, you need to focus on breathing out fully, since the more you breathe out the easier it is to breathe in. Breathing out should focus on the lower body and the sensation of the abdominal muscles – the belly – moving in towards the spine and slightly upwards.

Finally, you can work on the in-breath. Firstly, you need to ensure that the pelvic floor muscles – the ones you tense when you want to stop yourself from peeing – and the stomach muscles relax as you breathe in, so that the diaphragm can move down and the lower ribs can swing out. Then, you can work on strengthening the movement of the ribs and diaphragm.

There should be no tension either as you breathe in or out. Certainly there are muscles working, but there is a feeling of strength and power rather than tension when muscles are working well. Forcing is a waste of time.

Energy / Support

Vocal energy/support comes from muscular energy: from toned muscles working with confidence, commitment and ease. Two sets of muscles are responsible for vocal energy: the abdominal muscles and the lip and tongue muscles. The abdominal muscles support the voice, giving it power and strength, while the lip and tongue muscles shape the sound into speech, giving definition and clarity.

Both sets of muscles are toned through exercise just as with any muscles in the body. The two sets are best worked on separately. The attitude with which you work is very important. If you work tentatively there will be a lack of energy and you may find that you tense up and hold your breath, especially in the chest. If you work overeffortfully you will find that you are straining. If, however, you work with an attitude of confidence, purpose and ease, as you explored earlier in the chapter, you will find that the muscles will become more active, without excess effort.

Release

As well as toning the muscles, to develop vocal energy, it is important to release muscle tension, which might inhibit the voice or lead to vocal strain. Work on general posture has to come first and, then, specific work on releasing the neck, throat, jaw, tongue and lips, since these are all areas, which can block the voice.

It is also worth checking what is happening with your knees and your pelvic floor. If the knees lock, the belly and buttocks also tighten and this makes it harder for you to support your voice. The knees need to stay relaxed at all times. If the pelvic floor is tight, it inhibits a full and deep in-breath and can even lead to tightness in the throat. It is natural for the pelvic floor muscles to tighten towards the end of a full out-breath, or when you are speaking with vocal support, but they need to relax each time you breathe in.

Resonance

This is not about having a beautiful voice. It is about having a voice that is fully alive so that it touches you and the audience. Again, physical ease and physical tone are vital: if muscles are sluggish the voice will have a dull and muffled quality, whereas if the muscles are tense the voice will have a harsh and possibly sharp quality. Once ease and tone are in place, focusing on each area in the body where you want to increase your sense of vibration is very helpful. The more you build up the sense of vibrations throughout the bone and bony cavities of your upper body and head, the more power and richness your voice will have. The more it will be uniquely yours. To build up the sense of vibrations you need space and time. The space needed is in the mouth, throat and chest and is the result of good posture and a loose jaw. The time needed is on the vowels: sounding them for long enough to have a sense of the vibrations bouncing back and forth in the spaces you have created in the head, throat and chest.

Expression

Vocal expression is about variety: variety of pitch and pace. Vowel glides, where you glide up and down your range, are good for extending your pitch range. Working on different vowel lengths, and 'chunking' the text are good for varying pace [see pages 48 and 268]. In the end, of course, your vocal expression will be driven by your connection with what you are saying and what you want to do to the person you are speaking to [see pages 60 and 209].

Clarity

The lips and tongue give clarity and definition to what you are saying, so work on articulation helps here. It is important to stay connected to the sounds, words or phrases you are saying, otherwise you are practising dis-connection! Exploring vowels and consonants separately helps to build your awareness of the different sounds and your connection with them [see pages 48-56]. Working on the *Backward Circle* can help you to stay present and avoid gabbling if you have a tendency to rush. As with vocal expression, connection with what you are saying, and what you are doing to the person you are speaking to, is vital.

Daily Workout for Communicating Your Thoughts and Feelings Effectively

○ *Instead of making your whole journey by bus or train, walk part of it. Walking briskly for twenty to forty minutes a day will build up your physical Stamina.*

○ *Twenty minutes Yoga, Pilates or Callanetics each morning, can work on both Strength and Flexibility.*

○ *A twenty-minute daily voice warm-up – with one exercise covering each of the areas mentioned in the voice section – is better than a longer period once a week.*

Since the walking is part of a journey you're making anyway and probably won't extend your journey time by much, these exercises need not take up more than about forty minutes of your day.

Summary

Work on the three essentials: *Establishing Your 'Creative Bubble'*, *Developing and Using Your Imagination*, and *Communicating Your Thoughts and Feelings Effectively* will give you a strong technical basis and the confidence and freedom to trust and follow your instincts and produce your best work.

Below is a summary of the exercises in this chapter:

Establishing Your 'Creative Bubble'
Centring
Backward Circle
Spine Roll
360-Degree Vision
Purposeful Walk
Cameras Out

Developing and Using Your Imagination
Sharpening Your Senses
Noticing the Detail
Stepping Into Others' Shoes

Communicating Your Thoughts and Feelings Effectively
For each area choose a simple exercise or exercise sequence to work on that will take you forward. Once that exercise or sequence has achieved what you want choose another one.

Physical
Stamina
Strength
Flexibility
Connection

Vocal
Free Centred Breath
Energy/Support
Release
Resonance
Expression
Clarity

Are There Any Golden Rules?

THE THREE CONNECTIONS

On the whole I don't like rules when it comes to acting. They stop you thinking for yourself. However, there are sometimes useful rules that operate more as guidelines. They point you in the right direction and save a huge amount of time and effort. For me there are Three Connections which are valuable guidelines that can keep your acting on track and prevent a great many problems arising. So, what are these Three Connections? They are connecting with the text, connecting with the situation and connecting with the other actors. By making these Three Connections you will give yourself powerful anchors for your attention so that you will not be distracted by any doubts or sense of self-consciousness; in other words, these connections will keep your cameras firmly out. You will also find that you have a much deeper connection with the character you are playing, the world he/she inhabits and the words he/she speaks.

Connecting with the Text

This involves exploring the text so that you deeply understand its structures and rhythms, its language and imagery. In this way, the words become your own and at the same time take you into the world of the character and the play, as well as supporting you to honour the particular style in which the play is written. The chapters on modern text – **What Do I Say and How Do I Say It?** – and classical text – **And How the Hell Do I Say This?** – will show you how to connect with the text in a practical and enjoyable way.

Connecting with the Situation

This involves understanding the situations that your character is in so that you can relate them to your own experience. This is especially important in classical plays since the relevance of the situations can seem to be hidden by the language and settings. The chapters on character and situation – **Who Am I? Where Am I and When? What's Been Going On Before?** and **What's Going On Now?** – will give you ways of connecting with the character, and their past and present situations, that are effective and informative.

Connecting with the Other Actors

This involves focusing on the actors you are working with, both in rehearsal and performance: focusing on communicating with them, doing something to them. This allows you to be completely unself-conscious and also to be far more creative and original than if you are focusing on yourself. There will be work throughout on focusing outward rather than inward, which builds on the idea of *Cameras Out* that was explored in the last chapter. The chapter on identifying your character's objectives – **What Do I Want?** – will also be helpful.

Taking Your Time

Time after time I see actors beating themselves up because they are finding it difficult to connect and in most cases it is because they are rushing. It takes time to connect with what you are thinking, feeling, saying and doing. And with each new play, each new part, the connection has to start from scratch because the character, situation, text and action are different. If there is anything that marks out experienced actors it is that they take their time to make the connections. They may each do it in a completely different way, that may seem haphazard to the outside eye, but they know what it is they have to discover and the connections they need to make to play a part truthfully and engagingly. This does not mean that they are slow or indulgent in performance, but rather that they take time during the rehearsal period to connect, so that on stage they can go at whatever pace is required.

Backward Circle, *Changing Chairs* and *Phrase by Phrase* are especially effective in helping to slow everything down so that deeper connection is possible.

PART TWO

Text

What Do I Say and How Do I Say It?

HANDLING MODERN TEXT

The text is where you start. It is from what is said and not said, from the *structure* and *language* used, and the *way* they are used, that you can construct, consciously and subconsciously, your view of the characters, relationships, situations and journeys in a play. Yet, often, attention is moved away from the text too soon and returned to it too late, so that it gets buried under everything else that is being focused on.

One of the reasons for this is that although we may understand that the text gives us the *what* we often ignore the fact that it also gives us the *how*. By that I mean that the text not only gives us *information about* the characters, relationships, situations and journeys, it also gives us *tangible behaviour*. The words written by the playwright are more than just abstract psychological indicators. When spoken aloud they are concrete physical behaviours, and if you commit to these behaviours you will discover a great deal. Also, you will feel much more supported by, and connected to, the text and, as a result, much less self-conscious or tentative. The exercises in this chapter will enable you to explore the *how* of modern text in an effective and enjoyable way so that you can prepare for rehearsals, auditions and castings more thoroughly and confidently and, as a result, produce work that is powerfully truthful and deeply engaging.

The Text Demons

Before you start, however, I would like to mention two demons that can pursue actors when they begin to work on text. Both of them come from the relationship we may have had with text at school.

The first demon relates to early experiences of reading aloud. These usually take place when we are learning to read and still at the stage of making mis-

35

takes. It can be a painful time both for the child and the parents and teachers helping them. Often 'getting it right' becomes the main objective just because that is less painful for everyone. Reading aloud as adults can put actors right back in that fraught and pressured place. Fluency becomes the only goal and neither slowness nor stumbling is tolerated.

This is incredibly unhelpful for an actor, since focusing on fluency, in the early stages, means that little or nothing goes in. So drop the need for fluency and take the time to connect with the text. The actor who gives a slick performance at the read-through is often not the one who goes on to give the best performance in the end! The actor who takes his/her time often ends up with something far richer and deeper.

Note: Sight-reading for auditions and castings does obviously need a more polished read, but connection is still more important than empty fluency. We will be looking later at how to sight-read effectively [see page 254]. Everyone can learn to do it to a reasonable standard, and it's easier than you might think. The more you practise picking up a script and calmly connecting with it rather than worrying about fluency and correctness, the easier you will find it.

The second demon relates to our experience of analysing text in English Literature classes. There the emphasis was on understanding the text intellectually; on being able to discuss and describe structure and language use. Whether or not we were good at this, we are often left with the conviction that this intellectual understanding has to *precede* any work on a text. Now this may be so if you are going to write an essay, but it *isn't* necessarily so if you're acting. The kind of understanding you need to play a part is totally different, and it's often better if it comes slowly *whilst* you're working on the text.

So, rather than having to understand everything before you begin, it is more useful to start speaking the text aloud, taking your time to discover what is there. The exercises below enable you to do that in a structured way which is enjoyable and allows you to make a deep connection with both the *what* and the *how*.

Stop Acting, Start Talking

Speaking text is exactly that: speaking, talking to someone, communicating with him/her; *not* acting in a vacuum. So, from the start, make sure you know exactly whom, as your character, you are talking to and put all your focus on talking to them. This is important because it anchors your attention outside yourself and takes the focus and pressure off you: again it's a case of **Cameras Out**. It also brings to life the natural communicative energy we all have, when we truly want to communicate, and so it makes the text far more real and alive, both to speak and to listen to.

Note: If you are working alone, choose an object to represent the person you are talking to; or several objects if you are talking to several people. Talk directly to the object, or objects, even if you think that when you play the scene you will not actually be looking at the person or people. This will give you a sharpness of focus and keep your work active, because your words will always be spoken for and to someone. Where you are talking to yourself or to an imagined person, still choose an object to represent these, since, in reality, when we talk to ourselves or to an imagined person, we do so as if there were someone else actually in the room.

Exploring the Text Physically

All the exercises, as I mentioned in Part One, explore the text physically, because this takes you out of your head, helps you to commit and allows you to work more instinctively. It also means that your body will feel much more involved even if the speech or scene is eventually played completely still. The exercises are simple and clear. They allow you to explore the structures, sounds, words and images in the text in detail, layer by layer, so that you can notice for yourself what is there; rather than having to rely on anyone else to point it out to you.

EXPLORING STRUCTURES AND RHYTHMS

The first set of exercises looks at the various *structures* in the text and at the *rhythms* these structures give. There are no rules or right answers. These exercises are designed to help you become aware of what is there. Each actor will respond differently to what they find. However, all the responses will be valid and will honour the text because these responses will have grown out of what you have discovered there.

Note: I have included speeches for you to use whilst learning each exercise. Once you have a good understanding of how the exercises work you can then use them to explore whatever text you are currently working on. You can also do this work with scene partners.

The first speeches – one male, one female – we are going to use are from *The Way Home* by Chloë Moss. They are included below so you can have a quick read through before you start on the exercises. Each one is preceded by a brief description of where each character is, whom they are talking to and who and what they are talking about. Choose the one you want to work on and as soon as possible stand up and start exploring.

The Way Home [male]: Daniel is at Otterspool in Liverpool, where he likes to go to get away. It is shortly after his mother's funeral. He is talking to his new friend Bobby. They are telling each other about the dreams they've had. Daniel was born in Liverpool but still has a trace of an Irish accent. For the purposes of these exercises, it's fine to work in your own accent, allowing the way the text is written to dictate any shifts. The *** marks indicate where Bobby speaks and, at times, where Daniel replies to what Bobby has said. I have cut these lines so that the piece can flow as one speech here.

> DANIEL: I'm in the middle of the sea on one o' them whatd'yercallits
> – wha's the name for 'em? A – *** No. Not a fuckin' boat . . . I
> wouldn't forget wha'a boat's called, would I? Do I look like an eejit?
> [*Beat.*] A lilo. *** Just floating, that's all. [*Beat.*] Underneath a big
> black sky. [*Beat.*] Well, not black exactly but not blue either. Just
> kind of no colour. If you can think of the colour of nothing. [*Pause.*]
> Dirty dish water. So . . . it's sort of dark but light at the same time.
> [*Beat.*] I can definitely see the shape of me hand in the water and I
> can see beneath the water. Even though there's nothing there. Yer
> can tell that there's nothing there. *** I was lying on a lilo in the
> middle of the sea. And it's the end o' the world. That's not nothin'.
> Tha's quite a big fuckin' thing. *** I was just floatin'. [*Pause.*] It was
> quite nice really. [*Beat.*] I think I knew the lilo wouldn't last that
> long. It was one of those really cheap ones, like you get outside
> shops in Blackpool. [*Beat.*] By the time I woke up, the water was
> startin' to get into me eyes. *** I wasn't that bothered. I just
> thought it was . . . *** I dunno. Jus' . . . interestin' or somethin'.
> [*Beat.*] In the dream I couldn't swim. But it didn't really bother me
> like. I jus' let meself . . . it didn't bother me. [*Silence.*]⁸

The Way Home [female]: Ellie, Daniel's sister, is sitting with Daniel's friend, Bobby, a few days after her mother's funeral. She is telling him what it was like, seeing her mother after she had died. Again, Ellie has traces of an Irish accent, but it's best to work in your own accent and let the text lead to any shifts.

ELLIE: When I saw me mammy. Afterwards like. When she come back home. [*Beat*.] I stood by the door fer a while, just gettin' hold o' meself, kept sayin' over an' over in me head, "'S not really her, yer know wha' she looks like, tha's not her.' Got meself all knotted up expectin' somethin' . . . expectin' her t'look like . . . well y'know, what yer might imagine. Shut me eyes and took a breath an' went to her, opened 'em an' . . . She looked fuckin' gorgeous. [*Pause*.] Like the weight o' the world were off her shoulders. Twenty years younger. Didn't have a wrinkle on her face. [*Pause*.] Always frownin', she wa', me mam. Always had her forehead bunched up like she wa' worried sick about somethin'. [*Beat*.] She jus' looked like everythin' wa' grand. Like it'd all stopped. All the shite. An' I jus' thought . . . is this wha' it takes, like? This is the only peace yer get. She's struggled like a Trojan her whole life an' the best she's ever looked is lyin' in her coffin. [*Beat*.] Some shitty turn-up that is.

Walking the Sentences

To discover the rhythm, flow and energy of the thoughts in a text

I always start with this exercise when working on modern text. It helps you to connect with the rhythm and flow of the character's thoughts: to move away from your own rhythms towards those of the character. It also gives you a good sense of the way a speech is built up. In addition, it helps your breath because, as you begin to get a measure of each thought length, you automatically have a sense of the breath needed to match it and of where, within the thought, you can take a new breath, if necessary, without breaking the thought. Also, because you are up and doing immediately, you are able to commit from the very start rather than feeling tentative and self-conscious or piling on a lot of excess effort that stops the text from feeding you.

Below the speeches appear again but marked up to help you through the exercise. Read through the directions below before you start.

○ *Script in hand you are going to walk purposefully around the room saying the text.*

○ *Treat each sentence as a separate journey, so that you start walking as you start the sentence and keep walking without pause, ignoring all the commas, dashes, colons, etc. until you reach the full stop.*

○ *Then, stop to have a sense of having completed the journey of that sentence.*

○ Then, start off in another direction with the next sentence and again keep walking until you come to the next full stop.

○ As you walk, have a sense of someone in front of you to whom you are talking and really want to communicate with.

○ Make sure that you walk with a sense of focus, purpose and ease, as if you are going somewhere specific. Remember the Purposeful Walk on page 16. This will help you to journey through the thoughts, to move them forward rather than letting them become static.

○ Try the whole speech in this way.

○ Be extremely precise, always stop at the end of the sentence and always set off in a new direction for the next sentence.

Note: These particular speeches have Beats and Pauses that have been written in by the playwright. When these occur say 'Beat' or 'Pause', once you have stopped, and then move on to the next sentence. This is important because the beats and pauses are part of the overall rhythm.

DANIEL: I'm in the middle of the sea on one o' them whatd'yercalllits – wha's the name for 'em? [**stop**] A – [**stop**] No. [**stop**] Not a fuckin' boat . . . I wouldn't forget wha'a boat's called, would I? [**stop**] Do I look like an eejit? [**stop** – *Beat.*] A lilo. [**stop**] Just floating, that's all. [**stop** – *Beat.*] Underneath a big black sky. [**stop**] Well, not black exactly but not blue either. [**stop**] Just kind of no colour. [**stop**] If you can think of the colour of nothing. [**stop** – *Pause.*] Dirty dish water. [**stop**] So . . . it's sort of dark but light at the same time. [**stop** – *Beat.*] I can definitely see the shape of me hand in the water and I can see beneath the water. [**stop**] Even though there's nothing there. [**stop**] Yer can tell that there's nothing there. [**stop**] I was lying on a lilo in the middle of the sea. [**stop**] And it's the end o' the world. [**stop**] That's not nothin'. [**stop**] Tha's quite a big fuckin' thing. [**stop**] I was just floatin'. [**stop** – *Pause.*] It was quite nice really. [**stop** – *Beat.*] I think I knew the lilo wouldn't last that long. [**stop**] It was one of those really cheap ones, like you get outside shops in Blackpool. [**stop** – *Beat.*] By the time I woke up, the water was startin' to get into me eyes. [**stop**] I wasn't that bothered. [**stop**] I just thought it was . . . I dunno. [**stop**] Jus' . . . interestin' or somethin'. [**stop** – *Beat.*] In the dream I couldn't swim. [**stop**] But it didn't really bother me like. [**stop**] I jus' let meself . . . it didn't bother me. [*Silence.*]

*

ELLIE: When I saw me mammy. [**stop**] Afterwards like. [**stop**] When she come back home. [**stop** – *Beat.*] I stood by the door fer a while, just gettin' hold o' meself, kept sayin' over an' over in me head, "S not really her, yer know wha' she looks like, tha's not her." [**stop**] Got meself all knotted up expectin' somethin'... expectin' her t'look like... well y'know, what yer might imagine. [**stop**] Shut me eyes and took a breath an' went to her, opened 'em an'... She looked fuckin' gorgeous. [**stop** – *Pause.*] Like the weight o' the world were off her shoulders. [**stop**] Twenty years younger. [**stop**] Didn't have a wrinkle on her face. [**stop** – *Pause.*] Always frownin', she wa', me mam. [**stop**] Always had her forehead bunched up like she wa' worried sick about somethin'. [**stop** – *Beat.*] She jus' looked like everythin' wa' grand. [**stop**] Like it'd all stopped. [**stop**] All the shite. [**stop**] An' I jus' thought... is this wha' it takes, like? [**stop**] This is the only peace yer get. [**stop**] She's struggled like a Trojan her whole life an' the best she's ever looked is lyin' in her coffin. [**stop** – *Beat.*] Some shitty turn-up that is.

What did you discover? Did you notice how the shift in sentence length, and therefore thought length, gave the speech a specific rhythm? Did you get a sense of the structure of the speech? Of how each thought built on the one before? Did you notice how much easier it was to change thought and, therefore, pitch and tone of voice, because you separated each thought? Did you find it easier to feel 'on top' of the speech rather than it running away with you?

○ *Go through the exercise a couple more times making sure that you keep walking with purpose through each sentence and then turn in a completely new direction for each following sentence.*

○ *Notice how the different sentence lengths give each speech a specific rhythm and how each sentence builds on the one before, giving you a sense of journey.*

○ *Notice how you begin to get a sense of what the character may be thinking and feeling.*

This exercise will help you to have a sense of the *movement* of the thoughts. Thought is never static. It is always alive, always moving forward – even when it seems to go round in circles. By physically moving – walking with purpose – you will keep a speech alive and dynamic.

The more you practise this exercise on a speech or scene, the more the length and shape of the sentences and thoughts will become deeply embedded in you. This has two advantages. Firstly, you don't then need to think technically on stage. The sentence and thought integrity will be kept intact and your breath will sort itself out. Secondly, you will be pulled away from your own rhythms and enter deeply into the rhythms of the character. And, if you practise walking purposefully, but without rushing, your speeches will have energy without being frenetic.

Changing Direction

To discover the internal rhythm of each thought and the emotional to and fro of the text

Now we are going to look at the punctuation *within* each sentence. This gives a sense of the internal rhythm of each thought: the emotional ebb and flow. There may be two sentences of a similar length, but if one has hardly any punctuation and the other has a great deal, the effect will be very different.

Cicely Berry devised this wonderful way of exploring punctuation. Below is the description of how I use it.

Again, the text is included, marked up to help you out. As before, read through the directions before you start.

○ *Walk again as you speak the text: this time changing direction at every punctuation mark, including the full stops, without stopping at any point.*

○ *As before, it is important to have a sense of purpose, of forward motion and not to amble or rush.*

○ *Also, again, have the sense that there is someone in front of you to whom you are talking.*

○ *Try the whole text in this way, being very precise, so that you change on every punctuation mark – that includes all the dashes and dots!*

○ *Keep moving the whole time, so that you only stop when you reach the end of the speech.*

DANIEL: I'm in the middle of the sea on one o' them whatd'yercalllits – [**change**] wha's the name for 'em? [**change**] A – [**change**] No. [**change**] Not a fuckin' boat . . . [**change**] I wouldn't forget wha'a boat's called, [**change**] would I? [**change**] Do I look like an eejit? [**change** – *Beat.*] A lilo. [**change**] Just floating, [**change**] that's all. [**change** – *Beat.*] Underneath a big black sky. [**change** – *Beat.*] Well, [**change**] not black exactly but not blue either. [**change**] Just kind of no colour. [**change**] If you can think of the colour of nothing. [**change** – *Pause.*] Dirty dish water. [**change**] So . . . [**change**] it's sort of dark but light at the same time. [**change** – *Beat.*] I can definitely see the shape of me hand in the water and I can see beneath the water. [**change**] Even though there's nothing there. [**change**] Yer can tell that there's nothing there. [**change**] I was lying on a lilo in the middle of the sea. [**change**] And it's the end o' the world. [**change**] That's not nothin'. [**change**] Tha's quite a a big fuckin' thing. [**change**] I was just floatin'. [**change** – *Pause.*] It was quite nice really. [**change** – *Beat.*] I think I knew the lilo wouldn't last that long. [**change**] It was one of those really cheap ones, [**change**] like you get outside shops in Blackpool. [**change** – *Beat.*] By the time I woke up, [**change**] the water was startin' to get into me eyes. [**change**] I wasn't that bothered. [**change**] I just thought it was . . . [**change**] I dunno. [**change**] Jus' . . . [**change**] interestin' or somethin'. [**change** – *Beat.*] In the dream I couldn't swim. [**change**] But it didn't really bother me like. [**change**] I jus' let meself . . . [**change**] it didn't bother me. [*Silence.*]

*

ELLIE: When I saw me mammy. [**change**] Afterwards like. [**change**] When she come back home. [**change** – *Beat.*] I stood by the door fer a while, [**change**] just gettin' hold o' meself, [**change**] kept sayin' over an' over in me head, [**change**] "S not really her, [**change**] yer know wha' she looks like, [**change**] tha's not her.' [**change**] Got meself all knotted up expectin' somethin' . . . [**change**] expectin' her t'look like . . . [**change**] well y'know, [**change**] what yer might imagine. [**change**] Shut me eyes and took a breath an' went to her, [**change**] opened 'em an' . . . [**change**] She looked fuckin' gorgeous. [**change** – *Pause.*] Like the weight o' the world were off her shoulders. [**change**] Twenty years younger. [**change**] Didn't have a wrinkle on her face. [**change** – *Pause.*] Always frownin', [**change**] she wa', [**change**] me mam. [**change**] Always had her forehead bunched up like she wa' worried sick about somethin'. [**change** – *Beat.*] She jus' looked like everythin' wa' grand. [**change**] Like it'd all stopped. [**change**] All the shite. [**change**] An' I jus' thought . . . [**change**] is this wha' it takes, [**change**] like? [**change**] This is the only peace yer get. [**change**] She's struggled like a Trojan her whole life an' the best she's ever looked is lyin' in her coffin. [**change** – *Beat.*] Some shitty turn-up that is.

How did you find this exercise? Some actors get very irritated with it. They feel out of control and confused, as if the text is coming at them from all directions, but that is the point. That is often what happens to us as we think and speak. We feel bombarded by our thoughts; tossed to and fro on a turbulent sea whose current is constantly changing direction and speed.

○ *Try the speech again in the same way and pay attention to how the thoughts bob about. Allow yourself to be buffeted around by the shifting rhythms, noticing when you are constantly turning and when you walk in one direction for a longer period.*

Do you notice how, when there is a lot of punctuation, the thoughts are cut up and become staccato? Rather like being in a maze where you keep coming to dead ends and have to turn another away. The thought feels blocked.

Do you notice how, when there is less punctuation, the thoughts are more sustained and released? Suddenly you are less stuck; it is as if you can begin to find your way out of the maze, begin to go somewhere.

Do you notice how the rhythm is constantly on the move? What does it feel like when the speech changes from being staccato to being more sustained and released or vice versa? There's no right answer – it's simply a question of what you notice and what clues that gives you about how the character feels.

This exercise really thrusts you into the heart of the emotional movement of a speech or scene, and sometimes you realise that it is very different from how you thought it was. It is especially useful if you are finding it difficult to be spontaneous or emotionally free in a text; if it all feels a little too calm and well ordered.

You can use it when you begin your text work, as we have done here, and it can also be used later in rehearsal and performance, if things have become rather set, to bring back the freedom of the emotional ebb and flow.

Changing Chairs

To discover how each phrase builds on the one before, so creating a ladder of meaning in the text

We are now going to explore the punctuation within the sentences a little further. This is another excellent exercise of Cicely Berry's and, again the description below is simply how I use it.

○ *Place two chairs next to each other and sit on one of them.*

○ *Speak the text, changing chairs at each punctuation mark. You do not need to get right up, you can just shift across, but it is vital that you do not speak while you are shifting from one chair to the next, only when you are actually sitting still.*

○ *As with the earlier exercises, have a sense of someone in front of you to whom you are talking.*

○ *Use the same text as for the previous exercise and only read on once you've tried the exercise.*

How did you find this? Did you notice how the phrases build on each other? Were there any phrases you hadn't really noticed or connected with before? This exercise helps you to get in touch with the argument of a speech and to shape it. It is more rational. So, if you find that the emotion of a piece is running away with you, use this exercise to strengthen your sense of structure and journey.

It is particularly excellent if you tend to rush. It forces you to stay with each phrase and take your time! It is also excellent if you are working on a very witty piece of text, since it will help you to feel the cleverness of the construction and to make it your own.

Phrase by Phrase

To deepen the connection with the text

This exercise builds on the previous one and is the best way to deepen your exploration of and connection with the text. You will also find that it helps you to learn it.

○ *Sit in a chair with a lamp, plant or other object in front of you. The object represents the person you are talking to in the speech. [In both speeches from* The Way Home *that is Bobby.]*

Note: You can also do this exercise with another person sitting in front of you as your listener. I simply use a lamp, plant or other object because you can't always get someone to sit there when or for as long as you need them!

○ *Look at the text and take the time to absorb the first phrase – that is up to the first punctuation mark.*

○ *Then, look up and register the plant or lamp before you speak, as if you are taking a moment to connect with the person it represents.*

○ Then, speak the phrase really wanting to communicate it.

○ At the end of the phrase, pause for a moment as if to check that that phrase has been registered by the person you are talking to.

○ Continue through the whole speech in this way, taking the time to absorb each phrase, to look up and connect, to communicate and to check that what you have said has been received.

○ Again, use the text you used previously and only read on once you've tried the exercise.

What do you notice? Were you surprised at or struck by some of the phrases? Did you get more sense of the journey of the speech?

This exercise is a gentle but powerful way of connecting with a text. The more you approach it calmly and with full attention, taking your time to absorb each phrase and then communicate it without effort or artifice, the more you will discover and the more the text will be able to support you.

Note: This is a great exercise to do with a scene you are working on with others. When listening do not look down at your text to see when it's your turn to speak. Give your scene partner/s your full attention and, only when they seem to have finished, look down to see if you speak next. In this way you will really hear all they say and you will begin to discover how your lines grow out of theirs.

The four exercises – **Walking the Sentences**, **Changing Direction**, **Changing Chairs** and **Phrase by Phrase** – all explore the structures of the text. They give you a sense of the thought rhythms and within these a sense of both the emotional and the rational ebb and flow of the text: that is the movement of feeling *behind* the words and the way the sense is reasoned *through* the words.

I find these exercises the best to start with because they involve simple movement and so give you something concrete to do. They allow you to commit to speaking the speech from the start without forcing choices. They also allow for a great deal of discovery to take place. What's more, the discovery is organic and visceral. And because you explore through doing rather than discussing, the discoveries you make do not need to be consciously remembered, they will stay with you because you have experienced them: they'll be *in the muscle*.

You can return to these exercises at intervals throughout a rehearsal period and even during the run, since they will always bring fresh insights.

DISCOVERING THE EMOTIONAL FLOW

So far you have explored the rhythms that the *punctuation* yields. Now you are going to explore the rhythms that the *sounds* within the words yield and how these enable you to connect with the text.

Sounds can be divided into vowels and consonants. Vowels are the emotional river running through the centre of our speech. Try saying '*I've got toothache*' with just the consonants, so that the vowels are reduced to the shortest neutral grunts: '*uv-gut-tuthuk*'. It's very hard to express any pain just with the consonants! Now try the vowels on their own '*igh − o − oo − ay*'. This is much more satisfying emotionally: you can really let rip.

The consonants slot over the vowels: they bring definition and meaning. They shape the amorphous emotion to allow us to express ourselves more precisely. '*igh − o − oo − ay*' is very satisfying to say in terms of expressing our pain, and it will communicate how we feel. However, it doesn't allow us to communicate the precise reason for our pain or discomfort. For that we need the consonants as well. Together they enable full communication − sense charged with emotion, and emotion channelled through sense. The balance between the two is vital.

If the vowels dominate, the sense is drowned in a deluge of sound and feeling. You may have experienced performances where an actor is so engaged by the emotion that a speech becomes all 'sound and fury signifying nothing': the meaning becoming completely obscured. On the other hand, if the consonants dominate, the emotion is suffocated by the stranglehold of definition and reason. You may have experienced performances where the actor was so in the thrall of the sense that, although you understood every word, and perhaps even marvelled at his/her clarity, you remained utterly unmoved. In both cases the delicate balance between vowels and consonants, emotion and sense, heart and head has been lost.

You may be thinking that this all sounds very well in theory but that it would be impossible to work consciously to find this balance. However, this is not the case. It can take a while to feel confident with these exercises, but once you have mastered them you will have a simple but extremely effective way of connecting with the sound in text so that it feels extremely comfortable and truthful to speak.

Connecting with the Vowels

To connect with the emotional heart of the text

This exercise focuses on the vowels: isolating them so you can get a sense of their flow and rhythm. This allows you to connect with the emotional heart of the text and express it without force. The *flow* comes from the fact that the vowels are open, fluid sounds; the *rhythm* from the fact that vowels have different lengths.

Note: This is true whatever the accent, and often the length stays the same in different accents even if the vowel is pronounced differently. The one notable exception is the sound in 'bath', 'grass', etc. This is pronounced with a short 'a' sound in some accents and a long 'ah' in other accents. Both pronunciations are correct for their particular accents. The examples below are in what is known as a Standard English accent. I have included a word example for each vowel so that you can check if that vowel stays the same length in your accent. When you are working with a piece of text the vowels are, of course, pronounced in the accent in which that text is written and therefore any shift in length will be dictated by that accent.

There are three vowels lengths: *short, long* and *diphthong*. The first two are self-explanatory. The third – diphthong – is made up of two sounds, starting on one sound and moving to another ['diphthong' literally means *two sounds* in Greek]. For example, /ey/, as in 'they', starts on an /e/ sound and moves to an /i/ or /ee/ sound. Diphthongs, therefore, have a sense of *movement* as well as length. It's helpful to think of them as *travelling* vowels.

SHORT	LONG	DIPHTHONGS
/i/ as in pit	/ee/ as in peat	/ey/ [e + i] as in bait
/e/ as in pet	/ah/ as in part	/igh/ [u + i] as in bite
/a/ as in pat	/er/ as in pert	/oy/ ['o'+ i] as buoyed
/uh/ as in but	/or/ as in port	/oh/ [er + oo] as in bone
/'o'/ as in pot	/oo/ as in boot	/ow/ [ah + oo] as in pound
/'oo'/ as in put		/ear/ [i + 'er'] as in peered
/'er'/ as in final 'er' of other, etc. and the initial 'a' of again, around, etc.		/air/ [e + 'er'] as in paired
		/ooer/ [oo +'er'] as in truant

When working on vowel rhythm it is worth photocopying your text and taking the time to mark up the different lengths. I use a forward slash [/] to denote short vowels, a long dash [–] to denote long vowels, and a circle [O] to denote diphthongs:

/   O   —   /   / — O   O — / /
Sometimes she would let me stay while she undressed.

It is useful to mark up the text for two reasons. Firstly, you can see the rhythm: where the text is staccato [lots of short vowels], where it is more sustained [lots of long vowels] and where there is more movement [lots of diphthongs]. Secondly, it is easier to be precise when you come to practise because the rhythm is marked out rather like a musical score.

Marking the text does not tie you down to one way of saying it. Rather it encourages you to be more adventurous, to move away from your own rhythms and to commit strongly to the rhythmic shifts in the text which will give you greater variety.

Below are two new speeches: one from *Orestes: Blood and Light*, a version of Euripides' *Orestes* by Helen Edmundson, and the other from *Notes on Falling Leaves* by Ayub Khan-Din. They are included below with brief explanations. Once you have chosen which speech you want to work on, it's worth preparing by doing **Walking the Sentences**, **Changing Direction** and **Changing Chairs** before going on to the new exercises.

Orestes: Electra is in her mother's bedroom with her brother Orestes, who is sleeping. Six days earlier, with Electra urging him on, he murdered their mother in revenge for her having murdered their father many years earlier. They have taken refuge in their mother's palace and know it is only a matter of time before they are captured and killed. Electra is talking to herself, remembering being with her mother when she was young.

> ELECTRA: Sometimes she would let me stay while she undressed. Sometimes she would send the servants away and she would sit here while I brushed her hair. My mother. She would let me open jars and bottles, sniff and touch, she would let me uncover close things from drawers, treasures, and tell me where they came from. Tell me stories of a life before. Sometimes she would hold out her hands for me and I would rub them with oil, taking the rings off, one by one, feeling the deep lines on her knuckles, shifting her skin, gently, over veins and bone. I wanted to climb back inside her, always, and settle down behind her heart.[9]

Notes on Falling Leaves: The Man's mother is dying. He spent the previous night in the house where he grew up and she still lived until she went into hospital. He is talking to her but has no idea if she hears or understands what he is saying. In the speech he is describing standing in the coat cupboard smelling her old coats.

> MAN: I'm next to you again. The old you. The you I know. That makes me laugh. I put my head under your coat and breathe you in. All of you. All over. I can almost feel you warm by my side. You're with me, you're with me, you're with me, you're with me! I can smell you. I can smell you. I remember! I remember when our kid took you out . . . I got you ready. Helped you put your tights on . . . you kept trying to put both legs in the same hole, we shouted at each other, we fell on the floor and we laughed. We laughed like we'd laughed before. Before the lump. Before the dark. You put your arms around me and you kissed me. You looked at me and saw me. The last time, the very last time you were you and I was me. I remember . . . [10]

Now let's work through your chosen speech slowly and see what you discover from exploring the vowels. Phrases from both speeches are laid out side by side here, so simply work on whichever one you have chosen and ignore the other.

○ *Take the first phrase: 'Sometimes she would let me stay' or 'I'm next to you again.' Say it a few times so you are clear about what the actual vowel sounds in the words are.*

○ *Then, say the vowels on their own without thinking about them too much – almost as if you were inventing a language with a child:*

> /   O   — /   /   — O   O /   / — / /
> **uh – igh   ee 'oo'   e   ee ey   igh e   'er' oo 'er'e**
> Sometimes she would let me stay   I'm next to you again.

○ *Now add 'h' in front of each vowel. This will enable the vowels to release freely without any strain since the 'h' ensures that breath is flowing before any sound is made:*

> /   O   — /   /   — O   O /   /   — /   /
> **huh-high   hee h'oo'   he hee hey   high he h'er'   hoo h'er'-he**
> Sometimes she would let me stay   I'm next to   you   again.

○ *Say the vowels with the 'h' in front a few more times, committing to the different lengths so that the short vowels are really short, the long vowels really long and the diphthongs really travel.*

○ It is useful to mark the rhythm with your hand – doing quick downward movements for the short vowels, long horizontal movements for the long vowels and big rounded movements for the diphthongs.

Working physically allows you to make a greater differentiation between the vowel lengths and it creates more flow and commitment.

○ Once you have explored the first phrase move on to the second: 'while she undressed' or 'The old you.' As before, repeat the line a few times to get a sense of what the vowels do within the words. Then, say the vowels on their own with 'h' in front:

O — / /
high hee huh-he
while she undressed

/ O /
h'er' hoh hoo
The old you.

○ Again, repeat the vowels several more times, really committing to the different lengths and again making the corresponding movements.

○ Continue in the same way with the rest of your chosen speech taking it phrase by phrase.

ELECTRA:

/ O — / / — O O — / / / O — /
huh-high hee h'oo' he hee hey high hee huh-he huh-high hee h'oo'
Sometimes she would let me stay while she undressed. Sometimes she would

/ / — / / O / — / / O O O / —
he h'er' her-h'er' h'er'-hey h'er' hee h'oo' hi hear high high huh her
send the servants   away   and she would sit here while I brushed her

O O / / — / / — O / — / / / /
hair high huh-h'er' hee h'oo' he hee hoh-h'er' hah h'er' h'o'-h'er' hi
hair. My   mother.   She would let me open   jars and   bottles, sniff

/ / — / / — / / / O / / — /
h'er' huh hee h'oo' he hee huh-huh-h'er' hoh   hi   h'o' hor-h'er'
and touch, she would let me   uncover   close things from drawers,

/ / / / — O O O / / — — / / / O
he-h'er' ha he hee hair hey hey h'o' he hee hor-i h'o' h'er' high
treasures, and tell me where they came from. Tell me stories of   a   life

/ — / O — / O O — / / — / O /
hi-hor huh-high hee h'oo' hoh how her ha   h'er' hee er' igh 'oo'
before. Sometimes she would hold out her hands for   me and I would

/ / / O O / / / / / O / — / / — O
huh he   hi hoy hey-hi h'er' hi h'o' huh high huh hee-hi h'er' hee high
rub them with oil, taking the rings off, one   by   one, feeling the deep lines

/ — / / / // — / / / O / O / O
h'o' her huh-h'er' hi-hi her hi he-hi hoh-h'er' hey h'er' hoh
on her knuckles, shifting her skin, gently, over veins and bone.

O / / / O / / O — — O / / / O
high h'o'-he h'er' high ha hi-igh her hor-hey h'er' he-h'er' how
I wanted to climb back inside her, always, and settle down

/ O / —
hi-high her hah
behind her heart.

*

MAN:
O / / — / — / O / / — O O / O
high he h'er' hoo h'er'-he h'er' hoh h'oo' h'er' hoo high hoh ha hey
I'm next to you again. The old you. The you I know. That makes

— — O / O / / / — O / — — /
hee hah high h'oo' high he huh-h'er' hor hoh h'er' hee hoo hi
me laugh. I put my head under your coat and breathe you in.

— / — — O / O / — O — — — O O O
hor h'o' hoo hor hoh-h'er' high ha hor-hoh hee hoo hor high high high
All of you. All over. I can almost feel you warm by my side.

— / — — / — — / — — / —
hor hi hee hor hi hee hor hi hee hor hi hee
You're with me, you're with me, you're with me, you're with me!

O / / — O / / — O / / /
high ha he hoo high ha he hoo high hi-he-h'er'
I can smell you. I can smell you. I remember!

O / / / / O / / — O O / — / /
high hi-he-h'er' he how'er' hi h'oo' hoo how high h'o' hoo he-hi
I remember when our kid took you out...I got you ready

/ — / — O / — / O / / /
he hoo h'oo' hor high h'o' hoo he high-hi h'er' h'oo' hoh he
Helped you put your tights on...you kept trying to put both legs

/ / O O — O / / — / / — / / / —
hi h'er' hey hoh hee how-he ha hee huh-h'er' hee he h'o' h'er' hor
in the same hole, we shouted at each other, we fell on the floor

/ — — — — O — — / — / — / /
ha hee hah hee hah high hee hah hi-hor hi-hor h'er' huh
and we laughed. We laughed like we'd laughed before. Before the lump.

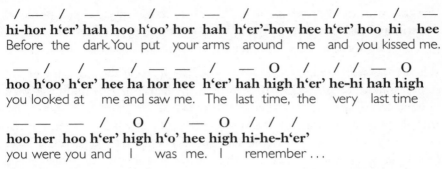

/ — / — — / — — / — — / — / —
hi-hor h'er' hah hoo h'oo' hor hah h'er'-how hee h'er' hoo hi   hee
Before the   dark. You put   your arms   around   me   and you kissed me.

— / / — / — — / — O / / / — O
hoo h'oo' h'er' hee ha hor hee h'er' hah high h'er' he-hi hah high
you looked at   me and saw me. The last time, the   very   last time

— — — / O / — O / / /
hoo her hoo h'er' high h'o' hee high hi-he-h'er'
you were you and   I   was me. I   remember . . .

○ *Once you have worked through your chosen speech exploring the vowels and
letting them have their own length, then speak it normally as always focusing on
communicating to someone in front of you.*

   ELECTRA: Sometimes she would let me stay while she undressed.
      Sometimes she would send the servants away and she would sit
      here while I brushed her hair. My mother. She would let me open
      jars and bottles, sniff and touch, she would let me uncover close
      things from drawers, treasures, and tell me where they came from.
      Tell me stories of a life before. Sometimes she would hold out her
      hands for me and I would rub them with oil, taking the rings off,
      one by one, feeling the deep lines on her knuckles, shifting her
      skin, gently, over veins and bone. I wanted to climb back inside her,
      always, and settle down behind her heart.

                                    *

   MAN: I'm next to you again. The old you. The you I know. That makes
      me laugh. I put my head under your coat and breathe you in. All of
      you. All over. I can almost feel you warm by my side. You're with
      me, you're with me, you're with me, you're with me! I can smell
      you. I can smell you. I remember! I remember when our kid took
      you out . . . I got you ready. Helped you put your tights on . . . you
      kept trying to put both legs in the same hole, we shouted at each
      other, we fell on the floor and we laughed. We laughed like we'd
      laughed before. Before the lump. Before the dark. You put your
      arms around me and you kissed me. You looked at me and saw
      me. The last time, the very last time you were you and I was me. I
      remember . . .

What do you notice? Is the speech easier to say; to commit to? Does it have
more flow? Do you have a sense of how the character is feeling?

Working with the vowels can be difficult at first. However, as you practise, you will find that this exercise becomes easier and therefore more helpful, so whatever is happening at the moment it is worth persevering.

When I was working on *Travesties* by Tom Stoppard at the RSC one of the actors came to me for help with a speech she had. She was finding it very difficult to engage with the speech and establish the character's mood and attitude. We worked through the vowels as I have described above and when we'd finished she said: 'That's it. I've got it. I don't want to describe it in case I lose it', and off she went. I knew exactly how she felt: she had located something and she didn't want to talk it away. She had no further problems with the speech, and her confidence in it and connection to it were evident in her performances.

So if you have any problems connecting with a piece, this is a good exercise to turn to. Also, if you find it hard to release emotionally or are often told that your work is somewhat cool then this exercise will help to free you up.

Working in this way, regularly, will also help you to build a habit of greater variety and flexibility, allowing you to mentally and vocally turn on a sixpence.

BALANCING SOUND AND SENSE

Having explored the vowels and established the flow of emotion through the centre of the text, let's look at the consonants and how you can work with these so that they shape and define without strangling the emotion or destroying its charge.

Work on articulation can make us feel that consonants are rather tiresome sounds that we have to make an effort to pronounce correctly but nothing could be further from the truth. Consonants are physically tangible. If you commit to them they can give your speech real bite and energy and like the vowels they can yield a great deal of information. You will also get strong feedback about the attitude and energy of the character and even about their physicality.

Note: Obviously if you're playing a character that mumbles or overemphasises you need to go some way in that direction, but that can come later and, to a degree, the quality of mumbling or overemphasising will be written into the text – if the writer is any good – and therefore as you commit to the text you will find that quality unfolding, without you losing the clarity or energy necessary to engage the audience.

By committing to the consonants you will move deeper into the physicality of the text and allow it to support you. The more you commit, the more you'll find and the less you'll feel self-conscious or awkward.

Connecting with the Consonants

To find energy, connection and commitment

As with the vowels, you are now going to isolate the consonants to explore their physicality and how they shape and define. The consonant-only versions of both speeches are included below. Continue working with whichever one you worked on earlier.

○ *Try saying just the consonants and allowing all the vowels to be reduced to the same neutral grunt. If a word is made up only of a vowel clap your hands or click you fingers for that word. These words are marked with a *.*

○ *Make sure that you say every consonant and, as always, focus on someone in front of you to whom you want to communicate the speech.*

Note: 'l' is pronounced differently when it comes at the start of a word or syllable from the way it is pronounced when it comes at the end of a word or syllable. An initial 'l' is called a clear 'l', and is made mostly by the movement of the tongue tip. A final 'l' is called a dark 'l' and the back of the tongue is also used. In the text they are marked as follows: clear – l   dark – ll

ELECTRA:
s-m-t-mz sh w-d l-t m st   w-ll sh ndr-st   s-m-t-mz sh w-d
Sometimes she would let me stay while she undressed. Sometimes she would

s-nd th s-vnts   w   nd sh w-d s-t h   w-ll * br-sht h   h
send the servants away and she would sit here while I brushed her hair.

m m-th   sh w-d l-t m   p-n j-z nd b-tlz sn-f nd t-ch
My mother. She would let me open jars and bottles, sniff and touch,

sh w-d l-t m   nc-v   cl-s th-ngz fr-m dr-z   tr-j-z   nd t-ll m
she would let me uncover close things   from drawers, treasures, and tell me

w   th c-m fr-m t-ll m st-r-z v * l-f b-f   s-m-t-mz sh   w-d
where they came from. Tell me stories of a life before. Sometimes she would

h-ld   t h h-ndz f   m nd * w-d   r-b th-m w-th ll t-k-ng th r-ngz f
hold out her hands for me and I would rub them with oil, taking the rings off,

n b   n f-l-ng th d-p l-nz n h   n-kllz sh-ft-ng h   sk-n g-nt-l
one by one, feeling the deep lines on her knuckles,   shifting   her skin, gently,

v v-nz nd b-n * w-nt-d t cl-m b-ck ns-d h   llw-z nd s-tll
over veins and bone. I wanted to climb back inside her, always, and settle

d-n b-h-nd h   h-t
down behind her heart.

*

MAN:
m n-kst t y g-n th lld y th y * n   th-t m-ks m
I'm next to you again. The old you. The you I know. That makes me

l-f * p-t m h-d nd y c-t nd br-th y n ll v y ll v
laugh. I put my head under your coat and breathe you in. All of you. All over.

* c-n llm-st f-ll y w-m b m s-d y   w-th m y   w-th m y
I can almost feel you warm by my side. You're with me, you're with me, you're

w-th m y   w-th m * c-n sm-ll y * c-n sm-ll y * r-m-mb
with me, you're with me! I can smell you. I can smell you. I remember!

* r-m-mb w-n * k-d t-k y   t * g-t y r-d h-llpt y p-t
I remember when our kid took you out . . . I got you ready. Helped you put

y t-ts n y k-pt tr-ng t p-t b-th l-gz n th s-m h-ll w
your tights on . . . you kept trying to put both legs in the same hole, we

sh-td t ch th w f-ll n th fl   nd w l-ft w l-ft
shouted at each other, we fell on the floor and we laughed. We laughed

l-k w-d l-ft b-f b-f th l-mp b-f th d-k y p-t y
like we'd laughed before. Before the lump. Before the dark. You put your

mz r-nd m nd y k-st m y l-kt t m nd s m th
arms around me and you kissed me. You looked at me and saw me. The

l-st t-m th v l-st t-m y w y nd * wz m * r-m-mb
last time, the very last time you were you and I was me. I remember . . .

I know this can be a very frustrating exercise to do. You can never get going.
But it does show you how the consonants work, how they cut up the flow of
the vowels. You can also feel how physical the consonants are. The act of
speaking is very much a physical, tangible event.

○ *Now read the whole speech through quite normally with your focus, as always, on*
   communicating it to someone in front of you.

ELECTRA: Sometimes she would let me stay while she undressed.
Sometimes she would send the servants away and she would sit
here while I brushed her hair. My mother. She would let me open

jars and bottles, sniff and touch, she would let me uncover close things from drawers, treasures, and tell me where they came from. Tell me stories of a life before. Sometimes she would hold out her hands for me and I would rub them with oil, taking the rings off, one by one, feeling the deep lines on her knuckles, shifting her skin, gently, over veins and bone. I wanted to climb back inside her, always, and settle down behind her heart.

*

MAN: I'm next to you again. The old you. The you I know. That makes me laugh. I put my head under your coat and breathe you in. All of you. All over. I can almost feel you warm by my side. You're with me, you're with me, you're with me, you're with me! I can smell you. I can smell you. I remember! I remember when our kid took you out . . . I got you ready. Helped you put your tights on . . . you kept trying to put both legs in the same hole, we shouted at each other, we fell on the floor and we laughed. We laughed like we'd laughed before. Before the lump. Before the dark. You put your arms around me and you kissed me. You looked at me and saw me. The last time, the very last time you were you and I was me. I remember . . .

What do you notice? Were you more aware of the consonants? Did your lips and tongue feel more alive? Did you feel more committed to the speech, as if you really owned the words?

Whatever you discovered, this is an excellent exercise to practise: it will encourage you to physically commit to the text and will bring energy and conviction to your work.

Mouthing the Text

To develop commitment, confidence and energy

This is another great exercise for getting in touch with the consonants: it is very useful if you are feeling self-conscious or unsure about a scene.

○ Mouth the text silently. Take your time to shape each consonant fully but without exaggerating.

○ Then, speak the text quietly, keeping your attention on the physical movements of the lips and tongue rather than on the sound and, as always, focus on communicating it to someone in front of you. Remember this is not about effort but rather about commitment, about being fully with each sound as you say it.

This will help to anchor you in a speech. It will also help you to stop listening to yourself because your focus will be on what you feel rather than on what you hear.

The more you focus on the physical act of speaking, and commit to that, the more you will find out about the character and situation. The spoken words of the text are, as I mentioned earlier, one of the behaviours of the character and by fully entering into this behaviour you will experience the character viscerally rather than intellectually.

'*But what about subtext?*' I hear you cry. '*Often, characters don't mean what they say; often they are not connected to what they are saying!*' This is true, and we will deal with subtext later. The difference between real life and a play is that with a play we start with the words. That is what the playwright gives us; and the rhythms and sounds he/she uses are a rich mine of information, which we can absorb through doing the work suggested here. This does not stop your character, later in the process, from having a different intention from what they are saying, but even if they do, the words are still there, they are still spoken and they still have to be heard by the audience.

All the work on the vowels and consonants is about paying more attention to what is there. Then, the sounds can support both feeling and meaning in the way that they do when we talk in real life. The text will feel more natural and yet at the same time you will be stretched to inhabit the rhythmic movement of it more completely. As always, once you have explored the text in this way, trust yourself and let all the work take care of itself.

CONNECTING WITH THE WORDS AND IMAGES

Having explored the structures and sounds in the text, and the rhythms these give, we are now going to focus on the words and the images behind them and on how to explore and connect with these.

Levels of Meaning

There is more than one level of meaning where words are concerned. Often in rehearsal the focus is put on the first level, and when this has been attended to, people think that they've finished the work on meaning. This is not the case. Indeed, the first level of meaning barely gives us half the story.

This first level is what may be called the *dictionary* level. This is the level at which words have *agreed* meanings, without which we couldn't use them to communicate. It's vital that we all agree that the word 'door' means a door. If I think the word 'door' means a table and you think it means a floor and someone else thinks it means a carpet, we are not going to get very far!

However, the crucial and exciting level in terms of acting is what may be called the *associative* one. At this second level, words become very personal. They do not mean the same to everyone. Let us take the word 'grief', for example. At the *dictionary* level we may all agree that this is the feeling of great sorrow we experience when we suffer a loss, particularly perhaps when someone dies. However, if we start to look at what the word 'grief' means to us personally, what it evokes for us, there is no longer agreement. The word will mean different things to each one of us, depending on our experiences of loss and on our personality: our way of dealing with experiences of loss, our way of grieving. Suddenly, the meaning splinters into as many interpretations as there are people. This is why a role will change depending on the actor playing it. Each actor will filter the words through his/her own experience, and, as a result, different aspects of the character will be highlighted.

So how do we make a connection with the associative level of meaning? Words are rather like railway engines and our associations are rather like railway carriages: when we speak in life, the 'carriages' are automatically attached to the 'engines'. However, with text what we have is a great many 'engines' with no 'carriages' attached, so we need to back up those 'engines' and hitch them onto our particular 'carriages': in other words, our particular associations.

This does not lessen the character by reducing it to our experience and personality; rather it *links* us with the character. Our experience informs the words, but also, as we begin to notice the specific words the character uses and link our associations with them, we are pulled into the world of the character, because their choice of words and their ordering of those words will be different from ours. In attending to the words and connecting with them we are taken beyond ourselves into the internal world of the character.

Three Times Through

To explore and connect with the words

The following exercise is the best one I know for connecting with the words at the associative level. It was created out of desperation many years ago when working with a young actor. I asked her to take the text in tiny chunks and repeat each one slowly and quietly three times. She did this and suddenly she connected. I have used this exercise a great deal since with actors of all ages, experiences and training, and it has never failed.

Below are two more speeches: one from *Shimmer* by Linda McLean and the other from *Mojo* by Jez Butterworth. Again, they are included with brief explanations so that you can read them through before going on to the exercise. As previously, it would be useful to swiftly go through *Walking the Sentences*, *Changing Direction* and *Changing Chairs*, *Exploring the Vowels* and *Exploring the Consonants*, or *Mouthing the Text* before going on to the new exercises.

Shimmer: Petal is on the way to Iona in Scotland with her mother and grandmother. Her grandmother believes that if they get there in time for midsummer, Petal, who has a terminal disease, will be cured. They have been stranded by flooding and taken refuge in a B&B. Petal is talking to herself. She is reinventing her past: imagining that her grandfather had been around when she was a child and had stopped her father from leaving.

> PETAL: . . . and in that instant my grandpa decides that even though he doesn't know my father as well as he'd like to, he is going to help him. Partly he's helping him because his daughter loves him and he wants her to be happy but part of it is because he thinks they might have a connection, given time and a bit of effort. So he stands in front of him and places his hand on his shoulder so that my dad has to look into his face. My grandpa looks straight at him and he says, 'This is the hardest time. It gets easier. I'll help you.' Not knowing that no one has ever said that to my father, not his own father, or grandfather, no one. And he was running away because he couldn't do it all on his own. Right there in the hallway he crumples and as he goes down, he sees me and realises that, of course, the one thing he's always wanted, was his daughter, and he swears there and then that he'll never leave us.[11]

Mojo: Baby is talking to Silver Johnny, who is hanging upside down in the middle of the room, gagged. Baby's father has been killed the night before and Baby has just avenged his death. Silver Johnny is a young singer and was the cause of the disagreement between Baby's father and his murderer. The play is set in 1958.

> BABY: . . . I was about nine, bit younger, and my dad tells me we're driving to the country for the day.
>
> He's got this half-share in this caff at the time, and it was doing really badly, so he was always really busy working day and night, so like, this was totally out of the blue.
>
> So I got in his van with him, and we drive off and I notice that in the front of the cab there's this bag of sharp knives. And like, a saw and a big meat cleaver.
>
> And I thought 'This is it. He's going to kill me. He's going to take me off and kill me once and for all.' And I sat there in silence all the way to Wales and I knew that day I was about to die.
>
> So we drive till it goes dark, and Dad pulls the van into this field. And he switches off the lights. And we sit there in silence. And there's all these cows in the field, watching us. And suddenly Dad slams his foot down and we ram this fucking great cow clean over the top of the van. And it tears off the bonnet and makes a great dent in the top, but it was dead all right. See we'd gone all the way to Wales to rustle us a cow. For the caff.[12]

Read through the directions first and then work through whichever speech you have chosen. I have divided each speech up to give you some idea of the best length for the chunks, since this is crucial to the success of the exercise. In some places I have gone with the phrase length and in some places I have divided the phrase up into smaller units. It is vital that the units are short. If they are too long some words will get lost, whereas if you keep them short every word will have a chance to resonate and connect with you.

○ *Sit comfortably in a chair or on the floor, with the text in front of you.*

○ *Look at the first chunk, then shut your eyes and slowly and quietly repeat it three times without overemphasis and without deciding how to say it.*

Note: This is the only exercise where you do not focus on talking to or communicating with anyone else. Instead you focus inward, allowing the words to resonate within you.

○ *Take your time so that the words have a chance to sink in.*

○ *Then, open your eyes and look at the next chunk of the text.*

○ *Shut your eyes and repeat that chunk quietly three times, again taking your time.*

○ *Continue in the same way through the text, saying each chunk three times and then leaving that chunk and moving on to the next.*

○ *Work quietly but avoid whispering. Take your time so that you can absorb the words and allow them to register and resonate. Connection will happen automatically.*

PETAL: . . . and in that instant/ my grandpa/decides that/ even though/ he doesn't know/ my father/ as well/ as he'd like to,/ he is going to/ help him./ Partly/ he's helping him/ because/ his daughter/ loves him/ and he wants her/ to be happy/ but part of it/ is because/ he thinks/ they might have/ a connection,/ given time/ and a bit of effort./ So he stands/ in front of him/ and places his hand/ on his shoulder/ so that my dad/ has to look/ into his face./ My grandpa/ looks straight at him/ and he says,/ 'This is the hardest time./ It gets easier./ I'll help you.'/ Not knowing/ that no one/ has ever said that/ to my father,/ not his own father,/ or grandfather,/ no one./ And he was running away/ because he couldn't do it/ all on his own./ Right there/ in the hallway/ he crumples/ and as he goes down,/ he sees me/ and realises that,/ of course,/ the one thing/ he's always wanted,/ was his daughter,/ and he swears/ there and then/ that he'll never leave us.

*

BABY: . . . I was about nine,/ bit younger,/ and my dad tells me/ we're driving to the country/ for the day./

He's got this half-share/ in this caff/ at the time,/ and it was doing/ really badly,/ so he was always/ really busy/ working day and night,/ so like,/ this was totally/ out of the blue./

So I got in his van with him,/ and we drive off/ and I notice that/ in the front of the cab/ there's this bag/ of sharp knives./ And like,/ a saw/ and a big meat cleaver./

And I thought/ 'This is it./ He's going to kill me./ He's going to take me off/ and kill me/ once and for all.'/ And I sat there/ in silence/ all the way to Wales/ and I knew that day/ I was about to die./

So we drive/ till it goes dark,/ and Dad pulls the van/ into this field./ And he switches off the lights./ And we sit there/ in silence./ And there's all these cows/ in the field,/ watching us./ And suddenly/ Dad slams his foot down/ and we ram/ this fucking great cow/ clean over/ the top of the van./ And it tears off/ the bonnet/ and makes a great dent/ in the top,/ but it was dead all right./ See/ we'd gone all the way/ to Wales/ to rustle us a cow./ For the caff.

What did you discover from that exercise? Did you notice how deeply you were able to connect with each chunk when you gave yourself the time?

This exercise is great to do at any stage in rehearsals or a run. If you do it at the beginning of rehearsals it will help you connect with the text quickly. It will also take you deep into the world of the character: since the language a person uses comes from their internal imagery and reflects their internal world, their internal psychology. This exercise will also help you to learn the text, although that should never be your focus of attention when you're doing the exercise. It is simply that you will make a deep and accurate connection early on and because you have associated the words with your own experience they will be easier to remember.

Later in rehearsals, this exercise takes you even deeper into the text, and brings to your attention words and phrases that may be crucial but that have, somehow, slipped by unnoticed.

During a run it can freshen up your connection with the words and bring the whole text alive for you again.

Physicalising the Words

To further explore, connect with and commit to the words

This is another great exercise for connecting with the words. It is a more active exercise than *Three Times Through* and so they make a good pair. It is based on an exercise of Cicely Berry's, but again I can only describe how I use it. Use the same text as you used for the last exercise.

○ *Prop the text up on a chair, or photocopy it and stick it to the wall, so that you don't have to hold it.*

○ *Stand in front of the text and explore each word separately. As you say each word make a physical movement that, for you, expresses the meaning of that word. The movement does not have to be clever, creative or witty, and it does not need to make sense to anyone else. This is exploratory work for you, so you simply have to fully commit, with your whole body, to whatever physical movement you make.*

○ *With some words you may find you only need to say them and do the movement once and you feel you have made a connection; with others you may find you need to explore them several times. Always explore by saying the word and simultaneously doing the movement rather than stopping and thinking!*

63

○ Include all the little words like 'in', 'the', 'a' and 'is' for these have their place in the journey of the sentence and the thought.

○ Accept the fact that the text will be broken up – you are exploring each word rather than working on the speech as a whole.

Note: Sometimes you may find that you can't completely connect with a word and you may have to leave it hanging and perhaps go and look it up in a dictionary or talk to someone about it.

○ Keep the exercise light and playful, make your gestures big and fully commit to them and ignore your inner critic [see page 241]!

How was that? Did you find that you had to search more deeply for what a word meant to you in order to find any movement at all? Did you notice how even the small words were important and moved the speech on?

This exercise is excellent for exploring the journey from word to word as well as for deepening the connection with each word. It can be a very liberating exercise that helps you to be much braver with the text. Play with it as a child might: enjoying the physical movement and the exploration of the word.

Three Times Through and *Physicalising the Words* allow you to make deep connections with each word so that when you flow the text together you can access those connections at speed and colour the words without being laborious or overemphatic.

STEPPING STONES THROUGH SPEECHES AND SCENES

We often worry about shaping a speech or scene. Certainly these do need to be shaped, but too often we do it externally, making analytical choices that can become frozen and lifeless.

However, if you pay attention to the words one by one: connecting with each word as you say it rather than lingering on the one before or anticipating the one to come, the twists and turns of the speech will take care of themselves.

Often certain words in the text hijack the whole. So, a strong word like sorrow may make all the words around it sorrowful whether they are or not. Similarly, if we decide a speech is a funny speech or that someone is angry during a speech, it can wash the whole speech in the same colour so that it ceases to travel anywhere. It becomes a blob of emotion and there is really no point in the audience listening after the first sentence since they are simply going to get the same information throughout.

So forget that a speech or scene is any *kind* of speech or scene. People on the whole do not stay stuck in just one emotional place. In reality they are very mercurial. Someone may be grief-stricken at the death of a partner or close friend or family member and yet, in the process of remembering a past time spent with that person, they may describe that event with joy, their voice and facial expression changing completely. You can be just as mercurial when you're acting. So, instead of pinning a speech down, if you stay with each word and allow its weight and colour to affect you, which it may do differently every night, you will end up with a far more varied and interesting whole.

Staying with each word does not mean stressing each word. That is where people often go wrong. Staying with each word means just staying with the act of saying each word, connecting with it as you say it and letting it have its unique colour. Now it's true that it is difficult to do this at speed at first, which is why you need to practise the *Three Times Through* and *Physicalising the Words* exercises and all the vowel and consonant work. If you do this you will then find you can talk at a perfectly normal speed and yet have time to rest your attention on each word. It is just a matter of learning to be specific.

Again, it was Cicely Berry who first made me aware of the potential here. She told me of her time working with Peter Brook and how he used to ask actors to 'attend to the word'. The more I thought about this phrase and played with it, the more I understood how brilliant it was.

Stepping Stones

To allow each word to have its own place and colour within the journey of the whole

This is another exercise which can help you to treat each word individually. It is best done after you have worked through all the previous exercises in this section and have a good knowledge of a speech or scene.

For now, continue with the same speech as you used for the previous two exercises. Read through the directions below before you start.

○ As always, imagine someone in front of you to whom you are talking.

○ Imagine each word as a stepping stone on the ground. Imagine you have a lot of choices of stones/words, so you have to choose where to step.

○ Choose your first 'stone' and step onto it as you say that word and let it have its full colour, unaffected by any words that follow. Then, look around for the next word/stone.

○ As you step onto this next one and say the word, let it be unaffected by either the word before or the word afterwards, but rather have its own full colour.

○ Continue in the same way with each word as if you are choosing the route of your journey across the room, from the beginning of the speech to the end and allowing each stone/word to be a completely unique step in that journey.

○ You will need to go slowly at first to be sure of connecting with each word.

What do you notice? Can you feel how much more individual the words are? Can you feel how much variety there is?

○ Now go through the speech at a more normal pace, but keep the individuality of the words as you do so.

This can be an excellent way to warm up a speech, before rehearsal or performance, especially if you work with the sense of choosing each word freshly.

INTERNAL GEOGRAPHY

When, in life, we refer to a place or a person we have a sense of where that place is or the situation in which we encounter that person. There is a specific geography. Even with abstract concepts we have a setting or reference in our heads. We have an internal geography, if you like. The words do not just float about.

However, when we come to a piece of text we have no internal geography unless we create it. We may refer to a place, we may even decide with the director and our fellow actors as to where that place is in relation to the stage, but it has no concrete reality for us. All the places and people and ideas float around in our heads rather like soup.

So we need to create a precise internal geography, which is what this next sequence of exercises enables you to do.

Geography Exercise

To anchor the places and people and ideas, which you refer to in a text, giving them a reality and relationship

Use any of the speeches you have worked on so far in this chapter. As always, read through the directions below before you start.

○ *Collect some objects. They should be of different sizes, weights, shapes and textures. I tend to use what is to hand in the room, e.g. a purse, some keys, a scarf or glove, a plastic cup or bottle, some string, a roll of tape, a book, a pencil. The more arbitrary the choice, the better. Just make sure that nothing you use is breakable!*

○ *Place the objects in front of you either on the floor or on a table. You are going to speak the text picking up an object for a key word or phrase.*

For example, if you are working on Petal's speech from *Shimmer* you may pick up one object up on 'and in that instant' and another on 'my grandpa'. Then, having put these objects down, you may pick another object up on 'decides' and another on 'that even though'. There is no right way to do this exercise. Whether you pick up an object for each key word or for each key phrase depends on what seems right to you at that point.

○ *Imagine that you are showing the word or phrase to the person you are talking to.*

○ *Make no attempt to choose relevant objects, simply pick up whatever comes to hand.*

○ *As before, imagine someone in front of you whom you are truly trying to communicate with.*

○ *The more playful you are with this exercise, the more you use the objects to represent the words and communicate what you mean to the person you imagine talking to, the better.*

How was that? Did you notice that you had more sense of the words in relationship to each other? Did you notice how the objects helped you to be more specific?

This exercise works because it physically recreates the mental act of choosing a word or phrase and using it to communicate with another person, to show them what you mean. Suddenly, the word or phrase becomes specific; it has a relationship with you and with the other words or phrases in the text.

This exercise is easier to do once you know the text, but you can use it in the early stages if you take it very slowly.

This is a great exercise to use when working on a scene with a partner or partners. Sit with the collection of objects between you and take it in turns to use the objects as each person speaks their lines. In this way you really find out how the language goes back and forth between the characters.

Museum Visit

To further anchor the places, people and ideas, which you refer to in a text, giving them a reality and relationship

This is a more mobile exercise and suits some speeches better than the more static exercise above. It's good if you want to energise a speech and make bolder choices.

My preference, however, is to use both exercises since they lead to slightly different discoveries. Use the same speech as you used for the previous exercise.

I call the exercise *Museum Visit* because you imagine that all the words and ideas in your speech are exhibited in the room, as they would be in a museum.

O *Move around the room touching, picking up or pointing to an object for a key word or phrase. Still have the intention of really communicating with someone as if you are taking them round because you want to show them what you are talking about, to take them on a journey through the speech with you.*

O *Sometimes you may choose objects that are near to each other, but feel free to run across the room to touch, pick up or point to something if that feels right. Need to choose the objects to get your words across. Want to move around the room taking the person you imagine talking to on a journey through your world.*

Note: If you are working with other people, you can actually lead them around the room.

How was that? Could you again feel the relationship between words? Did you notice the energy you gained from needing to move around the room to show someone the people and places and ideas that you were referring to?

This second exercise particularly tends to remove woodenness and encourage a natural flow of communication.

Summary

You've now looked at every aspect of the text: how sentence and other punctuation structures give you the thought rhythms of the character; how the vowels carry you to the emotional heart of a speech; how the consonants give energy, commitment and precision; how connecting with the words and images takes you deep into the psychology of the character and links your inner world with that of the character and the play.

Hopefully, you have found that these exercises enable you to harvest an enormous amount of information from the text and to make deep connections with it. Remember that it isn't necessary to consciously hold on to what you have discovered. If you've really committed to this work physically, if you've fully experienced it, you won't need to try to remember it because it will be in your physical and emotional memory. If, however, you've just read through the exercises and thought about them without doing them, they won't work at all. You have been warned!

In the next chapter we will look at classical text and at how these and other exercises can be used to unravel the seeming complexities of Shakespeare, his contemporaries, and Jacobean and Restoration playwrights.

In later chapters we will look at scene shape and dynamic, so if you are feeling I might have left out any work on text that you want, I am sure it will come later.

For now, here is a summary of the main points and exercises from this chapter.

Remember
Connection before fluency
Discover by doing
Stop acting, start talking

Exploring Structures and Rhythms
Walking the Sentences
Changing Direction
Changing Chairs
Phrase by Phrase

Discovering the Emotional Flow
  Connecting with the Vowels

Balancing Sound and Sense
  Connecting with the Consonants
  Mouthing the Text

Connecting with the Words and Images
  Three Times Through
  Physicalising the Words

Stepping Stones through Speeches and Scenes
  Stepping Stones

Internal Geography
  Geography Exercise
  Museum Visit

And How the Hell Do I Say This?

HANDLING CLASSICAL TEXT

Classical text can seem daunting – the strangeness and complexity of the language; the apparent remoteness of the characters, situations and stories; the seeming irrelevance to the modern world. So how do you handle it? How do you become comfortable with its complexity and get around its remoteness? How do you honour its language and form and yet, at the same time, own it, so that it becomes truthful and relevant, both for you and the audience?

As with modern text, you need to notice what's there; pay close attention to the structures and rhythms, the sounds, words and images. The more you can see these as supports rather than barriers, the more classical texts will open up for you, becoming exciting and invigorating to perform.

It is also important to connect with the underlying predicaments that the characters as *human beings* find themselves in. That is where the relevance lies: in the common human experiences of love and loss, ambition, fear, hatred, power, greed, vulnerability, courage, betrayal, heroism, compassion and so on – all of which are present in our lives and which infuse the stories that fill our newspapers and televisions screens on a daily basis.

The challenge always, with any text, is to breathe life into the language, situations and characters. If you can find the truth of human experience at the core, you'll be able to play the characters convincingly and the audience will want to watch them. It is a question of connection for both actor and audience.

The most important point to remember about classical text is not to be afraid of it. Yes, on the surface it's different. It can look complicated, it can seem incomprehensible and remote from 'real life' as you experience it, but once you engage with it in the ways suggested below you will find that you can not only handle it but also get a great deal of pleasure out of doing so.

In this chapter we are going to explore the text itself: its structures and rhythms, its sound and language patterns, its imagery and how these can become clues and supports. In a later chapter we will look at how you can contact the underlying situations so that you can find the relevance to your own experience. We will look at Jacobean and Restoration drama as well as Marlowe, Jonson, Wilde and Coward, but I will use Shakespeare's text for the exercises because that is the classical text you will most usually encounter.

Shakespeare's Text

Shakespeare's plays deal with human emotions and predicaments that are as true for us today as they were for the original audiences. What's more, his writing is such an accurate reflection of the way people think, feel and speak that it is breathtaking. But it can be difficult to appreciate this at first, owing to the complexity of the structure and the strangeness of some of the language. Once you have explored his text layer by layer and come to understand and feel able to handle it, you will find that he supports and stretches you as an actor. He really helps you to fly if you are willing to trust him and go with him.

As with the previous chapter we are going to focus on one element at a time, exploring each without bothering about any other elements. In this way you will get the chance to embed your discoveries and they will then stay with you even when you are focusing elsewhere. I cannot emphasise how important this way of working is. Firstly, it is easier and far more pleasurable. Secondly, you get a much clearer, deeper and more lasting sense of each element of the text, which will stay with you in performance so you can then simply focus on engaging with the other actors.

EXPLORING STRUCTURES AND RHYTHMS

The last chapter explored the structure and rhythm that sentence length and punctuation give. This chapter looks at the additional structure and rhythm that *verse* gives and at how the sense and verse rhythms weave together. Most of the chapter will focus on verse, so it is worth highlighting here the differences between prose and verse in terms of how this affects the way you work on them.

Dealing with Prose and Verse

Prose

Since prose has an *irregular rhythm* that *cannot be recognisably repeated* and *the end of the prose line is not fixed*, the rhythm and structure in prose comes from the *phrasing*, which is usually marked by the punctuation. Read aloud the prose examples below, noticing how the differing phrase lengths dictate the rhythm and structure of each piece. The first is from *A Mouthful of Birds* by Caryl Churchill and David Lan and the second from Shakespeare's *As You Like It*. As I said, the phrase lengths are dictated by the punctuation, and to accentuate these I have added double forward slashes.

> PAUL: When you stop being in love the day is very empty.// It's not just the one you loved who isn't exciting anymore,// nothing is exciting.// Nothing is even bearable.// So it wasn't till then that I left my wife and my job.// I can't stand small pleasures.// If there's nothing there's room for something to come.[13]

*

> ROSALIND: Love is merely a madness;// and,// I tell you,// deserves as well a dark house and a whip as madmen do;// and the reason why they are not so punished and cured is that the lunacy is so ordinary that the whippers are in love too.// Yet I profess curing it by counsel.[14]

The exercises in the last chapter on **Walking the Sentences**, **Changing Direction** and **Changing Chairs** will all enable you to explore and identify the rhythms within classical prose just as much as they do in modern prose. They are wonderful ways of getting to grips with such text, of breaking through the complexity so that it becomes manageable.

Verse

Since verse, by contrast, has a *regular pattern* that *can be recognisably repeated* and *the line ending is fixed*, the structure and rhythm comes from the *particular rhythmic pattern* used. Read aloud the verse examples below, being aware of the regular pattern and fixed line ending. The strong beats are marked in bold. If you gently emphasise those, the line will take care of itself and you will feel the rhythm. The first piece you may well know as a popular nursery rhyme. The second is the first four lines from a poem called *The Dead Beat* by Wilfred Owen and the third is from Shakespeare's *Romeo and Juliet*.

Humpty Dumpty sat on a wall
Humpty Dumpty had a great fall
All the king's horses and all the king's men
Couldn't put Humpty together again.

*

He dropped, – more sullenly than wearily,
Lay stupid like a cod, heavy like meat,
And none of us could kick him to his feet;
Just blinked at my revolver, blearily.

*

If I profane with my unworthiest hand
This holy shrine, the gentle sin is this:
My lips, two blushing pilgrims, ready stand
To smooth that rough touch with a tender kiss.

The exercises later in the chapter – *Moving the Metre, Walking the Verse* and *Exploring the Caesura* – will enable you to explore the rhythms and structures within the verse. To explore how the sense rhythms and structures interact with those of the verse you can use *Walking the Sentences, Using Colons and Semi-colons, Changing Direction* and *Changing Chairs*. Later you will have the chance to work through a Shakespeare speech using all these exercises, so that you can experience for yourself how they can help you.

Free verse, in which much modern poetry is written, *does not* have a regular rhythmic pattern, which can be recognisably repeated, but it does structure the lines on the page in a particular way chosen by the poet. Read through the example below being aware of how the writer has chosen to lay out the lines. It is part of a poem called 'The Horses' by Ted Hughes.

I climbed through woods in the hour-before-dawn dark.
Evil air, a frost-making stillness,

Not a leaf, not a bird –
A world cast in frost. I came out above the wood

Where my breath left tortuous statues in the iron light.
But the valleys were draining the darkness

Till the moorline – blackening dregs of the brightening grey –
Halved the sky ahead. And I saw the horses.

Some modern plays are written in free verse – for example, *Further Than the Furthest Thing* by Zinnie Harris, *stoning mary* by debbie tucker green and *strangers, babies* by Linda McLean. The exercises you would use for free verse are **Walking the Sentences, Changing Direction, Changing Chairs** and *Walking the Verse*.

Shifts between Verse and Prose

Whether a character talks in prose or verse, throughout a play or at certain points; whether whole scenes are written in prose or verse, these are choices made by the writer, so always mark these choices in the text and particular notice any *shifts* between the two. Ask yourself: *'Why might my character be using verse/prose here? Why might he/she be shifting from one to the other?'* There is no need to come up with immediate answers and there is certainly no single correct answer. If you have noticed which your character is using, you will find your own reason for that, and for any shift between the two, as you rehearse.

Iambic Pentameter

Most, though not all, of Shakespeare's verse is written in iambic pentameter. An iamb is a two-beat rhythm, where the first beat is *weakly* stressed and the second beat is *strongly* stressed.

'Pent' means five and 'metre' means rhythm. In other words, each line consists of five iambs, or 'weak-strong' pairs. I use 'ti' to denote the weak beat and '**tum**' to denote the strong beat. So a totally regular line in iambic pentameter would be written like this:

> ti-**tum** ti-**tum** ti-**tum** ti-**tum** ti-**tum**

This rhythm is very flexible and much closer to modern speech rhythms than, for example, the metre you find in nursery rhymes, limericks or ballads, which tend to have only three or four strong beats per line. Below I have given an example of each and of a regular iambic line.

Nursery Rhyme:
> **Hump**ty **Dump**ty **sat** on a **wall**
> **Hump**ty **Dump**ty **had** a great **fall** . . .

*

Limerick:

> There **was** an old **la**dy from **Hull**
> Who **found** all her **food** rather **dull** . . .

*

Ballad:

> There **lived** a **wife** at **Usher's Well**
> And a **wealthy wife** was **she** . . .

*

Iambic Pentameter:

> If **I** pro**fane** with **my** un**worth**iest **hand**
> This **ho**ly **shrine**, the **gen**tle **sin** is **this** . . .

○ *Speak each example out loud, putting the emphasis on the syllables in bold type, which represent the strong beats in that particular rhythm.*

○ *Notice how the extra strong beat in the iambic pentameter line makes it sound less predictable.*

Now there is nothing wrong with the rhythms of the other three in terms of the purpose they serve. They tended to be passed on orally and were much easier to memorise because the rhythm was strong and simple. The demands of drama, however, are for greater subtlety and flexibility, and the iambic pentameter allows for the twists and turns of thought and feeling needed.

So, if this rhythm is wonderfully flexible, why explore it at all? Why not get on with speaking the text and let the metre take care of itself? Because the rhythm acts like the bar count in music. It holds the text together. It underpins it. And, in fact, because this regular rhythm is there, the sound and sense rhythms can work in *counterpoint* to it. This produces a wonderful tension.

The task, therefore, is to establish the metric rhythm so strongly that you know it will be there when you return your attention to the sense and sound rhythms, just as the singer or musician needs to have the bar count strongly established so that, when they focus on singing or playing the melody, the bar count is still there underneath.

Moving the Metre

Stage One – To develop a strong sense of the iambic pentameter rhythm

It is best to start by exploring the rhythm in isolation before turning to Shakespeare's text. As in the previous chapter, the exploration is physical. This helps you to get the rhythm into your body and is much more effective and enjoyable than sitting and grappling with it mentally.

❍ *To mark the rhythm, say 'ti-**tum**' out loud and shift your weight from foot to foot: shifting on each weak beat and letting your foot hit the floor on each strong beat.*

❍ *Commit to the movement with your whole body as you might if you were responding to a rap or any dance music with a strong beat. Whatever you do, avoid being tentative or reverent!*

> ti-**tum** ti-**tum** ti-**tum** ti-**tum** ti-**tum** [*silent ti-tum*]
> *lift* hit *lift* hit *lift* hit *lift* hit *lift* hit *lift* hit

❍ *Practise several lines in this rhythm, with a silent 'ti-**tum**' between each line to separate it from the next. Continue shifting your weight on the silent beat.*

❍ *Note: It is important to separate each line from the next with a silent 'ti-**tum**' to keep each line in tact and so that you begin to have a sense of the verse shape, which we will look at in more detail later.*

> ti-**tum** ti-**tum** ti-**tum** ti-**tum** ti-**tum** [*silent beat*]
> ti-**tum** ti-**tum** ti-**tum** ti-**tum** ti-**tum** [*silent beat*]
> ti-**tum** ti-**tum** ti-**tum** ti-**tum** ti-**tum** [*silent beat*]
> ti-**tum** ti-**tum** ti-**tum** ti-**tum** ti-**tum** [*silent beat*]

❍ *Commit fully to the rhythm and to expressing it physically with confidence and sureness. You'll find that if you bash the strong '**tum**' beats out firmly, the weak 'ti' beats will take care of themselves.*

❍ *Keep playing with this until you feel utterly comfortable with the rhythm. Let it be playful and energetic as it might be if you were dancing or playing a sport.*

By working in this way you firmly establish the rhythm for yourself so that when you begin to work with text that rhythm is easy to hold on to.

Stage Two – To explore the iambic pentameter rhythm in the text

At this stage it's best to completely ignore the *sense stress*, which is pattern of stress that the *sense* gives, and instead simply pour the lines into the iambic pentameter rhythm, you have already established. For example, the *sense stress* of the following line from *Twelfth Night* would be:

Make me a **wil**low **cab**in at your **gate,**

Whereas the *metric stress*, dictated by the iambic pentameter rhythm, would be:

Make **me** a **wil**low **cab**in at your **gate,**

So the stress shifts from 'Make' to 'me'.

The reason for ignoring the sense stress and focusing on the metric stress is that it is the simplest and quickest way to feel the metric rhythm in the text. Once you have been through a speech or scene several times, pouring it completely into the rhythm, you can be sure that that beat will remain underneath the text when you return to the sense stress. What's more you will feel where the sense and metric stress flow together and where they run counter to each other. This can give interesting acting clues. Often, where they flow together the character is in greater harmony with him/herself whereas where they run counter to each other, the character may be more at odds with themselves and there will certainly be a greater tension. Also, as a result of the metric and sense stress running counter to each other, a word can be given greater emphasis, as is the case in the above example, where greater emphasis is thrown onto 'Make'. You will also find times when the iambic pentameter rhythm seems to break down completely for a few lines. This may well echo a breaking down for the character in some way.

To keep things simple I have chosen two short speeches – one female and one male – for you to use to explore the exercises in this chapter. Then, you can apply the exercises to a speech or scene of your choice. The speeches used here are one of Viola's from *Twelfth Night* and Claudio's from *Measure for Measure*. They are printed below together with a short description of the situation, who the character is talking to and what they are talking about. Read through which ever you intend to work on and then move on to the exercises.

Twelfth Night [Act 1 Scene 5]: Viola has been shipwrecked in a foreign country and to protect herself she has taken on the disguise of a boy and found a job as a servant to Count Orsino, with whom she has fallen in love. Orsino has sent her to woo Olivia, whom he loves. Olivia, however, says she cannot love Orsino. Fired by her own love, Viola tells Olivia that if she were Orsino she would not accept Olivia's refusal and, in the speech below, she describes what she would do to woo Olivia.

VIOLA: If I did love you in my master's flame,
   With such a suff'ring, such a deadly life,
   In your denial I would find no sense;
   I would not understand it.

OLIVIA: Why, what would you?

VIOLA: Make me a willow cabin at your gate,
   And cry upon your soul within the house;
   Write loyal cantons of contemnèd love,
   And sing them loud even in the dead of night;
   Hallo your name to the reverberate hills,
   And make the babbling gossip of the air
   Cry out 'Olivia!' O you should not rest
   Between the elements of air and earth
   But you should pity me!

OLIVIA: You might do much.[15]

Measure for Measure [Act 3 Scene 1]: Claudio is in prison in Vienna, sentenced to death for getting his girlfriend pregnant before they are married. His sister, who is intending to become a nun, has been to plead for his life. She has learned that only by sleeping with Angelo, who is in charge of Vienna in the absence of the Duke, can she save her brother. She returns to her brother and tells him to prepare to die, since she feels she cannot lose her virginity and risk her soul to save his life.

CLAUDIO: Ay, but to die, and go we know not where,
   To lie in cold obstruction and to rot;
   This sensible warm motion to become
   A kneaded clod; and the delighted spirit
   To bathe in fiery floods, or to reside
   In thrilling region of thick-ribbèd ice,
   To be imprisoned in the viewless winds
   And blown with restless violence round about
   The pendent world; or to be worse than worst
   Of those that lawless and incertain thought
   Imagine howling, 'tis too horrible.
   The weariest and most loathèd worldly life
   That age, ache, penury, and imprisonment
   Can lay on nature is a paradise
   To what we fear of death.[16]

○ *Before you add the text, shift weight to the rhythm again, to remind yourself of it.*

> ti-**tum** ti-**tum** ti-**tum** ti-**tum** ti-**tum** [*silent beat*]
> ti-**tum** ti-**tum** ti-**tum** ti-**tum** ti-**tum** [*silent beat*]
> ti-**tum** ti-**tum** ti-**tum** ti-**tum** ti-**tum** [*silent beat*]
> ti-**tum** ti-**tum** ti-**tum** ti-**tum** ti-**tum** [*silent beat*]

○ *Now, take the first line of your chosen speech and speak it in rhythm, shifting weight as you did on 'ti-**tum**'. Speak the syllables that fall on the strong stresses – in bold – as strongly as possibly, letting the weakly stressed syllables take care of themselves.*

○ *After the speeches you will find notes explaining how the sense stress varies from the metric stress in each of the lines below.*

VIOLA: If **I** did **love** you **in** my **mas**ter's **flame,**

*

CLAUDIO: Ay, **but** to **die,** and **go** we **know** not **where,**[a]

○ *Repeat your chosen line several times until the metric rhythm is clear. The less subtle you are the better; really beat it out.*

○ *Now, take the next line and beat that out strongly a few times. Again, focus on the strong beats and let the weak ones take care of themselves.*

VIOLA: With **such** a **suff**'ring, **such** a **dead**ly **life,**[b]

*

CLAUDIO: To **lie** in **cold** obs**truc**tion **and** to **rot;**

○ *Take the next few lines and beat them out strongly a few times, with a silent beat between the two lines to separate them.*

○ *The silent beat separates each line from the next, which makes it easier for you to keep track of the rhythm. It also helps you to begin to have a sense of the line structure which we will further explore later. Keep moving on the silent beat, as you will find this much easier.*

○ *Viola and Olivia share a line, so beat it out as a single line.*

VIOLA: In **your** denial **I** would **find** no **sense;** [*silent beat*]
      I **would** not under**stand** it.

OLIVIA: **Why,** what **would** you? [*silent beat*]

*

CLAUDIO: This **sen**sible warm **mo**tion **to** be**come** [*silent beat*]
A **knead**ed **clod**; and **the** de**light**ed **spir**it [*silent beat*]
To **bathe** in **fier**y **floods**, or **to** re**side** [*silent beat*]
In **thrill**ing **re**gion **of** thick-**ribbèd ice**, [*silent beat*][c]

○ *Now take the next four lines and beat them out strongly, with a silent beat between each line.*

VIOLA: Make **me** a **will**ow **cab**in **at** your **gate**, [*silent beat*]
And **cry** up**on** your **soul** with**in** the **house**; [*silent beat*]
Write **loy**al **can**tons **of** con**temnèd love**, [*silent beat*]
And **sing** them **loud** even **in** the **dead** of **night**; [*silent beat*][d]

*

CLAUDIO: To **be** im**pris**oned **in** the **view**less **winds** [*silent beat*]
And **blown** with **rest**less **vio**lence **round** a**bout** [*silent beat*]
The **pen**dent **world**; or **to** be **worse** than **worst** [*silent beat*]
Of **those** that **law**less **and** in**cer**tain **thought** [*silent beat*][e]

○ *Now take the last five lines and beat them out strongly, with a silent beat between the lines. Again, Viola and Olivia share a line, so beat it out as a single line.*

VIOLA: Hal**lo** your **name** to **the** re**ver**berate **hills**,
And **make** the **bab**bling **gos**sip **of** the **air**
Cry **out** 'Oli**via!'** **O** you **should** not **rest**
Be**tween** the **el**ements **of air** and **earth**
But **you** should **pit**y **me**!

OLIVIA: You **might** do **much**.

*

CLAUDIO: Imagine **howl**ing, 'tis **too hor**rible.
The **wear**iest **and** most **loathèd world**ly **life**
That **age**, ache, **pen**ury, **and** im**pris**onment
Can **lay** on **nature** is a **par**adise
To **what** we **fear** of **death**.[f]

When you return to the sense stress:

Note a: The first strong stress is likely to shift back from 'but' to 'Ay', so causing a rhythmic break at the beginning of the line. This makes great acting sense, since Claudio is likely to be in an agitated state and wanting to get his sister's attention.

Note b: There are two weak syllables between the strong beats of 'suff' and 'such'. This does not affect the overall rhythm. But there is a sense of extra being crammed in, of moving quickly on to the second half of the line, which might give a sense of urgency. See page 281 for more about lines with extra syllables.

Note c: The stress in the first line will move from 'ble' to 'warm'. This gives extra emphasis to warm, which is key in the line because the warmth of life is contrasted with the coldness of death. In the second line, 'the' will lose much of its stress which will give extra emphasis to 'delighted'. The stress in the third line will shift backward from 'to' to 'or' giving that an extra emphasis. In the fourth line it will shift forward from 'of' to 'thick', adding emphasis to that whole final phrase.

Note d: The stress will shift back from 'me' to 'make' giving the emphasis to the verb which is the answer to Olivia's question: 'Why, what would you?' Notice that, in the third line, in order that there are ten syllables, 'contemnèd' has three rather than two. This gives extra time and emphasis to the word, which means 'rejected' or 'despised', and shows Viola's identification with the pain of having your love spurned by another.

Note e: The stress in the third line will shift back from 'to' to 'or', again giving that extra emphasis.

Note f: The stress in the first line will shift from ''tis' to 'too', so giving that extra emphasis. In the second line it will shift from 'and' to 'most', again adding emphasis. In the third line, 'and' will keep its stress but extra stress will be added on 'ache' since he's pointing out that anything is better than death.

○ Now, work through the whole of your chosen speech beating out the rhythm strongly, and ignoring the sense stress. Remember to focus on the strong beats and let the weak beats take care of themselves.

○ Remember to shift weight with confidence, commitment and ease.

VIOLA: If **I** did **love** you **in** my **mas**ter's **flame**,
With **such** a **suff**'ring, **such** a **dead**ly **life**,
In **your** denial **I** would **find** no **sense**;
I **would** not **under**stand it.

OLIVIA: **Why**, what **would** you?

VIOLA: Make **me** a **wil**low **cab**in at your **gate**,
And **cry** up**on** your **soul** within the **house**;
Write **loy**al **can**tons **of** contemnèd **love**,

And **sing** them **loud** even **in** the **dead** of **night**;
Hallo your **name** to **the** reverberate **hills**,
And **make** the **babbling gossip** of the **air**
Cry out 'Olivia!' **O** you **should** not **rest**
Be**tween** the **elements** of **air** and **earth**
But **you** should **pity me**!

OLIVIA: You **might** do **much**.

*

CLAUDIO: Ay, **but** to **die**, and **go** we **know** not **where**,
To **lie** in **cold** obstruc**tion** and to **rot**;
This **sensible** warm **motion to** be**come**
A **kneaded clod**; and **the** delighted **spirit**
To **bathe** in **fiery floods**, or **to** reside
In **thrilling region of** thick-**ribbèd ice**,
To **be** imprisoned **in** the **viewless winds**
And **blown** with **restless violence round** about
The **pendent world**; or **to** be **worse** than **worst**
Of **those** that **lawless** and **incertain thought**
Imagine howling, 'tis too **horrible**.
The **weariest** and most **loathèd worldly life**
That **age**, ache, **penury**, and **imprisonment**
Can **lay** on **nature is a paradise**
To **what** we **fear** of **death**.

○ *Now speak your chosen speech normally as if you were talking to someone. Forget about the rhythm; let it take care of itself. If you are doing the Viola speech, include Olivia's half-lines.*

○ *As in the last chapter, choose an object to speak to so you have a sense of communicating rather than talking into a void. It's fine at this point if you are not absolutely sure of the meaning: that will come as we work.*

How was that? Did you find that the speech felt easier to say and that it flowed more? Did you have a sense of movement and energy as if the momentum of the rhythm was carrying you forward?

It's fine if you found yourself falling back too obviously into the rhythm. That can happen at first. However, in time you'll be able to speak the speech normally, while sensing the pulse of the rhythm in the background.

There are two great gifts which the iambic pentameter, or indeed any regular and yet flexible rhythm, gives the actor: *tension*, which I mentioned earlier, and *pace*. The fact that a regular beat exists, which the sense can flow with or against, gives an underlying *tension* that isn't possible to achieve in the same way in prose. And the regularly repeating beat keeps the text and the actor moving forward, so giving *pace*.

As with the work in the previous chapter, this is not something you have to worry about consciously in rehearsal and performance. As long as you have explored and experienced the metric rhythm thoroughly by going through this exercise regularly, you will find that the tension and pace are there without you thinking about them.

I find *Moving the Metre* an excellent way to start working on verse text. It stops you from worrying about the meaning, gets you up on your feet, committing to the text, and gives you the underlying beat along with the tension and movement which that brings. It gives you a preliminary shape without tying you down to an interpretation.

Note: On page 281, there is a section on irregular lines and shared lines, explaining what these are, how to identify and work on them and exploring what clues they give you.

Punctuation

With modern texts we can be pretty sure that the punctuation is that prescribed by the author. This is not so with Shakespearean text and indeed other texts of a similar date.

This leads some actors to disregard all the punctuation, especially in Shakespeare, on the grounds that 'we don't know what is and isn't his'. While in one way this makes sense, there are dangers in such an approach.

If you disregard the punctuation in Shakespeare's text, whose do you replace it with? It will tend to be your own and sentences will often be shortened as a result. This affects the energy of the text, breaking it up and making it less exciting and dangerous.

There are of course highly experienced directors, like Peter Hall, and actor/directors, like Mark Rylance, who do remove all the punctuation when working with Shakespearean text, but these directors and actors have worked with such text for years and have a profound understanding of how it works.

So what is the answer for you when working on your own with Shakespeare's text? Use either a well-edited version, such as the Arden, Cambridge or Penguin Shakespeare, or use the Folios and Quartos,[17] which are the earliest published versions of Shakespeare's plays, with the original punctuation, which may of course be the printer's rather than Shakespeare's. Applause Books publish First Folio editions in modern type, as do Nick Hern Books. The latter have the Folio version on one page and a lightly edited version on the facing page, which means you can directly compare them.

It is interesting to work with the Folio versions and an edited text and to compare them using the punctuation-based exercises – *Walking the Sentences, Using Colons and Semi-colons, Changing Direction* and *Changing Chairs* – noticing what differences the shifts in punctuation make. How do they affect the rhythm, and in what way does that rhythmic shift lead to an emotional shift as well as perhaps a meaning shift?

If you are working on a speech for yourself then you are free to choose whichever version you feel works best. If you are working with a director obviously the choice is up to them, but it can still be useful to explore other versions so that you have a more precise appreciation of the rhythms in the chosen version.

Note: If you are interested in understanding more about punctuation in general I would recommend Lynne Truss's book Eats, Shoots & Leaves. *It is an excellent and humorous read.*

Walking the Sentences

To discover the rhythm, flow and energy of the thoughts in a text

This exercise, as I mentioned in the previous chapter, focuses on the sentence structure, and gives us the rhythm of the thoughts. By working separately on this exercise and *Moving the Metre – Stage Two* you will find that both the metric and the thought rhythms establish themselves strongly in you. Then, when you come to performance, they will work together automatically, bringing great richness to the speeches without you having to think about it.

Note: For this exercise forget about the line structure. We will look later at how you keep the line intact rather than breaking it up.

Use whichever speech you worked on in the last exercise, reading through the directions first.

○ As in the last chapter, walk purposefully around the room as you say the text, treating each sentence as a journey, so that you start walking as you start the sentence and keep walking without pause, ignoring all the commas, dashes, colons, etc., until you reach the full stop.

○ Breathe whenever you need to, as long as you keep walking. As you work on this and the other punctuation exercises your breath will sort itself out.

○ At the end of each sentence, stop to have a sense of having completed the journey of that sentence.

○ Then, start off in another direction with the new sentence and again keep walking until you come to the full stop.

○ As you walk, have a sense of someone in front of you to whom you are talking and really want to communicate with. Avoid ambling or rushing; simply walk with purpose as if you were going somewhere specific.

Note: Say Olivia's lines as well as Viola's so you have a sense of the rhythm of the whole exchange between them.

VIOLA: If I did love you in my master's flame,
   With such a suff'ring, such a deadly life,
   In your denial I would find no sense;
   I would not understand it. [**stop**]

OLIVIA: Why, what would you? [**stop**]

VIOLA: Make me a willow cabin at your gate,
   And cry upon your soul within the house;
   Write loyal cantons of contemnèd love,
   And sing them loud even in the dead of night;
   Hallo your name to the reverberate hills,
   And make the babbling gossip of the air
   Cry out 'Olivia!' [**stop**] O you should not rest
   Between the elements of air and earth
   But you should pity me!

OLIVIA: You might do much. [**stop**]

How did you find that? How did you feel having to keep walking and keep the sentences going all the way to the full stop? What clues might the sentence lengths give you about how Viola is feeling at this point? Do you get a sense that this is an impassioned outburst, inspired by her own love rather than a cool and rational argument?

CLAUDIO: Ay, but to die, and go we know not where,
      To lie in cold obstruction and to rot;
      This sensible warm motion to become
      A kneaded clod; and the delighted spirit
      To bathe in fiery floods, or to reside
      In thrilling region of thick-ribbèd ice,
      To be imprisoned in the viewless winds
      And blown with restless violence round about
      The pendent world; or to be worse than worst
      Of those that lawless and incertain thought
      Imagine howling, 'tis too horrible. [**stop**]
      The weariest and most loathèd worldly life
      That age, ache, penury, and imprisonment
      Can lay on nature is a paradise
      To what we fear of death. [**stop**]

How was that? As you will have noticed, the first sentence is fairly long – eleven lines in fact. What did it feel like to have to keep walking and talking? What sense does that give you of how Claudio is feeling? Do you get the sense that this is an impassioned plea for his life rather than a cool and reasoned argument against dying? Even the second sentence, although shorter than the first, is four lines long and so to a degree continues his impassioned plea.

Walking the Sentences takes you away from your own rhythm and immerses you in the thought rhythm and journey of the character. It also helps your breath. When directors ask you to do a whole sentence on one breath it is usually because they want the thought to run through and not be broken up. If you walk the sentences without stopping, you will discover the shape of the unbroken thought, and your breathing will naturally organise itself so that you find the best places to breathe within the sentence without destroying the flow of the whole. After all, that is what you do quite naturally in real life! This does not mean that work on your breath capacity and control is unnecessary. It is simply that, in my experience, work on these alone will not allow you to sustain long thoughts successfully. You need to have a clear idea of how long a thought is and to have experienced sustaining it in order to handle the breath appropriately. *Walking the Sentences* is the best way to do that. So, your practice is simply to walk the sentences repeatedly until their lengths, and therefore the thought lengths, are embedded.

You may be wondering how the sentence structure fits with the verse structure. My general rule of thumb is that a sentence that begins in the middle of a line suggests a quicker pick-up; that is, the new sentence follows quickly on the one before. Whereas a sentence ending that coincides with a line ending suggests a less quick pick-up and perhaps even a pause. We will look at this in more detail when we do the *Walking the Verse* exercise.

Before we do that I want to examine the punctuation *within* the sentences so that we can weave that rhythm in with the metric rhythm and the thought rhythm we have explored so far.

Using the Colons and Semi-colons

To handle sentences with colons and semi-colons

In the last chapter we treated all the internal punctuation in the same way. However, colons and semi-colons need a special mention in classical text. Lynne Truss had this to say about them: 'Expectation is what these . . . are about; expectation and elastic energy. Like internal springs they propel you forward in a sentence towards more information . . . '[18]

I find the most useful way to consider colons and semi-colons in acting terms is as *potential* full stops, which are *overridden* because the character wants to add something further. What I mean by this is that the sentence *could* end at the colon or semi-colon, but the character *chooses* to go on; to add something to what they have just said, as I am doing now, rather than stopping and then starting a new thought.

This idea works brilliantly for an actor. It helps him/her to feel in charge of the text rather than the length of the sentences taking him/her by surprise.

O *Go through your chosen speech, walking the sentences as you did earlier.*

O *As before, stop at each full stop. Then, start off on a new sentence.*

O *When you come to the colons and semi-colons think: 'I could stop my sentence here but I want to add something' — as if you nearly pause and then interrupt yourself to carry on.*

I have marked the colons and semi colons with double forward slashes to help you see where they are. Continue to include Olivia's lines if you are working on Viola's speech.

VIOLA: If I did love you in my master's flame,
      With such a suff'ring, such a deadly life,
      In your denial I would find no sense;//
      I would not understand it. [**stop**]

OLIVIA: Why, what would you? [**stop**]

VIOLA: Make me a willow cabin at your gate,
      And cry upon your soul within the house;//
      Write loyal cantons of contemnèd love,
      And sing them loud even in the dead of night;//
      Hallo your name to the reverberate hills,
      And make the babbling gossip of the air
      Cry out 'Olivia!' [**stop**] O you should not rest
      Between the elements of air and earth
      But you should pity me!

OLIVIA: You might do much. [**stop**]

*

CLAUDIO: Ay, but to die, and go we know not where,
      To lie in cold obstruction and to rot;//
      This sensible warm motion to become
      A kneaded clod;// and the delighted spirit
      To bathe in fiery floods, or to reside
      In thrilling region of thick-ribbèd ice,
      To be imprisoned in the viewless winds
      And blown with restless violence round about
      The pendent world;// or to be worse than worst
      Of those that lawless and incertain thought
      Imagine howling, 'tis too horrible. [**stop**]
      The weariest and most loathèd worldly life
      That age, ache, penury, and imprisonment
      Can lay on nature is a paradise
      To what we fear of death. [**stop**]

How was that? Did it help you to handle the longer sentences? Did you feel more in charge of the text? This exercise, like the others, is worth doing regularly, since it helps the text flow much more easily and feel more natural and flexible.

Changing Direction

To discover the differing rhythms within each thought and therefore the emotional to and fro in the thoughts of the text

Now let the full stops and the colons and semi-colons take care of themselves for a moment while we return to explore the internal punctuation as we did in the last chapter. As I mentioned there, this is an excellent exercise of Cicely Berry's, which really helps you to find the emotional to and fro *within* the thoughts.

Continue using whichever speech you have used so far in this chapter, again speaking Olivia's lines as well as Viola's if you are working on that speech.

○   As before, walk purposefully as you say the text, but this time change direction, without stopping, at every punctuation mark – including all dashes, etc. The text is marked up below to make it clearer for you.

○   Let yourself loose in this exercise, so that you walk and change direction in a fluid way.

VIOLA: If I did love you in my master's flame, [**change**]
　　　　　With such a suff'ring, [**change**] such a deadly life, [**change**]
　　　　　In your denial I would find no sense; [**change**]
　　　　　I would not understand it. [**change**]

OLIVIA:　　　　　　　　　　　　Why, [**change**] what would
　　　　　you? [**change**]

VIOLA: Make me a willow cabin at your gate, [**change**]
　　　　　And cry upon your soul within the house; [**change**]
　　　　　Write loyal cantons of contemnèd love, [**change**]
　　　　　And sing them loud even in the dead of night; [**change**]
　　　　　Hallo your name to the reverberate hills, [**change**]
　　　　　And make the babbling gossip of the air
　　　　　Cry out [**change**] 'Olivia!' [**change**] O you should not rest
　　　　　Between the elements of air and earth
　　　　　But you should pity me! [**change**]

OLIVIA:　　　　　　　　　　　　You might do much.

*

CLAUDIO: Ay, [**change**] but to die, [**change**] and go we know
          not where, [**change**]
      To lie in cold obstruction and to rot; [**change**]
      This sensible warm motion to become
      A kneaded clod; [**change**] and the delighted spirit
      To bathe in fiery floods, [**change**] or to reside
      In thrilling region of thick-ribbèd ice, [**change**]
      To be imprisoned in the viewless winds
      And blown with restless violence round about
      The pendent world; [**change**] or to be worse than worst
      Of those that lawless and incertain thought
      Imagine howling, [**change**] 'tis too horrible. [**change**]
      The weariest and most loathèd worldly life
      That age, [**change**] ache, [**change**] penury, [**change**]
          and imprisonment
      Can lay on nature is a paradise
      To what we fear of death.

What do you notice? Can you feel the difference between the short phrases where you are constantly turning and the longer phrases where suddenly there's more release? Do you get an idea of how the character is feeling? Don't worry if you lose the sense. Here we are looking at the emotional back and forth, so it is good if you feel tossed around by the thoughts.

○ *Go through it again, paying attention to the difference between the short and long phrases and noticing what clues this gives you about how the character is feeling, about his/her emotional journey through the speech.*

This exercise is excellent for bringing a speech or scene to life emotionally so that it is not too rational or set. Enjoy the feeling of not being in control, of being tossed about by your thoughts. Allow yourself to be caught by surprise, then there's a chance that you might surprise the audience as well!

Changing Chairs

To discover how each phrase builds on the one before, so creating a ladder of meaning in the text

Having explored how the punctuation helps to give the emotional to and fro, let's look at how it helps you understand and experience the way in which each phrase builds upon the one before. Again, we are going to use an exercise from the previous chapter – another of Cicely Berry's excellent exercises – and again continue with the speech you have been using.

○ *Take two chairs and place them side by side. Sit in one of the chairs and imagine a person in front of you to whom you are talking. Speak the text, moving from one chair to the other on each punctuation mark.*

○ *You can shift quite rapidly from chair to chair but avoid speaking while you are moving.*

○ *Try the whole speech in this way, using the version marked up for the previous exercise. Again, include Olivia's lines if working on Viola's speech.*

How was that? Did the speech feel more manageable? Did it make more sense? Did you feel how one thought was added to another?

In my experience working through these five exercises – *Moving the Metre, Walking the Sentences, Using Colons and Semi-colons, Changing Direction* and *Changing Chairs* – you have a chance to explore the rhythms of the text and the way they interweave with each other. By focusing on each structure separately you can embed that rhythm clearly and without confusion. Once you go into rehearsal and performance you can then let the rhythms take care of themselves and play together knowing that they are all being honoured without you having to consciously think about them. And, indeed, the resulting interweaving is far more detailed and subtle than if you attempted to do it consciously.

Phrase by Phrase

To deepen the connection with the text

Having explored and begun to embed many of the structures and rhythms of the text, it is time to start work on understanding and owning it. We explored the *second stage* of this exercise in the last chapter. Before we move onto that stage here I want to look at the *first stage* – that is, working out what everything in the text means.

Stage One – Understanding the text

There is no easy exercise I can give you for this, but there are some ways of working that you may find helpful and these I have ordered into a process. You can add to or alter this process as you wish. I simply offer it as a framework.

I cannot stress enough how helpful it is to have gone through the metric, sentence and internal punctuation rhythms *before* you sit down and thrash out the sense, because in this way so much of the meaning starts to fall into place naturally, and it is then simply a matter of working on the parts that are still unclear.

○ *Always take each sentence separately and within the sentence take it phrase by phrase.*

○ *Look up any words you are unsure of in a glossary of Shakespeare's words such as* Shakespeare's Words *by David Crystal and Ben Crystal or* A Shakespeare Glossary *by C.T. Onions.*

○ *Use the notes in a good modern edition, such as the Arden, Cambridge or Penguin Shakespeare, to help you with phrases or sentences that are confusing. However, be warned: occasionally the explanatory notes are even more confusing than the phrase or sentence you are trying to unravel!*

○ *Use Lemprière's* Classical Dictionary *and Brewer's* Dictionary of Phrase and Fable *to look up people and places mentioned by your character.*

○ *Make sure you are absolutely clear who all the pronouns – he, she, it, you, they, etc. – are referring to.*

○ *Feel comfortable asking other people with more experience to help you out. They have been in the same position as you!*

Once you have a good idea of the meaning go on to Stage Two. This is vital as it helps to embed your understanding and begins the process of making the text your own.

Stage Two – Owning the text

○ *Sit with a plant or lamp in front of you. The plant or lamp represents the person you are talking to in the speech. This helps you to talk rather than act* [*see notes on this in the previous chapter*].

○ *Look at the first phrase on the page – that is, up to the first punctuation mark. Give yourself time to absorb it.*

○ *Then, look up and register the plant or lamp before you speak, as if you are taking a moment to connect with the person it represents.*

○ *Then, speak the phrase really wanting to communicate it.*

○ *At the end of the phrase, pause for a moment as if to check that that phrase has been registered by the person you are talking to.*

○ *Continue through the whole speech in this way, taking the time to absorb each phrase, to look up and connect, to communicate and to check that what you have said has been received.*

Note: For this exercise the lines may be temporarily broken up so that you can connect with each phrase. In later exercises, however, we will look at flowing each line through.

Use the speech you worked with in the previous exercises. I have marked the phrases with a forward slash so that you can see each one easily.

VIOLA: If I did love you in my master's flame,/
   With such a suff'ring,/ such a deadly life,/
   In your denial I would find no sense;/
   I would not understand it./

OLIVIA: Why,/ what would you?/

VIOLA: Make me a willow cabin at your gate,/
   And cry upon your soul within the house;/
   Write loyal cantons of contemnèd love,/
   And sing them loud even in the dead of night;/
   Hallo your name to the reverberate hills,/
   And make the babbling gossip of the air
   Cry out 'Olivia!'/ O you should not rest
   Between the elements of air and earth
   But you should pity me!

OLIVIA: You might do much.

*

CLAUDIO: Ay,/ but to die,/ and go we know not where,/
   To lie in cold obstruction and to rot;/
   This sensible warm motion to become
   A kneaded clod;/ and the delighted spirit
   To bathe in fiery floods,/ or to reside
   In thrilling region of thick-ribbèd ice,/
   To be imprisoned in the viewless winds
   And blown with restless violence round about
   The pendent world;/ or to be worse than worst
   Of those that lawless and incertain thought
   Imagine howling,/ 'tis too horrible./

> The weariest and most loathèd worldly life
> That age,/ ache,/ penury,/ and imprisonment
> Can lay on nature is a paradise
> To what we fear of death.

How was that? Did you have a greater sense of owning the phrases? Did the speech feel more manageable and meaningful? The more time you take with this exercise, the better. You need to give yourself the chance to absorb each phrase and connect with it *before* you attempt to communicate the phrase. Then, you need to focus on the plant/lamp and on communicating the phrase fully. Be prepared to say each phrase more than once if you feel you need to.

This is an excellent exercise to repeat at frequent intervals – as indeed are all the exercises so far in this chapter. By doing so you'll find that you start to remember the speech – although that should not be the objective of this exercise but merely a by-product.

Handling the Verse

Now that we have explored the rhythms and clarified the meaning, it is time to explore the *shape* of the verse and how that interacts with the other structures and rhythms within the text. This is exciting rather than daunting if you know how to approach it. You will find out just how much Shakespeare supports you through the verse shape: helping you with where to place the emphasis so that the text is easier to handle and to understand.

Walking the Verse

To experience the verse shape and how it interacts with the sentence shape

As I mentioned earlier, in verse the line ends at a specific point on the page. In free verse this point is chosen by the writer. In metric verse it is set by the metric rhythm used and how many beats that rhythm has per line. We have already paid some attention to the verse shape in *Moving the Metre*, where we used a silent beat at the end of each line to separate it from the next. Now we are going to explore the verse shape further and as usual we are going to make that exploration physical. Continue using whichever speech you have been working with so far.

○ *You are literally going to walk the verse line. By this I mean you are going to walk across the room in one direction as you say the first line and then back in the opposite direction as you say the next line and so on, back and forth across the room.*

○ *If the sentence end – that is, the full stop – coincides with the line end, stop after the last word in the line, before turning to start the next line.*

○ *If the sentence does not end at the end of the line, then turn immediately into the next line.*

○ *If there is a full stop in the middle of the line, keep walking but allow yourself to have time for the thought change into the new sentence.*

○ *The speeches are included again below with instructions to help you. As before, include Olivia's lines if you are working on Viola's speech.*

VIOLA: If I did love you in my master's flame, [**turn immediately**]
　　　　With such a suff'ring, such a deadly life, [**turn immediately**]
　　　　In your denial I would find no sense; [**turn immediately**]
　　　　I would not understand it. [**keep walking**]

OLIVIA:　　　　　　　　　　　　Why, what would you?
　　　　　　　　　　　　　　　　[**stop – then turn**]

VIOLA: Make me a willow cabin at your gate, [**turn immediately**]
　　　　And cry upon your soul within the house; [**turn immediately**]
　　　　Write loyal cantons of contemnèd love, [**turn immediately**]
　　　　And sing them loud even in the dead of night; [**turn immediately**]
　　　　Hallo your name to the reverberate hills, [**turn immediately**]
　　　　And make the babbling gossip of the air [**turn immediately**]
　　　　Cry out 'Olivia!' [**keep walking**] O you should not rest
　　　　　　　　　　　　　　　　[**turn immediately**]
　　　　Between the elements of air and earth [**turn immediately**]
　　　　But you should pity me! [**keep walking**]

OLIVIA:　　　　　　　　　You might do much. [**stop**]

*

CLAUDIO: Ay, but to die, and go we know not where, [**turn immediately**]
　　　　To lie in cold obstruction and to rot; [**turn immediately**]
　　　　This sensible warm motion to become [**turn immediately**]
　　　　A kneaded clod; and the delighted spirit [**turn immediately**]
　　　　To bathe in fiery floods, or to reside [**turn immediately**]
　　　　In thrilling region of thick-ribbèd ice, [**turn immediately**]

To be imprisoned in the viewless winds [**turn immediately**]
And blown with restless violence round about [**turn immediately**]
The pendent world; or to be worse than worst [**turn immediately**]
Of those that lawless and incertain thought [**turn immediately**]
Imagine howling, 'tis too horrible. [**stop – then turn**]
The weariest and most loathèd worldly life [**turn immediately**]
That age, ache, penury, and imprisonment [**turn immediately**]
Can lay on nature is a paradise [**turn immediately**]
To what we fear of death. [**stop**]

Can you feel how the verse structure works with the sentence structure? When the end of the sentence and the end of the line coincide, there is a sense of finishing, of resting slightly before you continue. Where the sentence flows over the line ending, the word at the end of the line is given an extra pointing or emphasis within the sentence. When the new sentence starts within the line, the new thought follows on from the previous one fairly rapidly, therefore keeping the flow of the line.

○ *Go through the speech again in the same way being aware of where the sentence and line stop together; where the sentence flows over the line ending and the last word of the verse line is given an extra pointing; and, in Viola's speech, where Olivia's sentences pick up rapidly in the middle of the line, flowing out of the Viola's.*

Can you feel how the shape of the verse works now and how it supports you in shaping the speech?

As always, it will, in the end, be up to the director to decide how strongly he or she wants you to adhere to this shape. However, in my experience this exercise, done outside the rehearsal room, will help you, whatever choice the director wishes to make, without in any way compromising their approach.

A word of warning though: you do have to practise the exercise a great deal to get the shape embedded. If you only do the exercise once this won't happen.

Clicking the Final Word

To understand how the final stressed word of each line is highlighted

This exercise builds on the previous one. It allows you to experience how the final stressed word of each line is highlighted and how this helps the sense both for actor and audience.

○ *Walk around the room with purpose as you speak the text.*

○ *Where a full stop and line ending coincide, stop for a moment, before setting out on the next sentence. Where a full stop comes in the middle of a line, keep moving and simply find the new thought as you move.*

○ *As you walk, click your fingers as you say the last stressed syllable of each line, which is written in bold.*

VIOLA: If I did love you in my master's **flame**,
      With such a suff'ring, such a deadly **life**,
      In your denial I would find no **sense**;
      I would not understand it.

OLIVIA: Why, what **would** you? [**stop**]

VIOLA: Make me a willow cabin at your **gate**,
      And cry upon your soul within the **house**;
      Write loyal cantons of contemnèd **love**,
      And sing them loud even in the dead of **night**;
      Hallo your name to the reverberate **hills**,
      And make the babbling gossip of the **air**
      Cry out 'Olivia!' O you should not **rest**
      Between the elements of air and **earth**
      But you should pity me!

OLIVIA: You might do **much**. [**stop**]

*

CLAUDIO: Ay, but to die, and go we know not **where**,
      To lie in cold obstruction and to **rot**;
      This sensible warm motion to be**come**
      A kneaded clod; and the delighted **spirit**
      To bathe in fiery floods, or to re**side**
      In thrilling region of thick-ribbèd **ice**,
      To be imprisoned in the viewless **winds**
      And blown with restless violence round a**bout**
      The pendent world; or to be worse than **worst**
      Of those that lawless and incertain **thought**
      Imagine howling, 'tis too **horri**ble. [**stop**]
      The weariest and most loathèd worldly **life**
      That age, ache, penury, and im**pris**onment

Can lay on nature is a **par**adise
To what we fear of **death**. [**stop**]

What did you discover from that? Did you notice that the words at the end of each line are important within the sense of each sentence? Did you notice that by highlighting them you were better able to shape each sentence and therefore to find and communicate its meaning more effectively?

As with the previous exercise, you need to practise this one over and over again to enable the verse and sentence structures to work together effectively.

Marking the Caesura

To understand how the caesura works within the line and how it can help to shape the text

Now we have looked at the verse line and the shape that it gives to the text, we are going to look *within* the line at the caesura, which shapes the line internally. The caesura is a slight break in the line that divides it into two parts. The break usually comes after the second or third iambic foot – that is, after the second or third strong stress in the line. The caesura is not equally strong in all lines. Indeed, in some lines it disappears almost completely.

What is the purpose of the break and why is it helpful to explore it? It gives further shape to the line and, if you attend to that shaping, you will have a better sense of how the line is built up.

Let's go through the speech you've been using and break each line into its two parts. In the speeches below the *possible* caesura is marked with a forward slash [sometimes there is more than one choice of position]. As I said earlier, some lines flow on with the caesura hardly noticed. As you do the exercise it will become clear to you where the break in the line is helpful and where it is better if the line flows on.

○ *Stand or sit as you prefer. You need your hands free, so stick the text on the wall or place it on a table in front of you.*

○ *As you say the first part of the line lift one hand – palm up – as if offering that part of the line.*

○ *Then, as you say the second part of the line lift the other hand – palm up – as if offering that second part.*

○ *Drop your hands at the end of the line and repeat the same procedure for the next line.*

99

○ *Continue in this way until you have worked through the whole speech.*

VIOLA: If I did love you/ in my master's flame,
        With such a suff'ring,/ such a deadly life,
        In your denial/ I would find no sense;
        I would not understand it./

OLIVIA: Why, what would you?

VIOLA: Make me a willow cabin/ at your gate,
        And cry upon your soul/ within the house;
        Write loyal cantons/ of contemnèd love,
        And sing them loud/ even in the dead of night;
        Hallo your name/ to the reverberate hills,
        And make the babbling gossip/ of the air
        Cry out 'Olivia!'/ O you should not rest
        Between the elements/ of air and earth
        But you should pity me!/

OLIVIA: You might do much.

*

CLAUDIO: Ay, but to die,/ and go we know not where,
        To lie in cold obstruction/ and to rot;
        This sensible warm motion/ to become
        A kneaded clod;/ and the delighted spirit
        To bathe in fiery floods,/ or to reside
        In thrilling region/ of thick-ribbèd ice,
        To be imprisoned/ in the viewless winds
        And blown with restless violence/ round about
        The pendent world;/ or to be worse than worst
        Of those that lawless/ and incertain thought
        Imagine howling,/ 'tis too horrible.
        The weariest and most loathèd/ worldly life
        That age, ache, penury,/ and imprisonment
        Can lay on nature/ is a paradise
        To what we fear of death.

How was that? Did you notice that in some lines the break helped the sense and that in others the break got in the way and you simply wanted to flow on? Did the break help you to understand how the second part of the line built on the first? Did it help you to shape the speech and to feel more in control of it?

Note: Full stops, colons and semi-colons within lines come at the caesura break. Also, if there is rhyme, or near-rhyme, within a line it will usually occur on the last word before the caesura break, as in this example from A Midsummer Night's Dream*:*

> Nor have love's **mind**/ of any judgement taste;
> Wings and no **eyes** figure unheedy haste:

O *Speak the speech normally now, forgetting about the break and letting the lines flow through. As always, remember to talk the speech to an object.*

VIOLA: If I did love you in my master's flame,
　　　　With such a suff'ring, such a deadly life,
　　　　In your denial I would find no sense;
　　　　I would not understand it.

OLIVIA:　　　　　　　　　　　Why, what would you?

VIOLA: Make me a willow cabin at your gate,
　　　　And cry upon your soul within the house;
　　　　Write loyal cantons of contemnèd love,
　　　　And sing them loud even in the dead of night;
　　　　Hallo your name to the reverberate hills,
　　　　And make the babbling gossip of the air
　　　　Cry out 'Olivia!' O you should not rest
　　　　Between the elements of air and earth
　　　　But you should pity me!

OLIVIA:　　　　　　　　　　　You might do much.

*

CLAUDIO: Ay, but to die, and go we know not where,
　　　　　To lie in cold obstruction and to rot;
　　　　　This sensible warm motion to become
　　　　　A kneaded clod; and the delighted spirit
　　　　　To bathe in fiery floods, or to reside
　　　　　In thrilling region of thick-ribbèd ice,
　　　　　To be imprisoned in the viewless winds
　　　　　And blown with restless violence round about
　　　　　The pendent world; or to be worse than worst
　　　　　Of those that lawless and incertain thought
　　　　　Imagine howling, 'tis too horrible.

> The weariest and most loathèd worldly life
> That age, ache, penury, and imprisonment
> Can lay on nature is a paradise
> To what we fear of death.

How did you find that? Did it help to have worked on the breaks previously? Could you feel yet more shape in the speech or maybe it simply felt a little easier to say? Often the shift is not huge. Each exercise simply moves you a little more deeply into a speech or scene so that it becomes more comfortable.

As with all the exercises, you never consciously put the caesura break in the lines in rehearsal or performance. If you have thoroughly explored it and how it supports you then the shape it gives will remain even though you are not focusing on it consciously.

We have now finished the exploration of the structures and rhythms within verse and prose text. Before we go on to look at sound, word and image, I want to say something about poetry and heightened text.

Poetry

Prose and verse relate to the *structure* of text, so where does poetry come in? Poetry relates to the *language* used and how it is used. Poetic language pays far more attention to sound and imagery; it is more descriptive and evocative. James Reeves describes poetry as 'vital, fresh and surprising language',[19] which I love because it gets away from the idea of poetry as being elaborate and remote. It returns us to the heart of what poetry is – namely, language that reverberates with many layers of meaning, which invokes in us a reaction that is not intellectually based but which rather involves our emotions and our senses. Indeed, Reeves describes poetry as 'felt thought'.[20]

It is important to understand that poetic language is not confined to verse. Prose and verse can both be more conversational or more poetic as you can see from the examples below.

○ *Speak them through several times and simply allow yourself to notice the different ways the language is used when it is poetic and when it is conversational.*

Conversational Prose: The Merchant of Venice
    PORTIA: If I could bid the fifth welcome with so good a heart as I can bid the other four farewell, I should be glad of his approach: if he have the condition of a saint, and the complexion of a devil, I had rather he should shrive me than wive me.

*

Poetic Prose: **Hamlet**
> HAMLET: What a piece of work is a man! How noble in reason, how infinite in faculties, in form and moving how express and admirable, in action how like an angel, in apprehension how like a god!

*

Poetic Verse: **Macbeth**
> MACBETH: To-morrow, and to-morrow, and to-morrow,
> Creeps in this petty pace from day to day,
> To the last syllable of recorded time;
> And all our yesterdays have lighted fools
> The way to dusty death.

*

Conversational Verse: **As You Like It**
> CELIA: Let's away
> And get our jewels and our wealth together,
> Devise the fittest time and safest way
> To hide us from pursuit that will be made
> After my flight.

Do you notice how the conversational examples use language in a more straightforward way? The meaning is more available on the surface. Whereas the poetic examples use language that is more evocative both of image and feeling, and there is greater depth of meaning.

We may not speak in verse in our ordinary lives but we do use poetic language, even though we are often not aware of doing so. We do this when a person or place or event or object moves us in such a way that we automatically search for a deeper way to express our experience.

We will look further at poetic language when we work on sound, word and imagery. For now I simply want you to be aware of the difference, and start to look out for shifts from one to the other in any text you are working on. And when you notice these shifts ask yourself: *'Why is my character using more conversational or more poetic language now?'* There is no need to come up with an immediate answer. If you notice the shift, and ask yourself the question, the answer will come up naturally during rehearsal. What is important, as always, is to notice.

Heightened Text

Often people will talk about heightened text. What do they mean by this? Are heightened text and poetry the same?

Heightened text is more *shaped* than everyday speech, so poetry, in that respect, is heightened. However, there are many ways of shaping a text. You could say that all plays have heightened text, to a lesser or greater degree, because the dialogue in all plays is shaped, even when it seems absolutely naturalistic. David Mamet's work is a wonderful example of this. The extract below is from the beginning of *Reunion*. Bernie is talking to his daughter, whom he hasn't seen for many years.

> BERNIE: I would have recognised you anywhere.
> It is you. Isn't it?
> Carol. Is that you?
> You haven't changed a bit.
> I would have recognised you anywhere . . .
> This is a very important moment.
> But there's no reason why we should have it in the hall so
>   let me take your coat . . .
> I feel like a racehorse. You ever go to the track?
> Well, that's what I feel like.
> If I was still drinking, I'd offer you a drink.
> If I was still drinking, you probably wouldn't be here.
> That's all right.[21]

This may have the appearance of everyday speech but Mamet uses punctuation, repetition and physical placing of the line on the page to create a specific rhythm. All the exercises in this chapter and the previous one ensure that you become aware of the specific ways each writer has shaped his/her text.

PATTERNS OF SOUND

Having looked at structure and rhythm and defined poetry and heightened text, let's move on to explore patterns of sound in classical text

Using sound effectively helps the listener to listen and understand. Shakespeare had a wonderful instinct for employing sound to underscore feeling and thought, so making his text more powerful for the actor to speak and the audience to hear.

Vowels and Consonants

We are going to start the work on sound by focusing on the vowels and consonants separately, as we did in the last chapter. Remember that vowels carry the emotion whereas consonants carry the sense. Achieving a good balance between the two is always important but doubly so with classical plays where so much is conveyed through sound. The following exercises will help you to find that balance. They will also allow you to hear the way the sounds work and how they create a pattern, or music, of their own.

Connecting with the Vowels

To experience how the vowels give rhythm and 'music'

As I pointed out in the last chapter, vowels have different lengths – short, long and travelling. Travelling vowels are traditionally known as diphthongs because they are, in fact, made up of two vowels. I call them travelling vowels because you have to move from one vowel to the other to make them. Below is an example of short, long and travelling vowels in a Standard English accent. In each case I have given an example of the sound in a word so that if you are working in another accent you can check whether the vowel stays the same length.

I have marked out the speeches below using the same marks as in the last chapter: a forward slash [/] to denote short vowels, a long dash [–] to denote long vowels, and a circle [O] to denote diphthongs.

If you have not read the previous chapter on modern text please look at page 48 for further explanation about vowels and how to work with them in text before you try the exercise on the speeches.

Continue working on the speech you used in the earlier exercises.

O Go through your chosen speech line by line saying only the vowels, remembering to commit fully to the different lengths.

O Add 'h' in front of each vowel to ensure that you are supporting the sound you are making with breath rather than the sound catching in your throat.

O It is useful to mark the rhythm with your hand – doing quick downward movements for the short vowels, long horizontal movements for the long vowels and big rounded movements for the diphthongs.

Note: I have chosen not to use phonetic symbols to identify the vowels because not everyone knows these symbols. Therefore, I have used the spelling which is as near as possible to a particular sound. Also, in connected speech we do not fully say all the vowels. Where they are unstressed they can be reduced to a more neutral 'er' or 'i'.

VIOLA:

/ O / / / — / O — / O
hi high hi huh hoo hi high hah-h'er' hay
If I   did love you in my master's flame,

/ / / / / / / / / O
hi huh h'er' huh-hi huh h'er' he-hi high
With such a   suff'ring, such a   deadly life,

/ — / O / O / O O /
hi hor hi-high-h'er' high h'oo' high hoh heh
In your denial   I   would find no sense;

O / / / / / /
high h'oo' h'o' huh-h'er'-ha hi
I   would not understand it.

OLIVIA:

O / / —
high h'o' h'oo' hoo
Why, what would you?

VIOLA:

O — / / / / / / — O
hay hee h'er' hi-hoh ha-hi ha hor hay
Make me a   willow cabin at your gate,

/ O / / — O / / / O
ha high h'er'-h'o' hor hoh hi-hi h'er' how
And cry upon   your soul within the house;

O O / / / / / / /
high hoy-h'er' ha-ho h'o' huh-heh-hi huh
Write loyal   cantons of contemnèd love,

/ / / O — / / / / O
ha hi heh how hee-h'er' hi huh heh h'er' high
And sing them loud even   in the dead of night;

/ — — O / / / — / / /
ha-ho hor hay h'er' h'er' hi-her-huh-huh hi
Hallo your name to the   reverberate hills,

/ O / / / / / / / O
h'er' hay h'er' ha-h'er'-hi ho-hi h'er' h'er' hair
And make the   babbling gossip of the   air

O   O   O / / /   O — /   /   /
high how hoh-hi-hi-h'er' hoh hoo h'oo' h'o' heh
Cry   out   'Olivia!'   O you should not rest

/ — / / / /   / O / —
hi-hee h'er' heh-h'er'-h'er' huh hair h'er' her
Between the   elements   of air and earth

/ — / / — —
huh hoo h'oo' hi-hee hee
But you should pity me!

OLIVIA:

       — O — /
       hoo high hoo huh
       You might do much.

*

CLAUDIO:

O / /   O /   O — O / O
high huh h'er' high h'er' hoh hee hoh h'o' hair
Ay, but to   die, and go we know not where,

/   O / O   / / / /   /
h'er' high hi hoh h 'er'-huh-h'er' h'er' h'er' h'o'
To   lie in cold   obstruction   and to rot;

/ / / / — O /   / / /
his heh-hi-h'er' hor hoh-h'er' h'er' hi-huh
This sensible   warm motion to   become

/ — / / / /   / O / / /
h'er' hee-heh h'o' h'er' h'er' hi-high-hi hi-hi
A   kneaded clod; and the delighted spirit

/ O / O   / — / — / / O
h'er' hay hi high-h'er'-hee h'oo' hor h'er' hi-high
To bathe in   fiery   floods, or to   reside

/ / / — /   / / / O
hi hi-hi hee-h'er' h'o' hi-hi-heh high
In thrilling region   of thick-ribbèd ice,

/ — / / / / /   — / /
h'er' hee hi-hi-huh hi h'er' hoo-huh hi
To   be imprisoned in the   viewless winds

/ O / / /   O / / O / O
h'er' hoh hi heh-h'er' high-h'er'-h'er' how h'er'-how
And blown with restless   violence   round about

```
  /     /      /    —   —    /     —   —   /     —
h'er' heh-h'er' her  hor h'er' hee  her   ha   her
The   pendent world; or  to   be worse than worst
  /     O     /    —    /    /    /    —    /    —
h'er' hoh h'er' hor-h'er' h'er' hi-her-h'er' hor
Of  those that  lawless   and    incertain thought
  /  /   /    O    /   /    —    /  /   /
hi-ha-hi how-hi  hi hoo ho-hi-h'er'
Imagine howling, 'tis too   horrible.
  /     O    /   /    /    O   O    /   —   /   O
h'er' hear-hi-h'er' h'er' hoh hoh-heh her-hi high
The      weariest    and most loathèd worldly life
  /     O   O    /    /    /    /    /   /    /    /
h'er' hay hay heh-h'oo'-hee h'er' hi-hi-h'er'-h'er'
That  age, ache,  penury,    and   imprisonment
  /    O   /    O    /    /    /    /    /    O
 ha hay h'o' hay-h'er' hi h'er' ha-h'er'-high
Can lay on   nature  is   a      paradise
  /     /    —    O    /    /
h'er' h'o' hee hear h'er' heh
To   what we  fear  of death.
```

Do you notice how committing to each vowel, to its specific sound and length, creates a *music* in the text? Do you get a sense of how the character might be feeling from this music? It may be at this point that you are focusing so hard on doing the exercise that you can't pick up on the music or emotion. This is often the case at first. As you practise the exercise, it will become more and more comfortable. For now, choose for yourself whether you want to have another go at the vowel exercise or return to the whole speech.

○ Speak the text normally, letting the vowels take care of themselves.

○ Use the earlier unmarked versions on page 101.

How was that? Did you notice that you were naturally using the vowel lengths more, that they were more distinct?

This exercise is an excellent way of becoming aware of the specific music of each text. The point being, as I hope you have begun to discover, that the music of a piece may be harsh and abrupt just as often as it may be beautiful or lyrical. It reflects the feelings of the characters and can change as those feelings change: it is not a single overlaid melody.

You may already have begun to notice patterns of sound in the text, where certain sounds are repeated. We will look at such patterns and the clues they give you after the next exercise.

Connecting with the Consonants

To become aware of physically forming the consonants and how they add to the sound pattern of the whole

Now let's focus on the consonants. The speeches are marked with a consonant–only version. Continue working with the same speech as before.

Note: As mentioned in the previous chapter on modern text, 'l' is pronounced differently when it comes at the start of a word or syllable from the way it is pronounced when it comes at the end of a word or syllable. An initial 'l' is called a clear 'l', and is made mostly by the movement of the tongue tip. A final 'l' is called a dark 'l' and the back of the tongue is also used. In the text they are marked as follows: clear – 1   dark – 11

○ Speak the consonants only, allowing the vowels to be reduced to a neutral grunt.
  * marks words that only have vowels, simply click or clap on these to acknowledge that there is a word there.

VIOLA: **f* d-d l-v y   n m m-st-z fl-m**
If I did love you in my master's flame,

w-th s-ch * s-ffr-ng s-ch* d-dl   l-f
With such a suff'ring, such a deadly life,

n y   d-n-ll* w-d f-nd n   s-s
In your denial I would find no sense;

* w-d n-t nd-st-nd t
I would not understand it.

OLIVIA: **w   w-t w-d y**
                                 Why, what would you?

VIOLA: **m-k m * w-l c-b-n t y   g-t**
Make me a willow cabin at your gate,

nd c-ll p-n m s-ll w-th-n th h-s
And call upon my soul within the house;

r-t   l-ll c-nt-ns v c-nt-mn-d l-v
Write loyal cantons of contemnèd love,

nd s-ng th-m l-d v-n n th d-d v n-t
And sing them loud even in the dead of night;

h-l   y   n-m t th   r-v-br-t h-llz
Hallo your name to the reverberate hills,

  nd m-k th b-bl-ng g-s-p v th *
And make the babbling gossip of the air

cr   t   l-v * y   sh-d n-t r-st
Cry out 'Olivia!' O you should not rest

  b-tw-n th l-m-nts v * nd   th
Between the elements of air and earth

b-t y   sh-d p-t m
But you should pity me!

OLIVIA: **y   m-t d m-ch**
                                    You might do much.

                    *

CLAUDIO:

  *** b-t t d   nd g w n   n-t w**
Ay, but to die, and go we know not where,

t   l n c-lld bstr-csh-n nd t   r-t
To lie in cold obstruction and to rot;

th-s s-ns-bll w-m m-sh-n t b-c-m
This sensible warm motion to become

*** n-d-d cl-d nd th   d-l-t-d sp-r-t**
A kneaded clod; and the delighted spirit

t   b-th n f-r fl-dz * t r-z-d
To bathe in fiery floods, or to reside

 n thr-l-ng r-g-n v th-ck-r-bd   s
In thrilling region of thick-ribbèd ice,

t   b   mpr-z-nd n th   v-l-s w-ndz
To be imprisoned in the viewless winds

  nd bl-n w-th r-stl-s v-l-ns   r-nd   b-t
And blown with restless violence round about

th   p-nd-nt w-lld * t   b w-s   th-n w-st
The pendent world; or to be worse than worst

 v th-s th-t l-l-s   nd ns-t-n   th-t
Of those that lawless and incertain thought

m-g-n h-l-ng t-s t   h-r-bll
Imagine howling, 'tis too horrible.

th w-r-st nd m-st l-th-d w-lld-l l-f
The weariest and most loathèd worldly life

th-t dg   k   p-n-r-y nd mpr-s-nm-nt
That age, ache, penury, and imprisonment

c-n l   n n-t-ch z * p-r-d-s
Can lay on nature is a paradise

t   w-t w f   v d-th
To what we fear of death.

Working with the consonants in this way can feel very frustrating as if you can't quite get going. This is because it is the vowels that carry the flow, and the consonants that define and shape that flow. At the same time you are probably aware of the amount your lips and tongue are working. This gives – as Cicely Berry calls it – muscularity to the words. It gives energy and bite.

○ *Now speak the whole text, letting the consonants take care of themselves.*

VIOLA: If I did love you in my master's flame,
       With such a suff'ring, such a deadly life,
       In your denial I would find no sense;
       I would not understand it.

OLIVIA: Why, what would you?

VIOLA: Make me a willow cabin at your gate,
       And call upon my soul within the house;
       Write loyal cantons of contemnèd love,
       And sing them loud even in the dead of night;
       Hallo your name to the reverberate hills,
       And make the babbling gossip of the air
       Cry out 'Olivia!' O you should not rest
       Between the elements of air and earth
       But you should pity me!

OLIVIA: You might do much.

*

CLAUDIO: Ay, but to die, and go we know not where,
       To lie in cold obstruction and to rot;
       This sensible warm motion to become
       A kneaded clod; and the delighted spirit

To bathe in fiery floods, or to reside
In thrilling region of thick-ribbèd ice,
To be imprisoned in the viewless winds
And blown with restless violence round about
The pendent world; or to be worse than worst
Of those that lawless and incertain thought
Imagine howling, 'tis too horrible.
The weariest and most loathèd worldly life
That age, ache, penury, and imprisonment
Can lay on nature is a paradise
To what we fear of death.

Does the text feel easier to say, does it feel more defined? Do you get a more muscular sense of the words as you say them? Working in this way gives you a physical sense of the words and makes them much more comfortable and authentic to say.

If you practise the vowel and consonant exercises regularly you will find that you become more responsive to sound in all texts and therefore more able to honour it and make it your own. This in turn will help you to find the particular size and energy of a text in a way that is truthful and engaging. So, even if you're not sure what you're getting out of these exercises, they are worth persevering with.

Alliteration, Assonance and Consonance

You will probably already have become aware of certain sound patterns during the previous exercises, whether you know what they are called or not. Here we are going to consider them more closely and how they can support you as an actor.

The patterns all involve *repetition*. When we repeat a sound, or indeed a word, in everyday speech we are usually *aware* of repeating it, and that causes us to say the repetition in a different way: to give it a little more energy or emphasis if you like; and each time we repeat, we build the energy or emphasis a little more. Repetition of sound in text builds in the same way and further supports both sound and sense.

Alliteration

Alliteration is the repetition of the first consonant or consonant cluster in the word. There are several examples in Viola's and Olivia's exchange: 'my master's', 'such a suff'ring, such', 'Why, what would you?', 'Make me', 'might do much'; and also in Claudio's speech: 'know not', 'fiery floods', 'thrilling region of thick-ribbèd', 'worst than worst'.

○ Take Viola's line: 'With such a suff'ring, such a deadly life' and say it being aware of the repetition of the 's'.

○ Notice how the repetition gives energy and therefore emphasis to 'suff'ring' and the second 'such'.

The repetition does not always have to follow immediately and indeed the thread of repeated 's's set up in the line we have just looked at is picked up again at the end of the following line:

> With such a suff'ring, such a deadly life
> In your denial I would find no sense

○ Try the two lines, letting the repetitions build in energy and therefore emphasis.

Can you feel the build-up of energy and emphasis and how it climaxes on 'sense' and communicates Viola's feeling of frustration both in terms of her own hopeless love for Orsino and his for Olivia?

The repetition can be even further apart, as in the following example from Claudio's speech where it occurs at the same point in each of the lines:

> To be imprisoned in the viewless winds
> And blown with restless violence round about

○ Try these two lines, letting the repetition in the second line build in energy and therefore emphasis.

Do you notice how the emphasis given by the repetition supports the feeling and meaning of the lines?

There can also be different threads of alliteration going on at the same time. In Viola's speech: 'Write loyal cantons of contemnèd love,/ And sing them loud'; and in Claudio's speech: 'Imagine howling, 'tis too horrible', 'weariest and most loathèd worldly life'. These give energy and emphasis in a much more subtle way than would repeating the same sound four times in close proximity.

○ *Try these phrases a few times, letting both repetitions build and feeling how they weave into each other.*

Focusing on and using the patterns of sound helps to bind emotion and sense together in a way that is satisfying both for you and the audience. Once we have been through all three patterns I will suggest the best way to explore them when working on text.

Assonance

Assonance is the repetition of the vowels *within* the word. Again, there are several examples in Viola and Olivia's exchange: 'such a suff'ring, such', 'denial I would find', 'Olivia! O'; and in Claudio's speech: 'Ay, but to die', 'go we know', 'thrilling region of thick-ribbèd', 'round about', 'most loathèd', 'age, ache', 'lay on nature'.

○ *Try out some of the phrases above so you can notice the build and emphasis for yourself, and again how it supports the feeling and meaning.*

As with the earlier work on *Connecting with the Vowels*, focusing on the repetition of the vowels gives you a sense of the emotional build and release. It encourages you to be much braver and it connects you much more deeply to the text.

You may have noticed that some of the phrases have both alliteration and assonance. This gives the text a complexity and intensity that allows the hearer to receive the essence of the speech at a sound level as well as a sense level.

You may be wondering how you are going to weave these different threads of sound repetition together, but as always you won't have to focus consciously on them if you have explored them individually and raised your awareness of them. They will look after themselves and weave together far more subtly and effectively than if you tried to weave them consciously.

Consonance

Consonance is the repetition of consonants in the middle or at the end of words. Again, there are examples in Viola's lines: 'call upon my soul', 'cantons of contemnèd'; and in Claudio's: 'kneaded clod', 'restless violence', 'weariest and most'.

Here the repetitions tend to give a more subtle build and emphasis. Paying attention to consonance gives a greater sense of commitment to the feeling and meaning, a sense of following through.

○ *Try out the phrases above and notice how paying attention to the repetition of the consonants encourages you to commit to the sounds and therefore to the words.*

Sometimes the consonant near or at the end of a word will be the same consonant that starts the next word; whilst this is not strictly consonance it is worth considering here. Both Viola and Claudio have examples: 'deadly life', 'warm motion'. This repetition tends to make us separate the two words and therefore give them emphasis through giving them more space and time.

○ *Try these two phrases for yourself, notice how separating the words gives each phrase greater power and allows you to use the sound to convey the sense.*

Exploring Alliteration, Assonance and Consonance

To explore the sound patterns effectively in a text

Below is a simple and effective way of exploring the sound patterns outside rehearsal and performance.

It can be a good idea to photocopy the speech or scene you are working on so that your rehearsal copy doesn't become too busy with marks. It is also a good idea to mark the three different sound patterns in different colours so that they are easier to see.

○ *Go through a speech or scene marking all the alliteration. The characters may share alliteration so be aware of this.*

○ *Then, speak the scene being aware of each thread of alliteration and allowing the energy to build.*

○ *Then, do the same with the assonance.*

○ *Then, do the same with the consonance.*

○ *Then, speak the text, letting the sound patterns take care of themselves.*

Focusing on the sound patterns in this way helps you to connect more deeply with the sound shape or music in a text and also helps you to find the key words in terms of the argument of a speech or scene. Together with the earlier work on vowels and consonants it will draw you closer to understanding *how* the sounds support the feeling and meaning. It is then much easier to commit to the language and because you have more sense of how it works, it becomes more fun to speak: you can really get your teeth into it. You will also begin to feel far more confident because you will get a clear sense of the clues that Shakespeare gives his actors and of the specific journey on which he takes the character.

Having looked at alliteration, assonance and consonance, there is a final sound pattern that we need to look at.

Rhyme

I am sure that you are familiar with rhyme, which consists of the repetition of the vowel sound and any following consonants in a word, while the preceding consonant is different. Therefore, '*grey*' rhymes with '*day*', '*laugh*' with '*scarf*', '*sign*' with '*pine*' and so on.

Note: Half-rhyme consists of the consonants in a word being the same and the vowel shifting: 'fall' *and* 'fail', 'laugh' *and* 'life', 'beat' *and* 'bite'.

In polysyllabic words, only the last syllable has to have the same vowels and any following consonant, although the writer may choose to rhyme earlier syllables as well, as Shakespeare does in the following couplet from Helena's speech in *A Midsummer Night's Dream*:

> Things base and vile, holding no quan**tity**,
> Love can transpose to form and dig**nity**.[22]

Rhyme helps to mark the end of a verse line, or group of verse lines, more strongly. There are many different rhyming patterns. The most common are *rhyming couplets*, where each pair of lines rhyme. This example comes from the same speech of Helena's:

> How happy some o'er other some can **be**!
> Through Athens I am thought as fair as **she**.
> But what of that? Demetrius thinks not **so**;
> He will not know what all but he do **know**.

There are also *quatrains with alternate rhymes* where, within four lines, the first and third line rhyme as do the second and fourth. This example is from a speech of Lysander's in *A Midsummer Night's Dream*:

> Fair love, you faint with wand'ring in the **wood**,
> And, to speak troth, I have forgot our **way**.

We'll rest us, Hermia, if you think it **good**,
And tarry for the comfort of the **day**.

Exploring the Rhyme

To understand how to work with the rhyme

So what do rhymes give us? Well, as mentioned, they use repetition, which creates a build-up of energy. In addition they give you a sense of set-up and completion.

Let's start with Helena's lines in rhyming couplets.

○ *As you say the lines, indicate the setting-up and completion of the rhyme physically by turning one of your hands palms upwards on the set-up of the rhyme and closing that palm on the completion of the rhyme.*

○ *Then, turn the other palm upwards on the next set-up and close it on the completion.*

> How happy some o'er other some can **be**!
> Through Athens I am thought as fair as **she**.
> But what of that? Demetrius thinks not **so**;
> He will not know what all but he do **know**.

How was that? Did you notice that the rhymes give an extra energy, so you spring off the set-up of the rhyme into the completion and then the completed couplet gives you an energy which springs you into the next couplet and so on?

Also, the rhymes make both listener and speaker more aware of the verse structure, as they highlight more strongly the end of the verse line. This gives a tighter framework for the content of the speech to push against. It also highlights even more strongly the last word in the line.

Now let's look at Lysander's alternate rhymes. Here you have two set-ups followed by two completions.

○ *Again, indicate the set-ups and completions with your hands as you say the lines. On the first set-up again turn one palm upwards and on the second set-up turn your other palm upwards. Then, on the first completion close your first palm and on your second completion close your second palm.*

> Fair love, you faint with wand'ring in the **wood**,
> And, to speak troth, I have forgot our **way**.

> We'll rest us, Hermia, if you think it **good**,
> And tarry for the comfort of the **day**.

How was that? Did you notice how different that feels? The rhyming is less obvious and you have to wait longer for the completion. With the rhyming couplets, each is a complete entity in itself, whereas with the alternate rhymes there is no completion until the fourth line.

○ *Try the two examples again in the same way and notice how they feel different for you and how they might lead to different thought and emotional energies.*

There is no right answer. As always, what is important here is to notice that there is a structural difference which is likely to lead to a difference in feeling and thought.

So how does rhyme interact with sentence structure? Where the completing rhyme and the full stop coincide, you get a greater sense of ending. Where there is no full stop you move straight from the completion of one rhyme into the set-up of the next. In this way variety is achieved, as one structure is played off against another and so predictability is avoided and tension increased. If you have separately explored the sentence, verse and rhyme structures through doing *Walking the Sentences, Walking the Verse* and *Exploring the Rhyme* you will naturally find the variety and tension when you rehearse and perform.

What happens when the whole or part of a scene is written in rhyme with the characters possibly sharing rhyming couplets?

The same tension between verse structure and sentence structure will be in evidence in scenes as it is in speeches. The added extra is the possibility of shared rhymes and also of breaking into or out of rhyme and therefore coming together with or moving away from the other character or characters.

*A word of warning: If you try to ignore rhyme it will stick out like a sore thumb. If, however, you immerse yourself in it and use it fully, it will seem wholly appropriate and real. This is true of every so-called artificial device or structure in a play – the more you embrace it, the more it will fit; the more you ignore or try to hide it, the more obvious and clumsy it becomes. Where a whole speech is in rhyming couplets, returning to **Walking the Sentences** and **Clicking the Final Word** will help you balance the rhyme structure with the sense structure and keep the speech flexible rather than emphatic.*

Rhyming couplets at the end of speeches and scenes help to finish the speech or scene firmly and give an extra energy to that end. Often they occur when a character has come to a decision: the rhyming couplet shows the decision, and the energy it releases takes the character forward into action.

The first example, from *Macbeth*, comes after Lady Macbeth has quelled Macbeth's doubts and he determines to kill King Duncan.

> Away, and mock the time with fairest show:
> False face must hide what the false heart doth know.

The second example, from *Measure for Measure*, comes after Angelo has offered to release Isabella's brother if she will sleep with him. She determines to tell her brother of this offer and that she cannot possibly agree so he should, therefore, prepare to die.

> I'll tell him yet of Angelo's request,
> And fit his mind to death, for his soul's rest.

The third example, from *Twelfth Night*, comes after Viola realises that Olivia has fallen in love with her in her disguise as a man.

> O time, thou must untangle this, not I;
> It is too hard a knot for me t'untie.

The final example, from *Richard III*, comes after Richard has succeeded, against all the odds, to woo Anne, whose husband and father he killed.

> Shine out, fair sun, till I have brought a glass,
> That I may see my shadow as I pass.

Notice rhyming couplets at the end of speeches and scenes and use them with confidence. They give tremendous energy, which is vital in transitions between speeches and between scenes. They are also great fun for the actor and audience whether in a light-hearted or blacker moment, so embrace them fully and let them help you and the audience on your way through the journey of the play.

Blank Verse

A great deal of Shakespeare's verse is not written in rhyme. As you may be aware this is known as blank verse. The structure of the verse is still there but is less strongly emphasised: there is less sense of completion than there is with rhyming lines.

The amount of rhymed or blank verse used in Shakespeare's plays varies. What is important, as with all the other patterns and structures in Shakespeare is to notice the shifts. Ask yourself: '*Why do I start or stop rhyming here? What difference does this make? What difference do I notice as I speak it? Is there a shift of thought or feeling or relationship?*'

CONNECTING WITH THE WORDS AND IMAGES

Having explored sound patterns, we are now going to move on to the words themselves: to connecting with them and the images behind them, as we did in the last chapter.

Levels of Meaning

As I explained in the last chapter, the first – or what I call *dictionary* – level of meaning only gives you the generally agreed sense of the word; it doesn't take you into the associations the word would have if you had chosen it for yourself. So it's important to find a way to go deeper into the words and make this associative connection. Many positive things happen when you do this. Firstly, you become more expressive since the images you connect with behind the words will colour them more profoundly. Secondly, the text becomes easier to remember since there has been a deeper exploration of each word and its place within the whole. Thirdly, the text becomes more comfortable to say: it feels more truthful and real, especially in the case of more obscure words that you would not use in everyday conversation.

As with modern text we will start with the *Three Times Through* and *Physicalising the Words* exercises, since these are simple and straight-forward ways of exploring and deepening your connection with the words and the images that lie behind them.

For the exercises in this section we are going to use two new speeches: one from *Romeo and Juliet* and the other from *Henry V*. Each speech is accompanied by a brief description of the situation and to whom the character is talking. It is worth preparing whichever speech you choose by going through the earlier exercises in this chapter.

Romeo and Juliet [Act 3 Scene 2]: Juliet has secretly married Romeo and is waiting for him to arrive so they can spend their first night together. She is by herself and talks first to the sun, imploring it to set quickly, then to the night, begging it to come quickly, then to Romeo, then to night again and lastly to herself.

JULIET: Gallop apace, you fiery-footed steeds,
        Towards Phoebus' lodging. Such a waggoner
        As Phaeton would whip you to the west
        And bring in cloudy night immediately.
        Spread thy close curtain, love-performing night,
        That runaway's eyes may wink, and Romeo
        Leap to these arms untalk'd-of and unseen.
        Lovers can see to do their amorous rites
        By their own beauties; or, if love be blind,
        It best agrees with night. Come, civil night,
        Thou sober-suited matron, all in black,
        And learn me how to loose a winning match
        Play'd for a pair of stainless maidenhoods.
        Hood my unmann'd blood, bating in my cheeks,
        With thy black mantle, till strange love grow bold,
        Think true love acted simple modesty.
        Come night, come Romeo, come thou day in night,
        For thou wilt lie upon the wings of night
        Whiter than new snow upon a raven's back.
        Come gentle night, come loving black-brow'd night,
        Give me my Romeo; and when I shall die
        Take him and cut him out in little stars,
        And he will make the face of heaven so fine
        That all the world will be in love with night,
        And pay no worship to the garish sun.
        O, I have bought the mansion of a love
        But not possess'd it; and though I am sold,
        Not yet enjoy'd. So tedious is this day
        As is the night before some festival
        To an impatient child that hath new robes
        And may not wear them. O, here comes my Nurse.

Enter NURSE, *with cords, wringing her hands.*

        And she brings news, and every tongue that speaks
        But Romeo's name speaks heavenly eloquence.
        Now, Nurse, what news? What hast thou there?
        The cords that Romeo bid thee fetch?[23]

Henry V [Act 3 Scene 1]: Henry is leading his army in an attack on Harfleur. Here he rallies them to attack once more. He starts by talking to them all, then addresses the nobles and then the common soldiers.[24]

> HENRY: Once more unto the breach, dear friends, once more,
> Or close the wall up with our English dead.
> In peace there's nothing so becomes a man
> As modest stillness and humility:
> But when the blast of war blows in our ears,
> Then imitate the action of the tiger;
> Stiffen the sinews, conjure up the blood,
> Disguise fair nature with hard-favour'd rage;
> Then lend the eye a terrible aspect;
> Let it pry through the portage of the head
> Like the brass cannon; let the brow o'erwhelm it
> As fearfully as doth a gallèd rock
> O'erhang and jutty his confounded base,
> Swilled with the wild and wasteful ocean.
> Now set the teeth and stretch the nostrils wide,
> Hold hard the breath, and bend up every spirit
> To his full height! On, on you noblest English!
> Whose blood is fet from fathers of war-proof;
> Fathers that, like so many Alexanders,
> Have in these parts from morn till even fought,
> And sheath'd their swords for lack of argument.
> Dishonour not your mothers; now attest
> That those whom you call'd fathers did beget you.
> Be copy now to men of grosser blood,
> And teach them how to war. And you, good yeomen,
> Whose limbs were made in England, show us here
> The mettle of your pasture; let us swear
> That you are worth your breeding; which I doubt not;
> For there is none of you so mean and base
> That hath not noble lustre in your eyes.
> I see you stand like greyhounds in the slips,
> Straining upon the start. The game's afoot:
> Follow your spirit; and upon this charge
> Cry, 'God for Harry, England, and Saint George!'[25]

Three Times Through

To explore and connect with the words

This exercise is excellent for when you want to sit quietly and work. It is a way of feeding the text into yourself and is one of the few exercises where you do not focus on talking to anyone. No decisions as to how to say the words are necessary. What you are doing here is noticing the words your character uses, the order in which he/she uses them and the images that these words evoke.

The key to the success of this exercise is in keeping the chunks short. I have marked up sections of the two speeches below to give you an idea of the ideal length of each chunk.

> JULIET: Gallop apace,/ you fiery-footed steeds,/
> Towards Phoebus' lodging./ Such a waggoner/
> As Phaeton/ would whip you/ to the west/
> And bring in/ cloudy night/ immediately./

*

> HENRY: Once more/ unto the breach,/ dear friends,/ once more,/
> Or close the wall up/ with our English dead./
> In peace/ there's nothing/ so becomes a man/
> As modest stillness/ and humility:/

Sometimes you will find that a longer phrase is broken into many bits. This is done so that you can take the time to explore all the words and not simply be drawn to what seem to be the key words. Read through the directions first and then work on your chosen speech.

○ *Sit comfortably in a chair or on the floor with the text in front of you.*

○ *Look at the first chunk, then close your eyes and say it slowly and quietly three times, allowing a slight pause between each time. Avoid deciding how to say the chunk, simply allow yourself to keep connecting more with what you are saying.*

○ *Once you have said the chunk three times, open your eyes and look at the next chunk. Take your time to absorb this new chunk and then close your eyes and allow yourself to say that chunk three times.*

○ *Continue through the speech in the same way, taking one chunk at a time. There is no need to add the chunks together. Simply explore them separately.*

○ *Work through at least the first half of your chosen speech before you move on.*

How was that? Did you notice that words and images leapt out at you and that the whole speech became much more tangible and that even the most unusual words started to feel more comfortable and connected?

This exercise is excellent with all text, but it is especially helpful with classical text because it allows you to take the time to own the words. It's enjoyable to do as well, since it's gentle and there's no need to come up with any external result. Just feed the chunks in and let the connection take place.

Physicalising the Words

To further explore, connect with and commit to the words

This second exercise offers a more active way of exploring and connecting with the words. It is based on an exercise of Cicely Berry's and is great for getting you to commit more to the words and feel confident handling them.

○ Prop up a copy of the speech you have chosen to work on, on a window ledge or suchlike so that you are free to move, rather than having the text in your hand.

○ Take each word individually and make a movement, large or small, which expresses that word for you. This is a private exercise for you, so it doesn't matter whether the movements would make any sense to anyone else, as long as they make sense to you.

○ Some words you may find you only need to explore once whilst others need to be explored several times, using either the same or different movements until you feel that you have connected with the word for yourself.

○ Include all the words – 'a', 'in', 'and', 'the', etc. – since these are also important in the journey of the speech. Also, pay particular attention to pronouns – 'I', 'you', 'they', etc. since it is important that you are crystal clear about who you are referring to.

○ Also, make sure that your movements, however large or small, are fully committed.

○ Work through at least the second half of your chosen speech before you read on.

How did you find that? Again, did you notice the words becoming more tangible and connected? Because you are moving, and doing so in a committed way, the words will also come out more confidently and expressively, since committing with the body leads to *vocal* commitment and release. It also shows up where you have no real idea what you are talking about! If that is the case, look the word up or ask someone about it.

INTERNAL GEOGRAPHY

As I mentioned in the last chapter, when we speak for ourselves, everything that we mention has a specific place or reference; whether it be a person or a place or an idea. However, when it comes to text, the people and places and ideas are less securely fixed and we need to create an internal geography, which specifically locates what we are talking about. This does not take away from the ambiguity that words often have. It simply allows us to have a much more precise sense of the words and the way they relate to each other.

The following two exercises – *Geography Exercise* and *Museum Visit* – are excellent ways of giving words a specific place or reference. They also help to deepen the connection with the text and the sense of owning and feeling comfortable with it.

It is easier to do these two exercises once you know the text, but nevertheless I often use it in workshops where people are unfamiliar with the text and are still having to refer to it. It is up to you whether you try it on one of the texts above or use a piece of Shakespeare you already know. If you are working with a text you don't know by heart then take your time rather than trying to keep the speech in one piece.

Geography Exercise

To anchor the places, people and ideas, which you refer to in a text, giving them a reality and relationship

○ Gather a group of objects with different textures – a scarf, some keys, a pen, a book, a hairbrush, a plastic bottle, a purse or wallet, etc. – and set them out in front of you on the floor or on a table.

Note: Seven to ten objects is sufficient since they can be used to represent more than one word or phrase.

○ If you need the text, place it beside the objects so that you can see it clearly without having to hold it.

○ Imagine that there is someone sitting opposite you that you want to communicate the speech to and that the objects in front of you represent the people and places and ideas you refer to in the speech.

○ Say the text picking up an object to represent the first key word or phrase as if the object is the word or phrase and you are showing it to the person you are talking to. Then, put that object down and pick up another to represent the next key word or phrase.

○ For example, in Juliet's speech you might pick up a first object for 'Gallop apace', a second object for 'fiery-footed' and a third for 'steeds'. In Henry's speech you might pick up a first object on 'Once more', a second object on 'unto the breach,' third on 'dear friends', a fourth on 'once more'.

○ Continue through the whole speech in the same way.

○ There is no need to make the objects fit what you are talking about; simply pick up whatever comes to hand.

How did you find that? Did you find that the words became more specific and that you could see the relationship they had with one another?

This exercise is great to do with a scene partner or partners. You begin to have a sense of the to and fro between the characters and of how each person's words relate to the others'.

Like many of the exercises this is worth coming back to at various points in rehearsal and even performance.

Museum Visit

To further anchor the places, people and ideas which you refer to in a text, giving them a reality and relationship

This exercise is similar to the last but is more active. It encourages commitment and increases the communicative energy as well as building the specific sense of place and relationship.

○ Imagine that the room you are working in is like a museum exhibition containing all the places and people and ideas that you refer to in your speech.

○ Imagine that you are dying to show someone round this exhibition: if you have someone you can work with, take them by the hand and literally pull them after you rather as a child might an adult.

○ As you say the speech, point to or pick up objects in the room as if they represent key words or phrases in the text.

○ Be prepared to run across the space to find the next object or to stretch up or crouch down, so that you are fully committing to showing the person the world that you are talking about.

How was that? Was it fun to do? Did you find you had more energy and felt more comfortable with the words? Did they become even more specific and begin to have even more of a relationship?

Like the last exercise this one is worth returning to throughout rehearsal and performance. It can be especially useful if you are feeling tentative about a speech or a scene or it has become stale. As with the last exercise you can do this one with scene partners so that whoever is speaking leads the other characters around their 'museum'. It is excellent for ensuring that each person drives the scene on, rather than letting the energy drop on their lines.

LANGUAGE PATTERNS

Now that we have explored the words and images I want to look at some of the language patterns and how being aware of them can help you to handle the text more easily and so make it more truthful and engaging.

Contrast [Antithesis]

Contrasts of words, phrases and ideas are very important to observe in a speech: these are the hinge points of the character's argument. The character, just as we do, moves through ideas, selecting and rejecting, refining and redefining, setting up one idea against another to reach a conclusion or an understanding or a resolution.

Antithesis is a particular type of contrast. Literally 'anti' means 'opposite' and 'thesis' means 'idea'. These opposite ideas are expressed in a way that creates a sense of balance as this line from Shakespeare's Sonnet 27 shows. He is talking about when he feels at odds with the world and how all the things he previously enjoyed now do nothing for him.

> With what I *most enjoy contented least*

The symmetry of form further highlights the difference between the two things being contrasted and so helps to communicate the predicament of the speaker.

Juliet's speech carries through it the contrast between day and night, light and darkness. The day, with its light, that she is so eager will pass in order that night and darkness can come. There is also a contrast between sight and blindness:

> Lovers can see to do their amorous rites
> By their own beauties; or, if love be *blind*,
> It best agrees with night.

In Henry's speech he contrasts peace and war and the behaviours that are appropriate to both:

> In *peace* there's nothing so becomes a man
> As *modest stillness* and *humility*:
> But when the *blast of war* blows in our ears,
> Then *imitate the action of the tiger,*

He also contrasts the possible lowly birth of the yeomen with the nobleness of their spirits:

> For there is none of you so *mean and base*
> That hath not *noble* lustre in your eyes.

By noticing these contrasts you will have a better understanding of the shape of a speech or scene and therefore of the character's thinking. As a result you will find it easier to take on that shape as your own.

Exploring Contrast

To experience the contrast in a speech or scene

You can work through Juliet's or Henry's speech or you can choose another speech to work on.

○ *Go through your chosen speech looking for and marking all the contrasts.*

○ *Choose objects to represent each. Therefore, in Henry's speech you would have an object to represent peace, another to represent war and so on.*

○ *As you speak the speech, pick up or point to the relevant object.*

How was that? Sometimes at first, it can be hard to co-ordinate but if you keep working at it you will find it easier and you will begin to feel how the contrast of words, phrases and ideas works: how one word or idea is held up against another.

What I hope you will realise is that with this work, as with all the rest, you are noticing what is there and how what is there works. I find that noticing the *what and how* is the vital element in all text work. Once you have noticed these you will naturally use them when you rehearse or perform a speech or scene: you won't be able to help it.

Repetition

Now we have looked at contrast let's move on to look at repetition. Repetition of word, phrase and idea has the same effect as repetition of sound, which we looked at earlier: it builds. Repetition in well-written text is fun to play with and, once you have noticed it, it will support you through speeches and scenes.

Obviously, repetition in badly written text is a completely different matter: it dulls rather than brings to life and moves away from truth not towards it. It in no way reflects how we use repetition in everyday life.

Repetition is natural to us when communicating. We use it all the time without being aware of it. We repeat what we have said to get attention, to make a point, to build an atmosphere or to build to a climax. We repeat what others have said to connect with them, to build on what they have said, to banter or to turn their words back on them.

Start to pay attention when you are talking and you'll notice it. Ask yourself: '*Why am I repeating here? Is it to clarify, to emphasise, to tease, to connect and so on?*' As you will discover, you are already an unconscious expert at repetition, so it is simply a question of now noticing the repetition that is in the text because once you have noticed it you will know what to do with it.

What you are going to do is look through Juliet's and Henry's speeches for repetition of word, phrase and idea, and explore what noticing and acting on that repetition gives you.

So let's start again with Juliet's speech. She says the word 'night' eleven times in twenty-nine lines. She repeatedly describes night calling it: 'love-performing night', 'civil night', 'sober suited matron, all in black', 'gentle night', 'loving, black-browed night'.

Four times she directly asks night to come and bring darkness so that she and Romeo can be together unseen. Twice she asks in other ways: 'Spread thy close curtain', 'Hood my unmanned blood . . . with thy black mantle'.

Why might she use this much repetition? When do you repeatedly ask someone to do something and address them with various complimentary names? When you want them to do something urgent and important for you! Juliet is desperate for Romeo to come to her so they can spend their first night together. Of course, there may also be nervousness at losing her virginity and about whether the reality of them being together will live up to her dreams – all the thoughts and emotions a young girl might feel on the brink of her first sexual encounter – but at the same time there is an eagerness and an urgency which is expressed in the repetition.

As I have already mentioned, repetition gives build. In Juliet's speech this build is increased because she adds different descriptions of night, just as you might add to the name of someone whose attention you were trying to get.

So what about repetition in Henry's speech? In the first line 'Once more' is repeated twice as Henry encourages his soldiers to yet again attack Harfleur. Later there is repetition: 'On, on' as he again urges them into battle. Then, he repeats the word 'fathers' as he encourages them to behave honourably. In the last line there is repetition of idea in that 'Harry, England, and Saint George' are all representations of what the soldiers are fighting for: their own country. Henry – here called Harry – as their king is the representative of that country, just as St George, the patron saint of England, is. The build in energy that the repetition gives here is added to by the fact that he starts with himself as king, then widens out to the country and then finally to the symbol of that country.

Exploring Repetition

To get to grips with repetition in speeches and scenes

Again, you can use Juliet's or Henry's speech for this exercise or one of your own choosing.

○ Go through the speech and mark all the repetitions of word and idea.

○ Choose an object to represent each word or idea that is repeated. If there are a lot of different words and ideas it's worth sticking a label on each object, with the word or idea written on it, so you can remember what each object represents.

○ As you speak the speech, pick up or point to the relevant object each time that word or idea is mentioned.

How did you find that? Did you notice the build? Can you sense how that helps the journey of the speech? You may already have noticed some of the repetition when you were doing *Geography Exercise* and *Museum Visit*, but it is always worth at least once focusing specifically on the repetition, especially with Shakespeare since you can be sure that the repetition is never accidental but rather beautifully constructed to help both the sense and the feeling of the speech.

Comparison [Simile and Metaphor]

We use these all the time in our everyday lives to communicate more accurately whatever is important to us: '*It's like* . . . ', we say, and find something that we can compare our idea or feeling or experience with, so that the other person will understand what we are talking about. As you may already know, this simple comparison, where one thing is compared with another, is called *simile*: 'Her hair was like golden sunlight.' The more compressed form of comparison, where the things compared become one, is called *metaphor*: 'Her hair was golden sunlight.'

So simile and metaphor in text are not sidetracks or nuisances that feel awkward or flowery. They are attempts by the character to find an even better way of communicating whatever it is that they want to communicate at that point.

Let's look at simile and metaphor in Juliet's and Henry's speeches. Juliet uses a metaphor to describe Romeo: 'thou day in night'. His presence, for her, will illuminate the night and make it bright, just as daylight would in the night. She packs this whole idea into four words. This is the advantage of metaphor, it can suggest so much in such a compact way.

Juliet follows up her metaphor by using a simile to further describe what it's like when Romeo's brightness interacts with the darkness of night: 'thou wilt lie upon the wings of night/ Whiter than new snow upon a raven's back'. Within this simile is another metaphor that is used to describe night: 'wings of night'. The suggestion here is that the darkness of night is a pair of huge wings spreading across the sky. Again, notice how much more powerful the metaphor is than the long-winded description.

Let's look at Henry's speech now. There are several similes and possibly one metaphor. In each case, Henry uses these to conjure up graphic examples of how he wants the soldiers to behave. The first simile, 'Let it pry through the portage of the head/ Like the brass cannon', describes how he wants their eyes to bulge out of their heads like canons do out of their defences. The second, 'As fearfully as doth a gallèd rock/ O'erhang and jutty his confounded base', describes how he wants their foreheads – perhaps furrowed in a fierce frown – to stand out just like the top of a huge rock protrudes much further than its base does. He goes on to talk of the base being 'Swilled with the wild and wasteful ocean', and this may be a metaphor: where the enemy soldiers are the ocean which is swilling around the base of the English soldiers in a wild and wasteful manner but is not doing any great damage. The third simile, 'like so many Alexanders', describes how tirelessly and relentlessly the soldiers' fathers fought just like the great soldier Alexander. The fourth simile, 'like greyhounds in the slips/ Straining upon the start', describes how he sees the soldiers standing in front of him so ready to go into battle that they are straining just like greyhounds might do at the start of a race.

These comparisons paint strong pictures that help both Juliet and Henry to summon up either what they are feeling or what they want those listening to them to feel and do.

Exploring Simile and Metaphor

To experience what similes and metaphors add to the text

Again, use either Juliet's or Henry's speech or one of your own choosing.

○ *Go through your chosen speech and mark all the comparisons. Remember the similes will be preceded by 'as' or 'like' ['like greyhounds in the slips'] whereas with metaphors what is being compared will simply have become the thing it is being compared to ['wings of night'].*

Note: Comparisons can also be indicated by the word 'than', *as in* 'whiter than new snow . . . '

○ *Speak the parts of the text where there are comparisons, leaving the actual similes and metaphors out for the moment. For example:*

> Come night, come Romeo, come . . . . ;
> For thou wilt lie upon . . . . night
> Whiter than . . . .

○ *Then, speak the same part of the text again, adding the comparisons back in, as if you have chosen them as the best way to communicate more clearly what you feel and mean. For example:*

> Come night, come Romeo, come **thou day in night**;
> For thou wilt lie upon **the wings of** night
> Whiter than **new snow upon a raven's back**:

How did you find that? Did you begin to feel that the comparisons – whether similes or metaphors – could be a help rather than a hindrance? That in fact they are essential to your character in communicating the ideas that he/she wants to communicate? The more you can embrace them in this way, the more they will become part of the whole rather than just a flowery nuisance or a mystifying jumble of words which hold you up.

Names and Titles

We often find having to say someone's name or title, like '*sir*' or '*my lord*', very awkward in classical text. It seems formal and interrupts the flow. This occurs because we are not aware of when and how we use names and titles in our normal conversation. It is quite possible to have long exchanges without using either names or titles, so, when do we use them and why, and how does this dictate the way we say them?

We use names when we want to get the other person's attention. By saying their name we hope they will focus a little more sharply on what we are saying at that point. We use titles in the same way, but we also use titles to raise or lower the status of the listener; to be polite, to show deference and respect, or quite the opposite, depending on the way we say it!

So a waiter may very politely say, '*Please sir/madam will you follow me*', and make the customers feel important and well treated, while a snooty waiter might use the same mode of address in such a way as to suggest that they are not worthy and not welcome.

Many couples play with names and titles. One partner may say, '*And what would Her Majesty like to do today?*' Or another may say, '*And what would sir like for breakfast?*' Depending on their relationship these words might be loving and playful or sarcastic and resentful. The point is that we do use names and titles more than we think and they are not awkward interruptions but an integral part of our communication with each other.

Let's have a look at how Henry uses names in his speech to the soldiers. In the first line he addresses them as 'dear friends'. In this way he moves from being their king, who is ordering them into battle, to being their fellow soldier, fighting alongside them and taking the same risks. He then addresses the nobles among his soldiers as 'you noblest English', playing on the fact that not only are they nobly born but also that they have behaved nobly and suggesting that they will behave nobly now. He follows this section by addressing the common soldiers as 'good yeomen', suggesting perhaps their strength and their sense of what is right. In each case the names he uses have a specific purpose, which is to bond the soldiers to him and inspire them to fight bravely, without hesitation.

As we have already discovered, Juliet frequently addresses night throughout her speech, each time adding different adjectives: 'love-performing night', 'civil night', 'gentle night', 'loving, black browed night'. Her use of these complimentary adjectives is part of her attempt to persuade night to come quickly. She uses the same strategy with her Nurse in an earlier scene where she wants news of Romeo: 'O honey Nurse', 'Now good sweet Nurse', 'good, good Nurse', 'sweet, sweet, sweet Nurse'.

As well as looking at the type of names used, the number of times a name is used and the shifting adjectives used, it is also worth looking for shifts in names from formal to intimate and vice versa. If you are interested in exploring this further there is an extract from *As You Like It* [on page 288], which is a good example of such shifts.

As always, the important point is to notice what is there and embrace it. In this way, as with everything else we have looked at, the names and titles will become a help rather than a hindrance and you will feel comfortable saying them.

Thee, Thou, Thy and Thine

As an end note to the work on names and titles I'd like to look briefly at the use of '*thee*', '*thou*', '*thy*' and '*thine*' as opposed to '*you*' and '*your*'. David and Ben Crystal point out that in Old English '*thou*' was singular and '*you*' was plural. Then, in the thirteenth century '*you*' started to be used as the polite form possibly due to French influence. Apparently, people would address their superiors using the formal '*you*' and their superiors would respond using '*thou*'. '*Thou*' was also used by the lower classes when talking to each other, whereas the upper classes tended to use '*you*' even with close relatives.[26]

So it is worth remembering that '*thee*', '*thou*', '*thy*' and '*thine*' are the more intimate form, and '*you*' and '*yours*', the more formal. Also, it is helpful to notice the shifts between the two forms in your text and what clues these give you about the shifts in the relationships between the characters. Again, see the scene from *As You Like It* for examples of the shift between the two.

Lists and Complex Sentences

These can be daunting in classical text. However, if you take them apart and build them up little by little, not only will you be able to handle them but also you will understand how they work within the text to build to a climax and what they tell you about a character's thoughts and feelings at that point.

Handling Lists

To get to grips with lists and how they build

Let's start by looking at lists, since these are simpler to work on. The following list comes from another speech in *Henry V*, where Henry is talking about the responsibilities laid on a king:

> Upon the king! Let us our lives, our souls,
> Our debts, our careful wives,
> Our children, and our sins lay on the king!

The best way to handle lists is to build them up one item at a time. In this way you can become fully aware both of the length of the list and the order in which it is constructed. This will enable you to handle it as you would if you had made the list up for yourself and it will therefore have the appropriate energy and build, and you will feel in control of it rather than lost in it.

○ *Take the main thrust of the sentence without any of the list and say that through a few times:*

> Upon the king! Let us . . . lay on the king!

○ *Then, add each item on the list one by one as follows:*

> Upon the king! Let us **our lives** . . . lay on the king!

> Upon the king! Let us *our lives,* **our souls** . . . lay on the king!

> Upon the king! Let us *our lives, our souls,*
> **Our debts** . . . lay on the king!

> Upon the king! Let us *our lives, our souls,*
> *Our debts,* **our careful wives** . . . lay on the king!

> Upon the king! Let us *our lives, our souls,*
> *Our debts, our careful wives,*
> **Our children** . . . lay on the king!

> Upon the king! Let us *our lives, our souls,*
> *Our debts, our careful wives,*
> *Our children,* **and our sins** lay on the king!

Do you notice how you now feel more in charge and build naturally because by adding one item at a time you have in fact gone through the process of constructing the list? On page 292 you will find a more complex list to explore.

Handling Complex Sentences

To get to grips with complex sentences and how they are constructed

Complex sentences are dealt with in a similar way. The only difference is that, instead of identifying each item in a list, you need to identify each subordinate clause, i.e. each chunk that can stand alone as a phrase and which can be removed from the sentence without destroying its main thread and thrust. These subordinate clauses can be thought of as tangents: they relate to the main thrust of the sentence, but they do not drive it forward. This is why they are so confusing: you can suddenly lose the sense of where you are going.

Here we will explore the first sentence of Claudio's speech from earlier in the chapter.

> Ay, but to die, and go we know not where,
> To lie in cold obstruction and to rot;
> This sensible warm motion to become
> A kneaded clod; and the delighted spirit
> To bathe in fiery floods, or to reside
> In thrilling region of thick-ribbèd ice,
> To be imprisoned in the viewless winds
> And blown with restless violence round about
> The pendent world; or to be worse than worst
> Of those that lawless and incertain thought
> Imagine howling, 'tis too horrible.

○ *Start by identifying the main thrust of the sentence.*

> Ay, but to die, ...
> . . . . 'tis too horrible.

○ *Now add in the subordinate clauses one by one, as follows:*

> Ay, but to die, **and go we know not where**,
> . . . . 'tis too horrible.

> Ay, but to die, *and go we know not where*,
> **To lie in cold obstruction and to rot**;
> . . . . 'tis too horrible.

> Ay, but to die, *and go we know not where*,
> *To lie in cold obstruction and to rot*;

This sensible warm motion to become
A kneaded clod; . . . .
. . . . 'tis too horrible.

Ay, but to die, *and go we know not where,*
To lie in cold obstruction and to rot;
This sensible warm motion to become
A kneaded clod; **and the delighted spirit**
To bathe in fiery floods, ...
. . . . 'tis too horrible.

Ay, but to die, *and go we know not where,*
To lie in cold obstruction and to rot;
This sensible warm motion to become
A kneaded clod; and the delighted spirit
To bathe in fiery floods, **or to reside**
In thrilling region of thick-ribbèd ice,
. . . . 'tis too horrible.

Ay, but to die, *and go we know not where,*
To lie in cold obstruction and to rot;
This sensible warm motion to become
A kneaded clod; and the delighted spirit
To bathe in fiery floods, or to reside
In thrilling region of thick-ribbèd ice,
To be imprisoned in the viewless winds
. . . . 'tis too horrible.

Ay, but to die, *and go we know not where,*
To lie in cold obstruction and to rot;
This sensible warm motion to become
A kneaded clod; and the delighted spirit
To bathe in fiery floods, or to reside
In thrilling region of thick-ribbèd ice,
To be imprisoned in the viewless winds
And blown with restless violence round about
The pendent world; . . . .
. . . .'tis too horrible.

Ay, but to die, *and go we know not where,*
To lie in cold obstruction and to rot;

This sensible warm motion to become
A kneaded clod; and the delighted spirit
To bathe in fiery floods, or to reside
In thrilling region of thick-ribbèd ice,
To be imprisoned in the viewless winds
And blown with restless violence round about
The pendent world; **or to be worse than worst**
Of those that lawless and incertain thought
Imagine howling*, 'tis too horrible.*

Again, can you feel the build? Taking complex sentences apart in this way helps you to understand how they are constructed and therefore how to handle them and make them your own rather than getting lost in them. Not only will this help you to feel more comfortable, it will also help the audience to grasp what you are saying.

On page 295 you will find a more complex speech to explore, with more explanation as to how to identify the main thrust and the subordinate clauses.

A COUPLE OF FOOTNOTES

All the exercises in this chapter will help you to make the text your own so that it sounds real for the audience. However, there are a couple of other important tools worth looking at to ensure that the text is fully alive as if being spoken for the first time.

Talking Not Acting

Often with classical text, actors consciously or subconsciously feel that they need to speak in a grander way. This can detract from the reality of the text and also rob it of its dynamism, making it heavy and ponderous. So how do you avoid this? Firstly, by exploring the structures, sound patterns, words, images and language patterns in your text, as you have done in this chapter, so that these are deeply embedded and you can feel confident that you are honouring the style of the text; and secondly, by focusing on the situation your character is in, which you will explore in the next chapters, and on communicating with the other character or characters. If you talk to the other characters rather than act in a grandiloquent bubble, the text will sound fresh, truthful and up-to-date.

Knowing Who You're Talking To

The second tool is to be *absolutely sure* to whom you are talking – especially with soliloquies. This may sound a stupid thing to say. But often, when I have been asked to deal with problems in rehearsal, the cause has been that the actor concerned was not clear to whom they were talking, so they felt uncomfortable and their work lacked energy, focus and, indeed, truth.

Before we look at the best way to nail down to whom you are talking, it's worth talking about soliloquies and the best way to play them. Soliloquies are a chance for the audience to be drawn into the private world of the character: to find out what he/she is thinking and feeling. Since the audience are the real star of any play, in that they are the ones who need to go on a journey, the ones who need to be provoked to think and feel, soliloquies offer a wonderful opportunity for the actor to engage the audience and almost literally hold them in the palm of his/her hand. So how do you handle a soliloquy in order to engage the audience? The best way is to think of the stage as your character's *public* place and the auditorium, where the audience are, as the character's *private* space. Then, when a character is alone, and speaking to him/herself, or to someone they imagine is there, he/she can speak to the audience *as if* the audience were him/herself or the imaginary person. In this way, the actor is never alone on stage, they always have someone to work with, to talk to, and the audience is drawn deeper into the play because the private world of the character has been directly shared with them.

The actor doesn't need to come out of the play, or out of character; rather, the audience is brought into the play, since the audience becomes whomever the actor is talking to.

Who Am I Speaking To?

To make clear who you are talking to and so bring focus and energy to the work

We are going to use two soliloquies: one is Juliet's that you were looking at earlier; the other is Edmund's from *King Lear*. They are included below, making it clear who you are speaking to and when, so that it is easy to make the shifts as you do the exercise. Prior to each is a summary of whom they are talking to and, in the case of Edmund's speech, a brief description of the situation. If you choose Edmund's speech you may want to go through the earlier exercises in this chapter to prepare.

Note: When Juliet talks to night and Edmund talks to nature they talk to them as if *they were people. Bearing this in mind helps you to keep the text alive and real.*

○ Choose different objects to represent each person you are talking to and place them apart from each other in the room.

○ Then, go through the speech talking to the appropriate object at the appropriate point. Ensure that you are specific about when you change from one 'person' to another.

Juliet addresses four different people. She starts by talking to the 'fiery-footed steeds' that pull the sun–god's chariot across the sky. Then, she talks to *night* for most of the soliloquy, with a couple of words addressed to *Romeo* within that. Then, at the end she talks to *herself*, and *her Nurse*.

JULIET: **[to fiery steeds]**
Gallop apace, you fiery-footed steeds,
Towards Phoebus' lodging. Such a waggoner
As Phaeton would whip you to the west
And bring in cloudy night immediately.

[to night]
Spread thy close curtain, love-performing night,
That runaway's eyes may wink, and Romeo
Leap to these arms untalk'd-of and unseen.
Lovers can see to do their amorous rites
By their own beauties; or, if love be blind,
It best agrees with night. Come, civil night,
Thou sober-suited matron, all in black,
And learn me how to loose a winning match
Play'd for a pair of stainless maidenhoods.
Hood my unmann'd blood, bating in my cheeks,
With thy black mantle, till strange love grow bold,
Think true love acted simple modesty.
Come night,

[to Romeo]
          come Romeo, come thou day in night,
For thou wilt lie upon the wings of night
Whiter than new snow upon a raven's back.

[to night]
Come gentle night, come loving black-brow'd night,

Give me my Romeo; and when I shall die
Take him and cut him out in little stars,
And he will make the face of heaven so fine
That all the world will be in love with night,
And pay no worship to the garish sun.
O, I have bought the mansion of a love,
But not possess'd it; and though I am sold,
Not yet enjoy'd. So tedious is this day
As is the night before some festival
To an impatient child that hath new robes
And may not wear them,

[**to herself**]

O, here comes my Nurse.

Enter NURSE, with cords, wringing her hands.

And she brings news; and every tongue that speaks
But Romeo's name, speaks heavenly eloquence.

[**to Nurse**]
Now, Nurse, what news? What, hast thou there?
The cords that Romeo bid thee fetch?

Edmund is the bastard son of Gloucester. Because he is a illegitimate he cannot inherit his father's land, which will all go to his legitimate brother, Edgar. In the speech, Edmund embraces nature as the goddess he will worship and bemoans the fact that his bastardy deprives him from inheriting. He swears that, using a letter – which we later learn is false – he will get his legitimate brother's land and prosper.

In the soliloquy he addresses three different 'people'. He starts by talking to *nature*, then, he talks to his brother *Edgar* and finally, in the last line, he talks to *the gods*.

EDMUND: [**to nature**]
Thou, Nature, art my goddess; to thy law
My services are bound. Wherefore should I
Stand in the plague of custom, and permit
The curiosity of nations to deprive me?
For that I am some twelve or fourteen moonshines
Lag of a brother? Why bastard? Wherefore base?
When my dimensions are as well compact,

My mind as generous, and my shape as true
As honest madam's issue? Why brand they us
With base? With baseness, bastardy? Base, base?
Who in the lusty stealth of nature take
More composition and fierce quality
Than does within a dull stale tired bed
Go to the creating of a whole tribe of fops
Got 'tween a sleep, and wake?

[to Edgar]

                        Well then,
Legitimate Edgar, I must have your land.
Our father's love, is to the bastard Edmund
As to the legitimate. Fine word, 'legitimate'!
Well, my legitimate, if this letter speed
And my intention thrive, Edmund the base
Shall top the legitimate. I grow, I prosper:

[to the gods]
Now gods, stand up for bastards![27]

How did you find that? Did it make the speech more specific? Was it easier to say? Did it feel much clearer and more manageable?

In real life we always know to whom we are talking, whether the person is there or not, whether they are real or imaginary. It is the fact that we are always addressing someone that makes what we are saying live. As soon as we lose that sense of talking to someone specific our words become hollow. We feel awkward saying them and the audience don't believe us. Whereas when we have a clear sense of who we are talking to, the text feels like our own and the audience is fully engaged with what we are saying.

Summary

We have looked at how to explore the various elements of Shakespeare's text: the structures and rhythms; the sound patterns; the words and the images behind them; the language patterns. If you work through the exercises, exploring each element one by one, you will find that you have a deep appreciation and understanding of the text that will allow you to own it in a way that is both comfortable and effective.

To give you an overview of this chapter I have listed the exercises below under their section headings.

Structures and Rhythms
Moving the Metre
Walking the Sentences
Using the Colons and Semi-colons
Changing Direction
Changing Chairs
Phrase by Phrase
Walking the Verse
Clicking the Final Word
Marking the Caesura

Patterns of Sound
Connecting with the Vowels
Connecting with the Consonants
Exploring Alliteration, Assonance and Consonance
Exploring the Rhyme

Connecting with the Words and Images
Three Times Through
Physicalising the Words

Internal Geography
Geography Exercise
Museum Visit

Language Patterns
Exploring Contrast
Exploring Repetition
Exploring Simile and Metaphor
Names and Titles
Thee, Thou, Thy and Thine
Handling Lists
Handling Complex Sentences

Knowing Who You're Talking To
Who Am I Speaking To?

OTHER CLASSICAL TEXTS

All the exercises listed above can be used on other classical text. Through the exercises you will discover the particularities of each text and how each playwright differs from the next. What follows is a little background information and some pointers as to which exercises I have found particularly helpful for certain playwrights and periods.

Marlowe

Christopher Marlowe and Shakespeare were born in the same year, 1564. However, Marlowe started writing plays some years before Shakespeare. It was in fact Marlowe who transformed iambic pentameter into a powerful dramatic tool, understanding as he did its potential for flexibility and marrying that flexibility to great power and movement. Nick de Somogyi, a scholar both of Shakespeare and his contemporaries, has described Marlowe's language as being full of 'passion, power and danger' and pointed out that in all his plays the main characters are somehow outsiders looking in, aspiring, grasping, always wanting more and yet ending up with nothing. Marlowe was killed in 1593 at the age of twenty-nine, in circumstances that were not entirely straightforward. An interesting book based on the circumstances surrounding his death, which gives a feel for the darker underbelly of the period, is *The Reckoning* by Charles Nicholl.

The exercises that I find particularly important when working on Marlowe are *Walking the Sentences* to access the immense arcs of thought in the text, and *Connecting with the Vowels* to discover the size of the vocal and therefore the emotional release. I still use all the other exercises, but I then return to these two and take them further, challenging the actors to use these exercises to embrace the size of Marlowe's 'mighty line', as it was dubbed by Ben Jonson.

Jonson

Ben Jonson, born in 1572, was also a contemporary of Shakespeare. He wrote more than fifteen plays, some in collaboration with other writers in a writing career that spanned the reigns of Elizabeth I, James I and Charles I. He is probably best known for three Jacobean comedies *Volpone*, *The Alchemist* and *Bartholomew Fair*; it is these plays to which the exercises below relate.

These plays, despite having the declared moral purpose of criticising the hypocrisy and deceit of city life, are anything but dry and dusty. They are full of fun and playfulness and require a great deal of zest and wit from the actor.

The exercises I find most useful are **Changing Chairs** and **Phrase by Phrase** to help shape the often quite dense text and bring out the wit; **Three Times Through, Geography Exercise** and **Museum Visit** to help get to grips with the language and own it; and **Handling Lists** and **Handling Complex Sentences** to help deal with the complexity of the text.

Again, it is important to work through all the exercises, returning to the ones I have highlighted for extra exploration. It also helps to have a version of the text with good notes, to be prepared to work through slowly and not be put off by the amount that you might not initially understand.

Jacobean Tragedy

Jacobean Tragedies are so called because they were written during the reign of James I [*Jacobus* is the Latin form of James]. He became king in 1603 following the death of Elizabeth I and ruled for twenty-two years until 1625. Two years after he came to the throne, a plot to blow up Parliament was foiled on November 4th. The Gunpowder Plot, which was planned by Guy Fawkes and Robert Catesby, is now remembered in a light-hearted way on November 5th, but its effect at the time was, as Nick de Somogyi has pointed out, probably similar to the effect of 9/11 in 2001. In addition there was a great deal of corruption and intrigue at court. England had become a darker place. It is no wonder then that the plays of this period inhabit a dark, neurotic, inward-looking and even psychotic world. The plots are concerned with power and political corruption, murder and madness. Nick de Somogyi suggests the plays have parallels with the films of Quentin Tarantino. They certainly exhibit grotesqueness and an apparent obsession with violence and blood.

Jacobean Tragedies are still largely written in iambic pentameter, but the language is more naturalistic both in terms of the vocabulary used and the structure.

The exercises I find most useful are **Moving the Metre** and **Walking the Verse** to keep the balance between the verse and sentence structure; **Connecting with the Vowels** to help the emotional size and release; **Connecting with the Consonants** to help the physicality of the language;

and *Three Times Through, Geography Exercise* and *Museum Visit* to help connect with the language used and the imagery evoked.

It is especially important to focus on the language and the images that the words conjure up, because these will take you deep into the world of the play and the inner world of the character. Also, by fully embracing the language and imagery through these exercises, you will find that the text becomes more comfortable to say and easier to inhabit truthfully.

Restoration Comedies

Restoration Comedies are so called because they were written after the restoration of the monarchy in 1660, when Charles II was invited to take the throne after the collapse of the regime established by Oliver Cromwell. The best-known playwrights of the period are Aphra Behn, William Congreve, George Etherege, George Farquhar and William Wycherley, but there are many others. Three excellent books relating to this period are J.L. Styan's *Restoration Comedy in Performance*, Fidelis Morgan's *The Female Wits*, and Liza Picard's *Restoration London*. As a good starting point see *Restoration Comedy* published by Nick Hern Books which, in addition to a useful introduction, contains three of the major plays of the period: *The Rover* by Aphra Behn, *The Country Wife* by William Wycherley and *The Way of the World* by William Congreve.

Restoration Comedies are comedies of social behaviour. They were written for an audience that shared the same values and experience and were performed in intimate spaces that were fully lit so that the audience were as much on show as the actors. They are very much plays of their time and yet they do have a relevance for us today in that they revolve around the game of social survival – a game that all humans are involved in to a greater or lesser degree – since we tend, on the whole, to want social interaction rather than to shun it.

I find it helpful to approach Restoration Comedies as games of social survival, played for serious stakes. This in no way takes away from the comedy and the need for wit and pace. Rather, it adds an underlying tension to the game, giving the brittle world an edge; an element of danger that makes it much easier for actors to play and audiences to engage with.

It can be useful to look at the characters in a Restoration Comedy and decide who plays the game well and who doesn't, and who *thinks* they play the game better than they actually do. There are many remarks in the plays that allude to how well various characters play the game and great fun is often made of those who can't play it well, especially if they think they can.

Restoration society, as depicted in these comedies, is a society that values social polish – it focuses on what people wear, how they carry themselves, what they say and do, and how they say and do it. This takes a great deal of work and yet has to seem perfectly effortless. So the characters are all the time having to work hard while seeming to be perfectly at ease and natural – artful artlessness. J.L. Styan points out that, under these circumstances, spontaneity is the enemy since it threatens a loss of control.[28] Now this does not mean that the characters are emotionless, just that they can't *show* their emotions. Styan suggests a helpful inversion to deal with this dilemma: the more strongly a character feels about something, the more they hide it; the less they feel, the more they can *pretend* that they feel very strongly. For example, if someone is in love with someone else they need to behave very coolly about it. However, if they are not at all in love with the person, they can pretend to be madly in love with them. So the serious is treated as if it is trivial and the trivial as if it is serious. This is all about control: the stakes are too high for unplanned disclosures. By working in this way a wonderful tension – between the unreality of the surface and the internal reality – is set up.

The language in Restoration Comedies needs to be handled precisely and skilfully. Working through *all* the exercises will help you to do this. The exercises I find most useful for extra support are *Walking the Sentences* to *sustain* the long arcs of thought; *Changing Chairs* to help *shape* those arcs; and *Geography Exercise* and *Museum Visit* to help the words to be handled with wit. There is also another exercise that I find very helpful, *Pointing the Word*, and this is described below.

Pointing the Word

To help highlight key words in a light but precise way

For this exercise we are going to use an extract from the Restoration Comedy *The Beaux Stratagem* by George Farquhar. Dorinda and her sister-in-law, Mrs Sullen, are comparing the behaviour of their two beaux, or would-be lovers. Read it through first. Notice that the lines work in pairs with Dorinda showing off about her lover's behaviour and Mrs Sullen topping Dorinda with her own remarks. Mrs Sullen is the more experienced of the two, which shows in her more suggestive remarks. This exchange between them is friendly, but they still play the game for all it's worth. It's simply that here the game is played to entertain themselves and not to score serious points.

DORINDA: But my lover was upon his knees to me.

MRS SULLEN: And mine was upon his tiptoes to me.

DORINDA: Mine vow'd to die for me.

MRS SULLEN: Mine swore to die with me. [*Orgasm was known as the little death; so Mrs Sullen is playing on words.*]

DORINDA: Mine spoke the softest moving things.

MRS SULLEN: Mine had his moving things too. [*Again, Mrs Sullen caps Dorinda's innocent sentiment with a sexual reference.*]

DORINDA: Mine kiss'd my hand ten thousand times.

MRS SULLEN: Mine has all that pleasure to come. [*Mrs Sullen suggests that she and her lover have already had sex and, so, all the play of courtship is still to come.*]

DORINDA: Mine offer'd marriage.

MRS SULLEN: O lard! D'ye call that a moving thing?[29]

○ *Take the text and a tennis ball. If you are working alone you will need a wall to throw the ball at. If you are working with a scene partner you can throw the ball between you.*

○ *Throw the ball in the air on every word you feel it is important for the other character/s to hear, catching it again each time. Then, throw the ball at the wall, or to whomever you are talking to, on the last word that is most important for them to hear.*

○ *If working with a partner they do the same on their lines, since they now have the ball. Then, they throw it back to you, on the last most important word of their lines. If you are working on your own, play both parts.*

It is useful to look for contrasts and repetitions, especially if these are contrasts with or repetitions of something that another character has said, since this is where a great deal of the sense of playfulness comes from.

Below the scene is marked up with italics on the words, where the actor might throw the ball in the air, and bold on the final important word where they might throw it to the other character, or at the wall.

DORINDA: But my *lover* was upon his **knees** to me.

MRS SULLEN: And *mine* was upon his **tip**toes to me.

DORINDA: Mine *vow'd* to **die** for me.

MRS SULLEN: Mine *swore* to die **with** me.

DORINDA: Mine *spoke* the *softest moving* **things**.

MRS SULLEN: Mine had his *moving* things **too**.

DORINDA: Mine *kiss'd* my hand ten *thous*and **times**.

MRS SULLEN: Mine has all *that* pleasure to **come**.

DORINDA: *Mine* offer'd **mar**riage.

MRS SULLEN: O *lard*! D'ye call *that* a **mov**ing thing?

Note: There is also the build through repetition of the word 'mine', so this will get more and more emphasis as it is increasingly repeated.

How was that? Did you notice that you did emphasise the words you threw the ball on but that this happened in a light and subtle way? Also, throwing the ball encourages the idea of a game. Indeed, the witty exchanges in these plays are often compared with a tennis match: one that needs to be played with alert attention, deadly precision, pace and ease.

Sheridan, Wilde and Coward

Although these writers come from later periods than the Restoration – Richard Brinsley Sheridan [1752-1816], Oscar Wilde [1854-1900] and Noël Coward [1899-1973] – I find that they can be approached in a similar way in terms of regarding their plays as games of social survival, with the same serious needs beneath the humour and seeming superficiality. So I tend to use the same exercises as I do for Restoration Comedies: *Walking the Sentences* to *sustain* the long arcs of thought; *Changing Chairs* to help *shape* the long arcs; *Geography Exercise, Museum Visit* and *Pointing the Word* to help the words to be handled with wit.

It is also worth noting the importance of adjectives and adverbs, especially in the plays of Wilde and Coward. Philip Prowse pointed this out when I worked with him on Wilde's *A Woman of No Importance* at the Barbican in the early 1990s and I have found it an invaluable observation. Focusing on and subtly emphasising the adjectives and adverbs helps to bring out the wit and playfulness in the plays and make the text great fun to handle, e.g.: It's *perfectly* clear . . . I *strongly* advise you . . . It's *extremely* exciting . . .

Texts in Translation

I have found that working with the exercises in this chapter helps you to connect with texts in translation and own them just as much as they help you connect with and own texts that were originally written in English. So whether you are working on a play by Lorca, Calderón, Pirandello, Chekhov, Ibsen, Strindberg, Goethe, Schiller or other more recent works in translation, these exercises will help you find the style and voice of that play and of your character within it.

It is worth mentioning a couple of points in relation to Greek plays. The dialogue between the characters or between a character and the Chorus takes the form of a debate in which the audience is the key player who must be won over to one side or the other. It is useful therefore to begin rehearsals facing where the audience will be and addressing the lines directly to them. Then, gradually turning in towards the character you are talking to, without ever losing a sense of appealing to the audience. In the end you imagine appealing to, engaging, persuading the audience *through* the other character.

Conclusion

I hope that these thumbnail sketches of some classical writers and texts other than Shakespeare will be helpful. My wish was to give you a little bit of context – a *hook* if you like – to make these texts less daunting.

Please remember that all classical texts were modern plays once: plays which were relevant to the lives of the audiences and fully understandable by them. And, although many of the superficial circumstances have changed dramatically, the underlying human preoccupations have altered less. Always embrace the text with confidence – using the exercises in this chapter to unravel the daunting complexities – so that you can connect with the truths underlying the text that are relevant for you and the audience today. When you put this text work together with the exploration of subtext covered in the following chapters you will find that you have a powerful way of connecting with and engaging audiences with all texts – classical or modern.

PART THREE

Subtext

Exploring Beyond the Text

Having explored the text – its structures and rhythms, its sound and language patterns and its imagery – we are now going to shift attention to what lies beneath and around the text. In other words: character, context, intention, background and situation. By exploring these you enable yourself to root your words and actions in a specific set of circumstances. As a result, your work will have greater depth, detail and resonance both for yourself and for the audience.

As I mentioned in Part One, it is sometimes suggested that there is no point exploring subtext in classical texts. In my experience this is not the case. Having a clear sense of who your character is, where they are, what they want, what has happened to them previously and what situation they are currently in helps you to connect with the underlying human experience, which is as relevant now as it was when the texts were written. In this way you will feel far more comfortable and confident playing the texts, and the audience will find the situations and characters far easier to connect and engage with.

As with the text work, we will explore each layer separately and then leave it to take care of itself on stage.

Who Am I?

BUILDING YOUR CHARACTER

How do you get under the skin of a character so that you can embrace the complexity of thoughts, emotions and behaviours and yet be able to play these simply and effectively? There are four key areas to explore: *Identity*, *Motivation*, *Rhythm* and *Language*. As with the work in the earlier chapters, exploring these areas individually will allow you to build up strands that can be weaved together unconsciously and give you a complexity, which can be played with clarity and ease.

As mentioned previously, what you are doing as you explore each area is asking *'What if . . . ?'*: *'What if I were in this context, with this identity, motivation and rhythm, using this language: what would I think and feel and do then?'* In this way you are pouring *your* experience through the *filter* of the character's circumstances and discovering how these shift you from your own way of doing and being to that of the character. In this way you can find the character or personal rules I talked about in Part One [see page 4].

Note: Remember to suspend all judgement of your character. The more you wholeheartedly pursue you character's goals, upholding his/her view of the world, whilst all the other actors do the same with their characters, the more dramatic tension there will be and the more the audience will be drawn in to the to and fro of the story being told. In this way a rich dialogue and debate can be created with each character fighting his/her corner and challenging the audience to constantly re-examine their opinion.

So let's work through each area, trying out the various exercises and discovering how they can support you.

IDENTITY

This is a simple and easy place to start. It takes you into the world of the character: looking at the facts known about them and the values and beliefs they express. The exercises below are based on questions that many actors are asked to look at when approaching a character. They offer a clear, simple and effective way of answering those questions.

Finding the Facts

To establish what facts the writer gives you about the character

This is a very important place to start since it is possible on a superficial reading of the text to overlook facts which might be immensely helpful in building up your sense of the character.

◯ *Choose a character to work on.*

◯ *Go through the text looking for all the facts about your character – age, family members, experience, etc. – and list these so that it is easy to scan through this list whenever you want. If the author wrote the stage directions, you can include any facts that you find there.*

Note: In many plays written before 1650, including Greek Tragedies, the stage directions have been added by modern editors.

I have compiled a list of facts for Claudio in *Measure for Measure* and Petal in *Shimmer* to give you an idea of exactly what I mean. I have written the list in the third person – 'he/she' – some actors prefer to write it in the first person – 'I'. Choose whichever you find most helpful.

Character Facts: Claudio

Parents dead – father respected as being a noble man.

Has a sister who is about to become a nun.

Loves Juliet and intends to marry her.

Has got Juliet pregnant.

Is in prison, awaiting execution, for getting her pregnant, as the Duke's deputy, Angelo, has reinstated an old law making it punishable by death to get anyone pregnant outside marriage.

Will be the first person to die under the reinstated law.

Character Facts: Petal

In her 20s.

Studying for a degree in psychology.

Knows how to listen.

Father left when she was a child.

Grandfather and uncle trampled to death along with many other men and boys at a football match before she was born.

When she was little and a film or book ended badly she'd go to bed and dream a new ending in her head.

She nearly drowned once – she was caught under a sail.

Loves flagstones.

Likes Tunnock's teacakes.

Main dream since she was about 13 is about her wedding, embarrassed about that.

Her hands tremble, they always have done.

Has a strawberry birthmark on the back of her head.

Has a dark shadow on her bladder.

The birthmark and the shadow are the same shape.

This 'thing' in her bladder is killing her.

Had almost a sense of relief when she heard [about her bladder disease] as she'd known something was wrong and 'there's a level of reassurance in hearing that what you know is true.'

Needs to pee regularly, can't hold it in, yet when she goes it only comes out drop by drop; she feels as if the pressure's building up and it's going to blow a hole in her back.

Her mother and grandmother have started telling her things she doesn't want to hear, things that they thought would upset her before.

Going to Iona with mother and grandmother because grandmother thinks they can 'catch a miracle there' and so cure her. She would rather have stayed at home.

○ *Take your time to read through the list you have written for your chosen character asking yourself: 'What if these were the facts of my life? How would that affect what I think, feel and do?'*

It may well be that no answers come at this point. However, by asking the question and taking the time to imagine, you will stimulate your mind to search and make connections.

○ *Return to this list regularly throughout rehearsals to refresh your memory and further stimulate your imagination. Also, to add to it as you become more familiar with the text and character.*

Owning the Opinions

To focus on the character's opinions about him/herself and about the other characters and the clues they give

Having identified what is factually true, it is useful to explore the opinions the character holds: firstly about him/herself and secondly about others. These give you clues about the values and beliefs of the character, about what is important to them.

○ *Go through the text, writing down everything the character says about him/herself and about other people, whether they appear in the play or not.*

○ *Create two separate lists, one listing the opinions about self and the other their opinions about others.*

Again, I have done this list for Claudio in *Measure for Measure* and Petal in *Shimmer* to give you an idea. The opinions are written as they are in the actual text.

Claudio's opinions of himself

'The most miserable have no other medicine.
But only hope:
I have hope to live and am prepared to die.'

'If I must die,
I will encounter darkness as a bride,
And hug it in my arms.'

[**Later**] 'I am so out of love with life that I will sue to be rid of it.'

Claudio's opinions of others and life in general

'Thus can the demigod Authority
Make us pay down for our offence by weight
The words of heaven. On whom it will, it will;
On whom it will not, so: yet still 'tis just.'

'As surfeit is the father of much fast;
So every scope by the immoderate use
Turns to restraint. Our natures do pursue,
Like rats that ravin down their proper bane,
A thirsty evil; and when we drink we die.'

'Death is a fearful thing.'

About his sister

                  ' . . . in her youth
There is a prone and speechless dialect,
Such as move men; beside, she hath prosperous art
When she will play with reason and discourse,
And well can she persuade.'

'What sin you do to save a brother's life,
Nature dispenses with the deed so far
That it becomes a virtue.'

Petal's opinions of herself

'I'm used to not having things turn out the way I want.'

'I try to smooth things over . . . I've been smoothing things over for as long as I can remember.'

'You don't stop dreaming, even if you think you're going to die.'

Petal's opinions of others and of life in general

'Most people are' [used to things not turning out the way they want]

'Some things are best forgotten.'

'Most of the time, without being aware of it, you're catapulted from one minute into the next. Before you know anything, the tail end of one minute becomes your past and the front end of the next minute takes you smack into the future. As if your life's some dot-to-dot puzzle that somebody else drew and everybody else can see, but is invisible to you.'

' . . . the past leaps up at the slightest opportunity.'

'We haven't a snowball's chance in hell of getting to Oban today.'

About mother and grandmother

'These two are about to fight. Faced with a new situation that's what they do.'

'And the truth is they need it [for Petal to be healed] more than me. They've been left too often already.'

'They can't face it' [the fact that the thing in her bladder is killing her].

'But at home there's no chance of them being happy.'

'They're scared. They can't cope.'

To/about her grandmother

'You should never have gone to see that fortune-teller woman.'

'She says stupid things like that as if she forgets that it's me who'll be dead later.'

About her mother

'You exaggerate.'

'She said that out loud [about a photo of her father and brother]. Which is the first sign of hope I've had that she can see past me.'

○ Again, take your time to read through the first list, asking: 'What if these were the opinions I held about myself?'

○ Then, read through the second list, asking: 'What if these were the opinions I held about others?'

Again, answers may not come immediately. The question focuses your mind so that answers can come up as you rehearse.

It is worth looking out for shifts in opinions either of self or others during the play since this may give you clues about the character's journey through the play.

○ Again, it is worth returning to these lists regularly, reading them through with the same or a similar question.

MOTIVATION

Now that you have explored the facts about your character and the opinions he/she holds, you have enough information to start exploring motivation. Identifying a core motivation for your character can give you a simple focus whilst at the same time hinting at greater complexity.

Finding Core Motivation

To establish an overall motivation for the character

This core motivation is *above and beyond* the circumstances of the play. It is the overriding *want* in the character's life, which can apply in any situation, and which leads him/her to think, feel and act in the way he/she does. For example, a character that wanted to be in control could act on this motivation both at work and with his/her friends and family. And, of course, the motivation implies that the character does not feel particularly powerful or secure, hence their need to assert control.

Finding the core motivation is a simple way of shifting from whatever drives *you* to whatever drives the *character*. Once this shift has occurred, you will be free to explore: to see how the character's motivation leads you to think, feel and behave in a different way. And, of course, once you have established this overall want then you can go on to identify the want within each scene, which will give greater colour, variety and depth. We will look at how wants within scenes are established in a later chapter. Now let's explore how you select and work with your character's overall want.

Stage One – Choosing the want

○ Calling to mind the exploration you have done on your character so far, ask yourself: 'What do I imagine my character might want, not in terms of the situations in the play, but overall in life? What is his/her overall motivation? What drives him/her to feel, think and behave in the way he/she does?'

○ Write down every idea you have. Work fast and avoid editing, that comes later.

Obviously the possibilities are endless so the following are just ideas to give you a flavour:

'I want to win'	'I want to be secure'
'I want to avoid conflict at all costs'	'I want to be different'
'I want to be in control'	'I want to love'
'I want to be the centre of attention'	'I want to be loved'
'I want to be appreciated'	'I want to be recognised'
'I want to be important'	'I want to be successful'
'I want to be understood'	'I want to be involved'
'I want to look after everyone'	'I want to be left alone'
'I want to be looked after'	'I want to be independent'

○ Look through your ideas, grouping similar ones together. You may notice a theme and that many of the wants are different ways of expressing the same thing.

○ Identify the want or wants that seem to you to be most essential to the character and most useful to you. Then, form these into a strong simple statement that begins with 'I want ...' E.g. 'I want to feel secure and loved' or 'I want to win whatever the cost.'

Note: There is not one right way to answer this question. Different actors may choose different wants and arrive at equally valid and effective versions of the character. The core motivation is simply a device *to shift you away from what drives you to what might drive the character.*

○ Say the statement to yourself and notice how it feels. If it feels ponderous and dull then you need to think again. If it feels interesting and makes you curious then you know you are on to something you can use.

Stage Two – Exploring the effect of the want

You are going to focus on the want and on wanting that want with various parts of your body. You may wish to record the instructions in the box below so that you can play them back to yourself while you do the exercise. If you do that, leave a pause between each instruction so you will have time while doing the exercise to focus on each part.

Want the want with your feet.

Want the want with your ankles.

Want the want with your lower legs.

Want the want with your knees.

Want the want with your upper legs.

Want the want with your hips.

Want the want with your groin.

Want the want with your belly.

Want the want with your buttocks.

Want the want with your spine.

Want the want with the whole of your back.

Want the want with your ribs.

Want the want with your chest.

Want the want with your shoulders.

Want the want with your upper arms.

Want the want with your elbows.

Want the want with your lower arms.

Want the want with your wrists.

Want the want with your hands.

Want the want with your fingers.

Want the want with your thumbs.

Move your attention back up to your shoulders and onto your neck.

Want the want with the back of your neck.

Want the want with the sides and front of your neck.

Want the want with your scalp.

Want the want with your forehead.

Want the want with your eyes and eyelids.

Want the want with your nose.

Want the want with your cheeks.

Want the want with your lips.

Want the want with your mouth.

Want the want with your jaw.

Want the want with your chin.

Then, let your attention settle on your breath in your belly and want the want with your breath.

○ *Sit or lie in a neutral position: one that is not too personal to you.*

○ *Close your eyes and either listen to your recorded instructions and respond to those or simply move through your body, slowly, from the feet upwards, wanting the want with each part.*

○ Have a completely open mind as to what will happen and trust that shifts will occur, without you needing to make them happen.

○ Once you have gone through each part of the body, repeat the want silently a few more times whilst imagining wanting it with your whole body.

○ Then, slowly get up, still repeating the want in your head and still wanting it with your whole body.

○ Begin to move around doing daily tasks, picking things up and moving them, putting on or taking off an item of clothing, packing a bag, etc. As you do so, keep repeating the want in your head.

○ Then, begin to experiment with a full body gesture that expresses the want, rather like a statue. Keep moving in and out of different positions until you find one that feels right. When you find one that does, stay in it for a few breaths to get a strong sense of it.

○ Then, release from the position and find your script, still repeating the want as you do so. Find a speech or scene to go through.

○ Keeping the want in mind speak the speech or scene. Notice what happens and how the want affects what you feel, think and do.

○ Now, relax and jot down anything that might be helpful. Draw a picture or doodle if that feels more appropriate than words. Or you may simply want to take a moment to reflect on what you have discovered without putting it into words or pictures.

○ Now, stretch and shake out thoroughly to let go, because this work can be very strong.

You can return to the full exercise whenever you want to or simply return to the gesture you found. The gesture allows you to contact the core motivation very quickly and may be useful as part of your preparation just before rehearsal or performance. When you are playing more than one character, using this process to produce a strong gesture for each character is very helpful. Then, all you need to do before you go on stage is to access that gesture and you will find that you click into that character's motivation.

A word of warning: This exercise is very strong. If ever you are working on a very disturbed character, do not do this work on your own. Do it with someone else around so that they can monitor the exercise and help you let go of it if it gets too strong.

mean you need to be scared of the exercise. I have worked with it a
and never had any problems. However, I keep a close watch, and if
someone has worked on a strong and disturbing want, I ensure it doesn't get out of
hand and that they release from it fully at the end of the exercise. Just treat the
exercise with respect and you will be fine.

RHYTHM

Rhythm is one of the key issues when taking on a character. Often when an
actor is having problems it is because there are profound rhythm
differences between the actor and the character, which the actor is not fully
aware of.

Working on the punctuation-based exercises *Walking the Sentences, Changing Direction* and *Changing Chairs* helps to establish the character's rhythm,
as does *Connecting with the Vowels* and *Connecting with the Consonants*.
Here I would like to look at another way of exploring character rhythm
which I find very helpful. It is based on the work of Rudolf Laban [1879–
1958], a dancer, choreographer and movement theorist, who was one of the
founders of Modern Dance.[30] Laban believed that movement of the body
and of the mind was the basis of all human activity and he searched for a
basic vocabulary of expressive movement that came out of everyday actions.
It is the connection between the movement of the body and the movement
of the mind that particularly interests me. Working on external physical
rhythm allows you to shift internal mental rhythm easily, as well as shifting
vocal rhythm and quality.

Laban identified three variables in terms of rhythm:

Weight – whether *heavy* or *light*

Flow – whether *sustained* [*continuous*] or *staccato* [*starts and stops*]

Focus – whether *direct* [*focused*] or *indirect* [*unfocused*]

There are eight different rhythms, which Laban called *Effort Actions*. They are
characterised using the above variables: weight, flow and focus. The following chart shows the eight effort actions. Each one has a unique combination
of the three variables.

	Sustained	*Staccato*	
Heavy	**PRESS**	**PUNCH**	*Direct*
Heavy	**WRING**	**SLASH**	*Indirect*
Light	**GLIDE**	**DAB**	*Direct*
Light	**FLOAT**	**FLICK**	*Indirect*

Press is Heavy, Sustained and Direct.

○ *Practise by pressing against a wall or down on a table.*

○ *Notice the heaviness this action has, that it can be done continuously and that your attention has a directness of focus.*

Punch is Heavy, Staccato and Direct.

○ *Practise by punching an imaginary punchball in front of you.*

○ *Notice that this action is also heavy and that your attention is again directly focused. However, since you have to pull your arm back after each punch before you can punch again, this action has a staccato quality.*

Wring is Heavy, Sustained and Indirect.

○ *Practise by wringing your hands together.*

○ *Notice that this action is also heavy, that it can be sustained without interruption, but that your attention is less directly focused.*

Slash is Heavy, Staccato and Indirect.

○ *Practise by slashing out to the side with your arms one after the other, almost as if you were fighting off an attack.*

○ *Notice that this action is also heavy, that it has a staccato quality like Punch, and that, like Wring, your attention is less directly focused.*

Glide is Light, Sustained and Direct.

○ *Practise by stretching your arms out to each side at shoulder level, with you shoulder blades relaxed, and moving around as if you were a glider.*

○ *Notice that this action is lighter than the previous four, that the movement can be sustained and that you have regained the focus of attention you had with Press and Punch.*

Dab is Light, Staccato and Direct.

○ *Practise by imagining that you are dabbing gently with a cloth, perhaps to clean a fragile object.*

○ *Notice that this action is also light, that it has a staccato quality like Punch, and that again your attention is focused.*

Float is Light, Sustained and Indirect.

○ *Practise by imagining that you are a piece of paper or a leaf being gently blown about by the wind.*

○ *Notice that this action is also light, that it has a sustained quality like Glide, but that, as with Wring, your attention is less focused.*

Flick is Light, Staccato and Indirect.

○ *Practise by imagining you are flicking fluff off your clothes or swatting away flies.*

○ *Notice that this action is also light, that it has a staccato quality like Dab, and that, as with Float, your attention is less focused.*

Exploring the Laban Rhythms

To experience the different rhythms and how they affect thought rhythms, physicality and voice

○ *Once you have a sense of the quality of each rhythm, take the time to explore each one more thoroughly, starting with the movements as described above, then involving more and more of your body.*

○ *Keep checking with the chart to make sure that you have the correct weight, flow and focus for each one.*

○ *Then, still doing the movement, say some lines of text, noticing the effect of the movement on your thought, rhythm and voice.*

It is worth noting which rhythms are more alien to you and then taking the time to explore them further physically until they become more familiar and available to you.

These rhythms are not tied to particular emotions. Any emotion can be expressed through any rhythm.

○ *Take an emotion and explore expressing it through each of the different rhythms.*

○ *Notice how the different rhythms change the quality of the emotion.*

This is extremely useful work, since it is often difficult to comprehend how a particular emotion could be expressed differently from the way you express it.

Rhythm Workout

To increase your ability to access the rhythms and to shift swiftly between them

Apart from exploring any rhythms which are alien to you and working with the emotions, as suggested above, it is a good idea to play with all the rhythms regularly so that it becomes easy to access them and to switch from one to another.

When you are playing with rhythms it is important to go back to the chart and check the weight, flow and focus so that you know the rhythms are precise.

Here is my suggestion for a regular *Rhythm Workout*.

◯ *Take each rhythm and begin to move in that rhythm, ensuring that the weight, flow and focus are accurate. Have the chart at hand so you can easily check.*

◯ *Work with your whole body committing to the rhythm you are exploring completely and with great ease.*

◯ *Once you have worked on each rhythm individually then alternate between them.*

◯ *Alternate slowly at first so that you are sure that you are getting accurate shifts of weight, flow and focus.*

◯ *Then, speed up so that you can change swiftly between the rhythms without losing accuracy.*

◯ *Then, speak some text shifting swiftly between the rhythms without losing accuracy.*

Working in this way will give you a great deal of flexibility – physically, mentally and vocally – and it will help you access those characters whose rhythms are radically different from yours.

Applying the Rhythm Work

To identify and explore a specific character's rhythms

Having worked on all the rhythms, and developed a sense of them and an ability to access them accurately and swiftly, you can begin to apply these rhythms to a particular character.

The following exercise allows you to identify the differences between your own and a particular character's rhythm, and gives you a way of working on those differences once identified.

Continue working with whichever character you chose for the earlier exercises in this chapter.

Stage One – Identifying the character's, and your, rhythms and the differences between them

○ *Imagining that your character can only have one rhythm, choose which, from Laban's eight, it would be. For the moment choose instinctively rather than considering weight, flow or focus.*

○ *Once you have chosen one rhythm choose a second one in the same way.*

○ *Then, choose a third in the same way. Make sure that you have noted these three rhythms down.*

Note: I usually find three rhythms are a good and workable number, but if you feel you need more, fair enough. I choose them one at a time, because I find this the simplest and most effective way. As with the motivation there is no one right answer. Choosing the rhythms is a device for helping you to identify the differences between you and the character.

○ *Now, consider yourself for a moment. Again, imagining that you can only have one rhythm, choose which it would be. As before, choose instinctively.*

○ *Then, pick a second rhythm.*

○ *Then, pick a third. Again, note these three rhythms down.*

Now that you have the two lists of possible rhythms you can analyse and then compare them. Start with your character's list and refer to the chart as necessary.

○ *Note whether the character is predominately heavy or light.*

○ *Note whether the character is predominately sustained or staccato.*

○ *Note whether the character is predominately focused or unfocused.*

For example, if for Petal we chose *Glide, Float* and *Dab*, that would make her completely light, predominately direct and predominately sustained.

If for Claudio we chose *Punch, Wring* and *Glide* that would make him predominantly heavy, direct and sustained.

○ *Now go through the same process with your own list.*

For example, if the actor playing Petal identified her *own* rhythms as *Glide*, *Wring* and *Slash*, she would be predominantly heavy, indirect and sustained.

If the actor playing Claudio identified his *own* rhythms as being *Punch*, *Float* and *Dab*, that would make him predominantly light, direct and staccato.

○ *Now compare the analyses of yourself and your character. Look for differences in weight, flow and focus between the two.*

For example, the actor playing Petal would notice that Petal is lighter than her and more direct.

The actor playing Claudio would notice that Claudio is heavier and more sustained than he is.

Simply identifying the differences can be very helpful and is often enough for the actor concerned to make the necessary rhythmic changes.

Stage Two – Exploring the character's rhythms physically

This stage allows you to take the rhythm work further by physically exploring the rhythms you have chosen for your character and what clues they give you about the character's external and internal movement.

○ *Start by taking each of the character rhythms individually and exploring it physically, ensuring that you are committing fully to the specific combination of weight, flow and focus of that rhythm.*

○ *Then, move between the different character rhythms exploring how they work together.*

○ *Rest for a while and consider what you have learnt about the character and the way he/she moves, thinks, feels, etc. Make notes or draw images if that is helpful to you.*

○ *Then, return to the strong physical exploration of these three rhythms and begin to speak the text, shifting from one rhythm to the next as feels instinctively appropriate.*

Always keep the choice of which rhythm you use for which part of the text free, rather than setting it in any way. You are simply exploring possibilities: '*What if these were the rhythms I used?*'

Working with the rhythms is particularly useful when you have to play more than one character.

○ Firstly, establish the rhythms for each character.

○ Then, look for the main differences in rhythm between each of the characters you are playing.

○ Focus on these differences and explore them physically.

○ Then, still working physically, practise switching from one character to another, slightly exaggerating the rhythmic differences.

As always, this is exploratory work, which you then allow to take care of itself once you are back in rehearsals and performance.

Double Layers of Rhythm

There can be two layers of rhythm in play at the same time: with one, if you like, covering, and so hiding, the other. Typical examples of this are where there is internal *Press* or *Wring*, with *Glide* or *Float* overlaying. This might be the case where someone was attempting to hide an intensity of thought or emotion by appearing to be lighter on the surface.

Any rhythm may be either a hidden or covering one and can be different at different points in the play.

Exploring Double Layers of Rhythm

To discover how the double layers of rhythm interact

So once you have done your initial character work, ask yourself the following questions:

○ 'Are any of the rhythms I have identified and explored hidden either all or some of the time?'

○ 'Are there any other rhythms that the character might have hidden beneath the ones I have explored?'

If it is not possible to answer these questions immediately, carry them with you as you rehearse and note what arises.

Once you have identified that there is an underlying or hidden rhythm you can work on it in the following way:

○ Take the hidden rhythm first and explore it fully physically, committing to its specific weight, flow and focus.

○ Then, allow that hidden rhythm to be expressed simply by your hands as if they were showing what is occurring internally.

○ Now, explore the covering rhythm fully physically, committing to its specific weight, flow and focus.

○ Then, explore the two rhythms together: expressing the hidden rhythm with your hands and the covering rhythm with the rest of your body.

○ Explore how these two rhythms work together. For example, allowing the hidden rhythm to grow so it threatens to be revealed and then allowing the covering rhythm to exert itself and drive the hidden rhythm deeper.

By working in this way you are exploring possibilities, which will allow you to make accurate choices subconsciously during rehearsal and performance.

It is a good idea to return to the physical exploration of your character's rhythms regularly in order to strengthen the shift away from yourself and your way of being and doing to that of the character. The more you explore this work the more you will find that you make discoveries that are fresh and authentic rather than clichéd and superficial.

LANGUAGE

The final area to explore is the language the character uses. This reflects the inner world of the character.

The exercises in Part Two exploring connection – *Three Times Through*, *Physicalising the Word*, *Geography Exercise* and *Museum Visit* – all help you to explore your character's language and imagery. It's also revelatory to list the key language your character uses throughout the play and the threads of words and images that run through that language.

Finding the Threads

To connect more deeply with the inner world of the character through the language and imagery they use

○ Go through each scene, noting down key words and phrases that the character uses.

○ Trust your instinct and simply note down whatever jumps out at you, even if you're not sure why.

Again, below is a possible list of Petal's key words and phrases from the first twenty pages of *Shimmer* to give you some idea.

Petal's key words and phrases

I'm used to things not turning out the way I want.

Most people . . .

Statistically speaking . . .

A lot of people . . .

. . . lot of people.

. . . try to smooth things over.

I've been smoothing things over . . .

. . . been mostly statistics.

. . . interventionist, I'm told.

. . . intervention comes in many forms.

That was gentle intervention . . .

. . . empirically . . .

It's empirical.

Something in the way I say . . .

. . . which is a bland statement of the obvious,

. . . has hit the guilt button in the two of them.

Something in my voice . . .

You can't tell strangers I'm dying . . .

. . . or miracle. Don't say miracle.

Do you have to say that?

I do actually need a pee and it's not as if I can hold myself in. You know that.

Some things are best forgotten.

You exaggerate.

Already it's falling apart.

It's not as if they don't remember.

. . . if only they'd have faith.

And now I'm going to burst apart at the seams; the fear that I would wet myself, would make a public show of myself, is secondary to the burning that's starting to grip me.

I need to go.

He doesn't say that out loud.

Drip.

Drip.

One minute, desperate. Next minute, dripping. One measly drop at a time as if it's liquid gold that can only be extracted by burning an acetylene torch on the pocket of tissue that's keeping it back so that it trickles out with a red bodyguard and a cry of relief.

Did I cry out loud?

He didn't say that out loud.

I'm sure he didn't mean it that way.

There are faces in those rocks.

She didn't say that.

Is that really true?

But she doesn't say that out loud. Believe it or not.

They don't all want to go [about people who leave].

Everybody knows now.

I don't mind.

I really don't mind.

I found myself imagining the top of his thighs. I didn't say that out loud, did I?

○ *Read through the language you character uses, giving yourself time to build up the images behind the words and phrases where they are particularly descriptive Ask yourself: 'What if this were the language and imagery I used?'*

How did you find that? It's likely that any discoveries and resulting shifts will come slowly and gently, and that often you won't be able to articulate them. That is fine. Simply trust that regularly reconnecting with the language your character uses will inform your work in a profound and useful way.

Summary

The work on *Identity* allows you to enter the world of the character and have a sense of how he/she interacts within that world. The *Motivation* work gives you a sense of what drives the character. The *Rhythm* work gives you a sense of the shifts you need to make to move away from your own rhythms. Lastly, the *Language* work allows you to enter the internal or psychological world of the character, the images behind their words. By exploring all these areas and asking, '*What if this was my identity and I was driven by this motivation, with these rhythms and using this language?*', you will develop a deep, instinctive sense of how the character might behave in the various situations within the play and how his/her behaviour may differ from yours. This will allow far greater flexibility and subtlety in your character work.

Below is a summary of the exercises in this chapter.

Identity
>   *Finding the Facts*
>   *Owning the Opinions*

Motivation
>   *Finding Core Motivation*

Rhythm
>   *Exploring the Laban Rhythms*
>   *Rhythm Workout*
>   *Applying the Rhythm Work*
>   *Exploring Double Layers of Rhythm*

Language
>   *Finding the Threads*

Where Am I and When?

ESTABLISHING PLACE AND TIME

The clearer you are about the context in which a play is set, the more truthful and imaginative you can be in your rehearsal and performance work. There are two contexts to explore: the larger and the more immediate. The larger context refers to the place, time and culture in which the play is set. The more immediate context refers to the precise on- and offstage geography and conditions of each scene.

THE LARGER CONTEXT

In researching this context you need to find information that feeds and fires your imagination. You need the time, place and culture to come alive for you, so that you can begin to sense what it would have been like to live in those circumstances instead of the ones you inhabit. Again, we are dealing with *'What if . . . ?'*: *'What if I lived in this place, in this time, in this culture with this set of beliefs and customs; what would I think and feel and do then?'* In this way you can build up a detailed sense of situation, your situational rules that I referred to in Part One, in the same way that you built up a detailed sense of character rules in the last chapter.

You are searching for information about *external experience* and *internal beliefs*. What would you see, hear and feel around you in this world? What would people be doing? What would be their customs and beliefs? What would be important to them and what would be taboo?

Note: Directors often set the plays of Shakespeare in a period other than the one in which they were written: what is the best approach in this case? It is useful if you have an understanding of the beliefs about the world that existed in Elizabethan and early Jacobean times, since these were the beliefs that surrounded Shakespeare as he wrote. How much research you do into the period in which the play is set will depend on the director. Your main focus will be on the immediate context: the on- and offstage geography and conditions of each scene.

Many people start by *reading* about the place and time and culture. [If this doesn't suit you, other ways of gathering information are suggested below.] If you are reading straight factual accounts they need to be ones which bring those facts to life. Read the first paragraph or so: if you can begin to sense the place or time being described, then the book will help you. If the words conjure up a blank for you, it's better to look elsewhere. In the case of fictionalised accounts they need to be based on accurate research, so that, although the characters may not have existed or the events occurred, they are typical of what might have happened and therefore give an accurate flavour of the world concerned.

Start by reading through whatever you have chosen without making any notes. As you read, allow yourself to step into the place and time you are reading about as if you were there, experiencing what is being described. Give yourself the time to build up a sensory experience which is as detailed as possible. Once you have done this, then you can start to gather some useful notes.

Observing and Noting Key Details

To gather key information that will support your intuitive knowledge and highlight key differences between your world and the world of the play

○ *Once you have read as much as you want to read, answer the questions below. In each case what you are looking for are the key differences between the world you are exploring and your own world. So, rather than having huge amounts of information, focus on the striking differences.*

○ *What can be seen and heard and felt in the world you are exploring? How is it different from what you see and hear and feel in your own world?*

○ *How do people behave in the world you are exploring? What are the accepted behaviours and what are taboo behaviours? In other words, what are the rules of that world and how do they differ from the rules of your world?*

○ *What are the beliefs and values people in that world have: about what is important, about gender roles, class roles, the importance of the group or individual, etc.? What are the key differences between their beliefs and the beliefs in your world?*

Here you are exploring the world as a whole. Later you can compare the work you've done on your character with your findings here to discover whether your character shares the behaviours, values and beliefs of this wider world or rebels against them in some way.

Eventually, reduce your answers to these questions to key words or phrases so that they are all on one page and can be easily read through before rehearsal or performance. This can help you to drop in to the world of the play quickly and effortlessly.

Looking, Listening and Experiencing

To feed your imagination through other stimuli

There are other ways of feeding your imagination in regard to time and place.

You can look at paintings and photographs, which date from the same era in which the play is set. There may be films or documentaries that will feed you visually, and allow you to go deeper into the world of the play. With so many television channels available, look out for relevant programmes. Also, many period classics are available to buy or rent on DVD.

○ *Look at the pictures, photos or films in a relaxed way and imagine stepping into them.*

○ *Ask yourself: 'What would it be like if that were my world? If that was what was around me or that was how I was dressed?'*

You can listen to music from the time, place and culture of the play and you can also listen to soundtracks. It may be that the soundtracks come from a film and that you simply shut your eyes so that you can focus on the sounds alone.

○ *Again, allow yourself to step into the world as you listen to the music or soundtrack and ask yourself: 'How would it be if that were the music or sound that I heard around me?'*

The National Sound Archive is a good source of sounds, and also a good source for accents, should you need them. It is now part of the British Library, and their website has a list of the sound recordings they own: www.bl.uk.

If none of the above methods work for you, find someone who can talk to you about the larger context, either because they have personal experience or because they have studied it extensively.

○ *Allow yourself to step into the world as they describe it, perhaps recording what they say rather than taking notes, so that you begin to experience it and can allow that experience to feed your imagination.*

Many museums not only exhibit objects from a certain time or place; they also place them in a setting that evokes the world from which they came. This can give you an excellent sense of the surroundings and, where relevant, the living and working conditions within these worlds. In London, the recreated rooms from various periods at the Geoffrye Museum and the costume collections at the Victoria and Albert can be particularly valuable. For general information about museums in Great Britain visit: www.museums.co.uk.

○ *As always, allow yourself to step imaginatively in to the world depicted, asking: 'What would it be like to live in these conditions, or wear these clothes or handle these objects?'*

Where it is sensible and safe to experience the tastes and smells of the world in which the play is set these can give you imagination further stimulus. They are especially important if you character refers to them a lot. For example, if there are certain foods your character loves or hates and you have never tried them, it might be a good idea to do so. Or if you character talks about a smell that is particularly important to him/her – the smell of a flower or wood smoke, of newly mown grass or a particular food, etc. – then it might be worth seeking out these smells so you have a strong and clear sense of them.

○ *As always, activate your intuition by asking yourself: 'What if these were the tastes and the smells that were around me a great deal of the time?'*

Note: Of course, the Internet can be a great source not only for written information but also for pictures and sounds. Useful sites for historical information are www.channel4.com/history, www.bbc.co.uk/history, and www.britannia.com/history. For geographical information, including a wide range of pictures, www.geographica.com is a good place to start. Otherwise, the best place to begin your search is at www.google.co.uk or www.wikipedia.org.

So, there are plenty of ways of gathering information and feeding your imagination in order to build a sense of the time and place in which the play is set. The richer this sense is, the more comfortable you will feel, especially in worlds that are very different from the one that you inhabit. As you feel more comfortable you will also find it easier to believe in the situations in the play and to play them truthfully.

THE IMMEDIATE CONTEXT

Having looked at the larger context, let's look at the more immediate one: the on- and offstage geography and conditions. This relates specifically to where the play takes place, over what space of time, whether the scenes are indoors or out, domestic or formal, public or private and at what time of day, season of the year and so on they take place in.

On- and Offstage Geography

To be clear about the exact location of each scene

In real life, apart from when we are in a strange or new environment, we enter a room knowing where that room is in relation to the surrounding rooms and to the building as a whole. We also know where the building is in relation to the city or town or village or countryside around it. Similarly, if we go outside we know where we have come from and what we're expecting to see around us. In a play it can be easy to lose a sense of what is beyond the scene, of its exact location and it is even possible to be hazy about the on-stage geography, especially if there is little or no scenery and the details of the onstage space have to be imagined.

Vagueness, about on- and offstage geography, takes away from the reality of the situation both for you and for the audience. Whereas clarity will enable you to produce more detailed, specific and original work, which is far more interesting for the audience.

Onstage Geography

O Make yourself a plan of each scene, noting any details that are added in rehearsals. It does not need to be to scale or drawn with any degree of skill. It is simply your map of the space.

O This plan should include not only what is actually present onstage but also whatever is to be imagined.

O Spend some time in the rehearsal or performance space, walking around and physically and mentally allotting a particular place for everything, whether real or imaginary, and being clear about the relationship between one thing and another.

Offstage Geography

O Now decide what surrounds the scene. If you are 'inside', what other rooms are nearby or further away? Where and what is outside? What can you see from any windows?

○ If you are 'outside', are there buildings or open space beyond where you are? Are there different types of building or countryside in different directions?

○ As with the onstage geography, draw yourself a detailed plan of the offstage space so that you have a precise sense of what surrounds the scene.

○ Again, you might find it useful to walk around the edges of the performance space imagining what is beyond and exactly where it is.

Note: It is also important to give a definite location to offstage people and places that you refer to, even if they are further away than the eye can see.

The clearer you are about the on- and offstage geography the more you will behave in a truthful and authentic way as you enter, inhabit and leave the space in which the scene takes place. You will also find that you move around the stage more easily, since you have a much more secure sense of where you are.

Time, Temperature and Light

To be clear about the time of day, temperature and light

The last exercise explored the details of where; this one explores the details of when and the effects this has in terms of temperature and light.

○ Start by asking yourself about the time of year and the weather outside. What season is it? How hot or cold, wet or dry, sunny or cloudy is it?

○ Also, ask yourself about the time of day: whether it is light and, if so, how light? Is it dawn or midday or dusk? If it is dark, how dark is it? Are there any stars? Can you see the moon? Are there any other light sources: fires or torches or lamps?

○ If the scene takes place outdoors, imagine what you would feel. Can you feel sun or wind or rain?

○ If the scene takes place indoors, go on to imagine the light and temperature inside the room. Is the light in the room natural or artificial? Is the temperature constant or changing? How does it contrast with outside? How aware is your character of the weather and light and temperature outside?

○ Can you hear any sounds outside the room? What sounds are inside the room and how are they different from the ones outside?

○ How does the room feel to be in: is it familiar or unfamiliar; comfortable or awkward?

○ Are there any smells or tastes?

○ *Once you have gathered this information you might want to write it in your script at the beginning of each scene so that you can quickly remind yourself of these details before you enter the scene.*

As with the on- and offstage geography, the details concerning time of year and day will help you to inhabit the space more truthfully, pulling both you and the audience deeper into the world of the play.

Linking the Scenes

To identify the shifts in place and time between one scene and the next

Once you have identified the where and when for each scene you can look at how they link together.

○ *Firstly, go through the script noting the length of time between the scenes. When do they follow on from each other: are they hours or days or years later?*

○ *Note these gaps at the beginning of each scene.*

In a later chapter we will look at exploring what may have occurred in the intervals between scenes. Here all that is necessary is to identify the length of the gap.

○ *Then, go through the script noting the shift in where the scenes take place. Are all the places familiar to the character or are some of them new? What scenes are domestic and/or private and what are more formal and/or public?*

○ *Ask yourself how comfortable or awkward your character might be in each place.*

○ *Again, note these details at the beginning of each scene.*

By identifying the difference in time and place from scene to scene you give yourself the situational journey of the play. This is the backdrop against which your character makes his/her personal journey through the play. This is important because it allows you to respond more accurately and authentically and gives more detail to the steps of your journey and so makes it more interesting for the audience.

Note: It's always worth wearing clothes and shoes in rehearsal that resemble what you are going to wear in performance. Countless times I have seen an actor's whole performance be lost, in dress rehearsal and previews, because the clothes changed so much that it was too late to integrate them with the rest of the performance.

Summary

Knowing where and when you are establishes the circumstances that surround you, giving you an experience much closer to the one you have in real life. This organic way of working produces the best performances on stage. Again, it is a question of *'What if . . . ?'* Approaching a character in this way will always produce work that is more secure and satisfying for you, and more truthful and interesting for the audience.

Below is a summary of the exercises in this chapter.

The Larger Context
Observing and Noting Key Details
Looking, Listening and Experiencing

The Immediate Context
On- and Offstage Geography
Time, Temperature and Light
Linking the Scenes

What Do I Want?

IDENTIFYING YOUR
CHARACTER'S OBJECTIVES

Having established who you are, where you are and when, you can focus on what your character wants to achieve: in other words, what his/her objectives are, both in the play as a whole and in each individual scene. These are the character's drivers *within* the play whereas the core motivation, which we looked at earlier, provided the character's driver *above and beyond* the play. The core motivation helped you understand your character's overall want and identify how he/she was different from you. The play and scene objectives give purpose to your journey through the play: they give your work focus and energy.

PLAY OBJECTIVE

The *play objective* is whatever your character wants from early on in the play that drives everything he/she does for the rest of the play. This objective can be present from the beginning, in which case it is likely to have been triggered by an event or circumstance that occurred before the play started. Or it can be triggered in the early scenes of the play as a result of an event or circumstance that occurs there. It is important to identify the *triggering event or circumstance* because it gives meaning to the objective.

Let's take some of the characters whose speeches we looked at in earlier chapters and identify possible *play objectives* and *triggers*: I say 'possible' because of course there are always many interpretations. The point is to find an objective that helps you play the character effectively. Also, it is not fixed and may well change during rehearsals. It simply gives you a focus, something your character is working towards, and if what you've chosen is not the most helpful this will become clear in rehearsals and you can easily find another. What *is* crucial, as always, is that you ask the questions.

Edmund's *play objective* in *King Lear* could be to disinherit his brother. The *triggering event or circumstance* is his realisation that, as the bastard son, he will never have the status Edgar does. This event would have occurred before the start of the play and therefore his *play objective* would be present from the beginning of the play.

Electra's *play objective* in *Orestes: Blood and Light* could be to die nobly with her brother. The *triggering event or circumstance* is the killing of her mother by her brother at her instigation, which, again, happened before the play started. This killing in its turn was triggered by the earlier killing of her father by her mother and her lover, which was in turn triggered by earlier events. And *all* these earlier *triggering events* would need to be taken into consideration.

Man's *play objective* in *Notes on Falling Leaves* could be to reconnect with his mother. The *triggering event or circumstance* being his mother's declining health, which means she can no longer communicate or be communicated with. Again, this occurred before the play started.

Note: If the play objective is triggered during the early scenes of the play, choose a prior objective to focus on until the play objective is triggered, so that you still have something to drive those early scenes. For example, Juliet's play objective, which could be to find a way to be with Romeo, does not begin until she meets him and falls in love with him. In this case, her prior objective might be to enjoy herself and not be bothered with growing up too quickly. It is good if the prior objective contrasts with the play objective so that the triggering event can cause a shift of direction and focus.

The *play objective* is always external: something the person is striving to achieve in the outside world. Often this external objective is linked to a deeper and more internal objective that is important to the character psychologically. In Edmund's case the *deeper need* may be for recognition that he is of equal worth to his brother; in Electra's case it may be to be utterly united with someone at last; in the Man's case it may be to go back to the relationship he had with his mother before she was ill; and in Juliet's case it may be to choose her own destiny.

Once you have identified your play objective, as well as the event or circumstance that triggered it and any connection to a deeper need, the following exercises will help you to bring these to life so that they can support you in rehearsal and performance.

Connecting with the Trigger

To connect with the event or circumstances that triggered the play objective

I start here because this is where the play objective is created.

○ Once you have identified the trigger event or circumstance, make sure that the details of this are clear in your mind. If the event or circumstance occurs in the play go over that scene carefully. If it occurred before the play or in between scenes look for any references to it in the play, and then fill in the gaps yourself based on what is most likely to have occurred.

○ Take the time to imagine the trigger event or circumstance in detail. See what the character saw, hear what the character heard, feel what the character felt.

○ As in previous chapters, you are using the 'What if . . . ?': 'What if, as this character, this event or circumstance had happened to me?'

○ Once you have done this, bring the play objective to mind and notice how the triggering event or circumstance gives meaning to that objective.

Strengthening the Play Objective

To make the play objective as tangible as possible

In order to maintain a strong sense of purpose it is important that the play objective is as real and concrete to you as possible. This exercise will help that.

○ Having identified your character's play objective, take the time to imagine what it would be like if this objective were achieved. What would you see and hear and feel?

For example, if you were playing Edmund in *King Lear*, you might imagine having inherited your brother's land and titles and the resultant recognition you would be getting from others – how they would be treating you and how you would feel.

○ *Fill in as many details as possible so that your sense of the play objective is very strong.*

It is irrelevant, at this point, whether or not the character actually achieves his/her objective during the course of the play. Here you are simply making sure that the objective your character is working towards is as tangible as possible, so that it is easier to hold on to.

Connecting with the Deeper Need

To link the play objective with the deeper need

○ *Having identified the character's deeper need, take the time to ask yourself: 'What would it be like if I had this particular deeper need?'*

○ *Once you have a sense of connection with this need, ask yourself: 'How would this need affect my play objective? Would it make it stronger or more urgent or more vital or more frightening, etc.?'*

As always, trust that an answer will arrive at some point even if you are not entirely conscious of it. It is the question that is important because it triggers your mind to consider the issue and make the necessary connections.

Establishing Present Circumstances

To establish the difference between where your character is and where they want to be

Having strongly established where your character wants to end up and why, it is also important to be clear about where they start, so you have a sense of the gap between the two.

○ *Identify the facts of your character's circumstances at the start of the play.*

○ *Having identified these, take the time to connect with these in as much detail as possible.*

For example, if you were playing Edmund, the present circumstances would be that although your father recognises you as his son, you carry the stigma of being the bastard son and cannot inherit his land or titles, which will all go to your brother who is legitimate.

○ *Having built a strong sense of the present circumstances, explore the gap between them and where your character wants to end up. Ask yourself: 'How far away from the play objective do I feel? How possible or impossible does the objective seem?'*

Charting Your Progress

To note whether your character is moving towards or away from his/her play objective in each scene

Once you have connected with where your character is and where he/she wants to be and what it was that triggered this objective and the deeper internal need, then it's a good idea to chart the progress of the objective from scene to scene; possibly putting this on paper in some way.

○ *Go through each of your scenes and ask yourself: 'Does this scene take me closer to or further away from my play objective?'*

In this way you will get a sense of when the character feels they are moving forward and where he/she feels blocked or frustrated.

It is a good idea to ask this question afresh every time you rehearse since the way the scene is played may shift as new discoveries are made and this may affect your character's ability to move towards his/her objective.

On the following page is a chart for Edmund.

1.1	1.2	2.1	2.2	3.3	3.5	3.7	4.2	5.1	5.3
His father introduces him as his bastard son, says he's been away for nine years and is about to go away again.	Edmund convinces his father that his brother, Edgar, is plotting against him and convinces Edgar that he has displeased his father.	Persuades Edgar to flee. Persuades his father that Edgar wanted to murder him. * Taken into the service of Duke of Cornwall.	In the service of the Duke of Cornwall.	His father Gloucester confides in Edmund, giving him the ammunition to betray his father to the Duke of Cornwall.	Rewarded for betraying his father by being made the new Earl of Gloucester.	Tasked with escorting Goneril back home.	Goneril promises herself and quizzes him about his relationship with her sister. *	Regan wants Edmund once she has got rid of her husband. * He decides it's up to them to sort out which of them has him. He also swears to give no mercy to Lear and Cordelia.	Orders Lear and Cordelia's death. * Confronted by Albany for committing adultery with his wife. * Challenged to fight and killed by Edgar.
Very far from his objective	Good step closer	Good step closer	Staying on course	Chance for another step forward	Big step forward	Chance for another step forward	Big step forward	Some complication there, but staying on course	Almost there, then brought down at the last moment.

SCENE OBJECTIVES

Having identified the play objective, it is worth looking at your individual scenes and identifying the objective for each. These smaller objectives are the drivers for each scene as the character pursues his/her larger objective. For example, Edmund's objective in his first scene might be to show himself as an obedient and respectful son. Electra's objective in her first scene might be to remind herself why it was right that her mother should be murdered.

Establishing Scene Objectives

To clarify the objective of each scene

○ *Take each scene and ask yourself: 'What is it that the character wants to achieve in this scene that will further his/her play objective?'*

○ *Once you have identified the scene objective, build a strong sense of it by imagining what you, as the character, would see, hear and feel once that objective were achieved.*

Of course, as mentioned earlier, the character may or may not achieve their objective during the course of a scene.

○ *Then, focus on your character's circumstances at the beginning of the scene so you have a sense of the gap between where your character is and where they want to be.*

The exercise *My Corner or Yours* in the chapter on internal dynamics [see page 225] allows you to work physically on your scene objectives with your scene partner/s.

Summary

As I said earlier, the point of the work on objectives is that it gives you focus, energy and purpose, just as having a clear objective does in life. It also allows you to work with more confidence, because you have a clear sense of what your character is attempting to achieve, and it allows you to be more responsive in rehearsal and performance, because you will have a sense of whether you are getting nearer or further away from the objective you are striving to reach. All of this will give your performance a sharpness and sense of forward movement, which will engage the audience and keep them moving with you.

Below is a summary of the exercises in this chapter.

Play Objective
Connecting with the Trigger
Strengthening the Play Objective
Connecting with the Deeper Need
Establishing Present Circumstances
Charting Your Progress

Scene Objectives
Establishing Scene Objectives

What's Been Going On Before?

FLESHING OUT THE BACK STORY

The last area to explore, before looking at the scenes themselves, is what was going on before the play started. In life we carry our history with us. Everything we have thought, felt and experienced is stored very precisely. In a play, however, it is very easy for scenes to exist in a vacuum. Yes, we have some sense that important events have occurred before the play and between our scenes, but that is very different from having a strong connection with these as we would if they had really happened to us. So we need to create 'memories' of these important events.

The important events fall into three categories: firstly, key events that occurred before the play, which are referred to directly or indirectly by your character during the play; secondly, key events that occurred in any gap between your present scene and your previous one; thirdly, what has taken place *immediately* before each of your scenes.

Note: Obviously, where one scene runs straight into the next, the first scene will be the back story to the second, so it is not necessary to create a memory in this case.

Identifying Important Events

To select the events which need to be explored and connected with

○ Go through your script making three lists, corresponding to the three categories:

      1. Important events which occurred before the play started

      2. Important events which occur between your scenes

      3. What has taken place immediately before each of your scenes start?

By 'important events' I mean, of course, events that have significance for your character.

In the case of Baby in *Mojo*:

1. The important events before the play are [i] the discovery of the singer Silver Johnny, who has been working in his father's club and bringing in a lot of money and [ii] the proposal Mr Ross, a local gangster, has made to take over Silver Johnny.

2. The important event between the first and second scenes is the murder of Baby's father, Ezra; and between the third and fourth scenes it is Baby killing Mr Ross, who was responsible for his father's murder.

3. Immediately before the last scene of the play – which the speech we looked at earlier comes from – Baby has found out that Mickey, who worked for his father, knew Mr Ross was going to kill him and had made a deal with Mr Ross.

In the case of Viola in *Twelfth Night*:

1. The important events before the play are the shipwreck and the presumed loss of Viola's brother as a result.

2. The important events tend to happen in the scenes rather than between them.

3. Immediately before Act 1 Scene 5, from which the speech we looked at earlier comes, Viola, having fallen in love with Orsino, has been sent by him to woo Olivia for the first time.

Once you have the three lists you can work through them using either or both of the exercises below.

Creating the Memory Internally

To connect with the event through imagining it internally

○ *Take your time to imagine the event you want to connect with. See what your character might have seen, hear what he/she might have heard and feel what he/she might have felt, filling in as much detail as possible.*

O Revisit this sensory experience of the event that you have built up, from time to time, in order to reconnect with it and strengthen it.

Creating the Memory Externally

To connect with the event through external methods

O If you prefer to work externally you can draw a picture of the event, write about it or improvise it.

O It is simply a matter of what is most enjoyable and effective for you.

If you do choose one of these external methods it is important to keep in mind that any pictures or writing or improvisations you do are ways of feeding you, of exploring the event so that you can create the memory. They do not have to be interesting or meaningful for others, they simply have to be useful to you!

Keying In

To connect with what has just occurred before you start a scene

Once you have created the 'memories' it is useful to practise keying into them, so that once you come to performance you can very quickly access them just before you start each scene.

O Take up your starting position for a scene.

O Choose a place in the space around you to locate the created memory you wish to key into.

O Recall your created memory of that event: seeing what you imagined seeing, hearing what you imagined hearing and feeling what you imagined feeling.

If you practise this regularly, then it will be easy and swift to access the created memory during rehearsal and performance.

Summary

By creating memories in the way I have suggested you will never have the sensation of starting a scene cold or feeling that you are working in a vacuum, and, as a result, you will feel more comfortable and at ease and more able to respond truthfully rather than forcing your actions and reactions.

Below is a summary of the exercises in this chapter.

Identifying Important Events
Creating the Memory Internally
Creating the Memory Externally
Keying In

What's Going On Now?

EXPLORING THE INTERNAL DYNAMICS
OF A SCENE

Having established character, place and time, objectives and back story let's explore what is going on *within* each scene, beneath the level of the words: the emotions, thoughts and actions underlying the text. It is useful to think of these as the *internal dynamics*, the constant inner shift that keeps a speech or scene alive. There are four aspects worth exploring: *Bringing the Situation to Life*, *Identifying Shifts Within Your Character*, *Identifying Tension and Shifts Between Characters* and *Exploring the Scene Journey Spatially*.

As with all the work it's helpful to explore each aspect separately, trusting that they will weave themselves together of their own accord, giving a rich underlying tapestry to the scene and allowing you to play with clarity and ease.

BRINGING THE SITUATION TO LIFE

The more you connect with the situation underlying a speech or scene, the easier it is to respond accurately and intuitively in terms of emotions, thoughts and actions. The following exercise brings the situation to life by identifying all the people and elements, real or imaginary, individual or group, which are, explicitly or implicitly, involved in a speech or scene. This allows you to have a sense of all the influences on the character.

Connecting with the Situation

To bring to life the people and elements influencing a speech or scene

To help you I have identified the various influences in four different speeches, two modern and two from Shakespeare, all of which were explored in the earlier text chapters. Try out the exercise described below on at least one modern and one Shakespeare piece. Then, try it out on your own speeches or scenes.

Daniel in *The Way Home* has been to his mother's funeral. He is sitting with his friend Bobby at Otterspool: a place he likes to go most days. Before you go any further, see page 38 if you aren't familiar with the speech and the situation he's in.

The people and elements to focus on in this speech are: *his dead mother*; *his sister,* who keeps crying all the time; *his father*, who's in a state and has spent all his money on the funeral; *his aunt*, his mother's sister, who is constantly at loggerheads with his father; *all the people who've been visiting since his mother died* so he can't get any peace in the caravan; *Bobby*, his friend, whom he's beginning to trust even though he's not a traveller; *the non-traveller community*, who he senses are prejudiced against travellers; *the present situation*, which he feels he's trapped in – 'this shitehole'.

Edmund in *King Lear* is alone on stage bemoaning the fact that being illegitimate prevents him inheriting his father's land, and planning to discredit his legitimate brother and gain the land. Again, if you're not familiar with the speech or the situation Edmund is in, then see page 141 before you go on.

The people and elements to focus on in this speech are: *the Goddess Nature*, whom Edmund turns to because she doesn't discriminate against illegitimacy; *Edmund's father, Gloucester*, who despite his love for his illegitimate son can't give him land or titles; *his brother, Edgar*, who because he is legitimate will inherit everything; *his mother*, who is presumably dead; and *a representation of the religion and custom of society*, which dictates that illegitimate children cannot inherit or be recognised as true heirs. Edmund's mother is not a character in the play and is only mentioned briefly and indirectly, but it can prove useful for some actors if she is represented.

Ellie in *The Way Home* is talking to her brother's friend Bobby, about seeing her mother after she had died. Before continuing, see page 39 if you aren't familiar with the speech and the situation she's in.

The people and elements to focus on in this speech are: *her dead mother*, whom she really misses and who looked peaceful when she was dead in a way she never did when she was alive; *her brother*, who has gone missing and she hopes has gone off to make a better life for himself; *her father*, who isn't coping well with his wife's death; *her aunt*, her mother's sister, who's been staying to help and whom she likes but her father doesn't get on with; *Bobby*, her brother's friend, who isn't a traveller, but whom she likes all the same; *the non-traveller community*, who she feels are judging her and her family the whole time and waiting for them to mess up.

Juliet in *Romeo and Juliet* has secretly married Romeo and is waiting for him so they can spend their first night together. See page 120 before you continue if you are not familiar with the speech or situation she's in.

The people and elements I would like you to consider in relation to this speech are: *the fiery-footed steeds*, who draw the chariot of the sun-god across the sky and therefore represent the day which she wants to end; *Night*, which she calls by many different names and which she is longing will come since it will allow Romeo to come safely to her; *Romeo*, whom she has married and is waiting to spend her first night alone with; *her first sexual experience* and losing her virginity; *her mother and father*, who know nothing about the marriage and would be horrified since Romeo is the son of their sworn enemy; *Romeo's parents*, who would be similarly horrified; *their wider families and servants*, who are also involved in the feud; and *the Nurse*, who is bringing the rope ladder that Juliet will lower to enable Romeo to climb up into her room, and whom Juliet is impatiently waiting to return.

○ *Choose the speech you are going to work on [and find it on the page numbered above].*

○ *Take the list of people and elements that influence the character in your chosen speech.*

○ *Place each person or element on the list in a specific spot in the room.*

○ *If you find it difficult to remember who/what is where, write each one on a separate piece of paper and fix these on the wall.*

This 'geographical' placing is very important since it relates to your unconscious understanding of the situation and the relationships between the people influencing your character in some way.

○ *Stand in the middle of the room.*

○ *Take your time to turn and consider each person, element, etc. and connect with how you, as your character, feel about them and their influence on the present situation.*

○ *Keep returning to each until you feel ready to say the speech.*

○ *As you say the speech, allow yourself to remain aware of each and their influence on your character's present situation. Turn to look at each, or move towards or away as feels appropriate.*

How did you find this exercise? Did it help to make the situations more tangible? Taking the time to connect with everyone/thing who could possibly have a direct or indirect influence on the scene allows you to create a richer understanding of and connection with the situation your character is in. This in turn makes the text more detailed and truthful.

The great joy with this exercise is that you do not have to worry about being 'right'. If someone/thing you have chosen to include turns out to be less relevant or if someone/thing is missing, you will discover this as you do the exercise. You are simply exploring and you will always learn something.

Connecting with the situation behind a speech or scene in this way is useful with any text, bringing depth and detail to your work. With classical plays it also makes seemingly remote situations tangible and relevant so that they are far easier to play and far more believable to watch.

IDENTIFYING SHIFTS WITHIN YOUR CHARACTER

The exercises in this section help you to explore and mark the various shifts that occur for your character during a speech or scene. Being able to mark these shifts physically allows you to have more variety and tension in your work, and so will make it more secure for you and engaging for an audience.

Spectrum

To explore simple shifts within a speech or scene

This is an excellent exercise for getting to grips with *potential* emotional shifts within your character during a speech or scene.

You can try this exercise out either on one of the speeches from earlier in the book or on one of your own choice.

○ *Choose one of the most obvious emotions in the scene.*

In Daniel's case it might be fascination; in Ellie's case, bitterness; in Edmund's case, resentment; and in Juliet's case, excitement. These may seem generalised, but that is fine because we are starting with broad brushstrokes.

○ *Search for another emotion within the scene that in some way contrasts with the first. Often this emotion is more hidden and implied rather than explicitly expressed.*

In Daniel's case it might be being fed up; in Ellie's case, confusion and grief; in Edmund's case, triumph or amusement; and in Juliet's case, fear.

○ *Imagine a line running across the room; place the first emotion at one end of the line and the second emotion at the other end.*

○ *Ask yourself: 'Where am I on the line when I start the speech or scene? Am I completely with one emotion or the other or somewhere between the two?'*

○ *Go through the speech or scene moving back and forth along the imaginary line as feels appropriate, trusting your instincts.*

Note: If you find it hard-going it usually means that there is insufficient tension between the two emotions. In which case you change one or both until you hit on a combination that really works. By which I mean it becomes easy and right to move back and forth along the line.

How did you find working on a speech in this way? Did it help you to feel some of the potential shifts in the scene? Did it yield any surprises? Did you notice that sometimes you were making small shifts and at other times you were moving a much greater distance? This is an excellent exercise for encouraging you to act on your instinctive responses since you have to commit and move.

The other great thing about this exercise is that there are no rights or wrongs. You will learn whatever happens. And you can explore more than one set of tensions, by changing the emotions at one or both ends. In this way you can establish a multiplicity of tensions within your character during the speech or scene.

The point of the exercise is that you are exploring ambiguity within your character. This ambiguity is what brings speeches and scenes to life and makes them interesting for an audience.

As with all the exercises, avoid fixing the points at which you shift. These are exploratory exercises that allow you to understand a speech or scene deeply. Whatever you learn will be stored by your unconscious and inform your rehearsal and performance work.

Note: You can also do this exercise with others in a scene you might be working on. It's fantastic being able to see all the different shifts that are occurring in the scene. When working with others, you each identify a separate line in the room and move up and down it not only when you are talking but also when you are listening.

Certain/Uncertain

To explore what your character is certain about and what they are unsure about

This exercise works in the same way as the *Spectrum*: however, instead of emotions, you place certainty at one end of the line and uncertainty at the other.

It came out of trying to solve a problem in a scene from *The Comedy of Errors*. In this scene a master and servant mistake a courtesan for the devil. She in turn mistakes them for their identical twins. Everyone is uncertain about what is going on, so the tendency is to play such a scene very uncertainly. However, what became clear when we did this exercise was that they have flashes of uncertainty and then make very certain assumptions that they cling to until the next event that confuses them. Using the

Certain/Uncertain line made the scene far more dynamic and revealed that the humour lay in the swift shifts from certainty to uncertainty and back again as they tried to make sense of the situation. This exercise works well with many texts and it is very interesting to try it on familiar speeches such as Hamlet's 'To be or not to be . . . ' or Hermione's 'Sir, spare your threats . . . ' It can bring surprises and blow away clichéd ways of playing.

As before, either work on one of the speeches explored elsewhere or on one of your own choice.

○ Choose one end of the room to represent complete certainty and the other end to represent complete uncertainty. Between the two lies a sliding scale of certainty.

○ Place yourself on the line according to how certain or uncertain you feel your character is at the start of the speech or scene.

○ Then, play the speech or scene moving back and forth depending on how certain or uncertain you feel at any point.

How was that? Were you surprised at what your character was and wasn't certain about? Did the possibility of shifting between the two make the speech or scene more dynamic?

Corners

To explore the possibilities within a speech or scene

This exercise builds on the *Spectrum*. It is called *Corners* because the first time I used it we took the four corners of the room to represent four different emotions. We were working on a stage adaptation of *Les Enfants du Paradis*, and the actor concerned was playing a dark, psychopathic character. He wanted to avoid being one-dimensional, so we created this exercise to allow him to explore varying emotional shifts. Since then the exercise has expanded so that an endless number of different emotions can be explored.

Note: In the end it is best in any speech or scene to focus on what you want – your objective – and how you go about getting what you want – your actions. Nevertheless, it is useful to explore the emotional shifts, especially early on, because it creates a greater sense of journey through the scene.

○ Write down all the possible emotions your character may have during a scene.

It is worth starting with the obvious ones and then looking for contrasts. For example, if a speech seems to be full of darker, more serious emotions, look for lighter ones that could be present. It doesn't matter whether they all get used; you are simply looking for any emotion that could be there, even for a millisecond.

Below is a list of the emotions that Ellie and Edmund might be feeling in their speeches:

Ellie: Sad, resentful, bitter, angry, confused, surprised, loving, happy. [*The last three may relate to feelings she has when she sees her mother at peace; they provide a contrast with the emotions you might expect to find in the scene.*]

Edmund: Bitter, resentful, angry, hurt, dismissive, excited, triumphant, gloating.

○ Take some sheets of paper and write one of the emotions on each piece of paper. Write these large enough to read from a distance.

○ Place the pieces of paper around the room as feels appropriate to you.

○ Also, place some blank pieces of paper amongst the rest.

○ Look at the papers and decide where you are at the start of the speech or scene. Then, go and stand by that particular piece of paper or between two or more if you think that you are feeling a mixture of emotions.

○ Say the first section of the speech or scene – which could be the first phrase or sentence or occasionally the first couple of sentences. Then, when you feel the need for a shift to a different emotion, look around to find one that seems right and move to that and say the next part. Continue in this way through the whole speech or scene, taking as much time as you need.

○ It is absolutely fine if you find that some of the papers never get chosen: they are simply there in case you need them. Equally, you may look round and realise that none of the papers has the emotion you want, so then you can go and stand by one of the blank pieces, name for yourself what emotion that is and then say the next part.

Note: Again, there is no right or wrong. If you make a choice and it doesn't feel right, simply make another choice and deliver that part again. A section could be several sentences, a single sentence, a phrase or even a single word. The point is that you move every time you sense there is a shift in emotion.

How was that? Did you find more shifts? Did those shifts give the speech greater variety and precision? This exercise and the two previous ones are all about exploring the *potential territory* of a speech or scene – what *might* be there – so that you have a rich choice of possibilities to draw on in rehearsals and performance.

Writing a Thought Script

To identify the thought bridges which connect across thought jumps

Having explored the larger shifts, this exercise helps you to begin to be more specific. By creating a *thought script* you identify the *thought bridges* that connect one thought to the next where there is a *thought jump*: that is, one thought does not necessarily follow on smoothly from the one before. Sometimes it will be useful to add a whole sentence; at other times a single conjunction such as '*and*' or '*but*' may be sufficient. There is no one right thought script for any speech or scene. It is simply a question of creating an underlying logic for your character. This will make the lines much easier to remember and much more convincing for the audience.

Modern Texts

This is one of the few cases where for Elizabethan and Jacobean texts it is best to work slightly differently, as I will explain later. For now, try the exercise on a short scene from *The Cherry Orchard* by Anton Chekhov, which is marked up here with a possible thought script.

The scene comes from the final act of the play when most of the characters are on the point of departure. The house and estate have been sold to Lopakhin, the son of a former servant, who is now a rich man. Varya, is the adopted daughter of Ranyevskaya who previously owned the estate with her brother Gayev. For two years everyone has been talking about Varya and Lopakhin getting married, and Varya does like him. Lopakhin, however, has never said a word. Just before this scene Ranyevskaya has spoken to him about Varya and he has agreed that he will ask her to marry him right now. So Ranyevskaya calls Varya. The thought script is in bold.

Offstage, a stifled laugh and whispering. VARYA finally enters.

VARYA: [**I'll pretend to look for something.**] [*Inspects the luggage at some length.*] That's strange, I can't find it anywhere . . .

LOPAHKIN: [**How am I going to do this?**] What are you looking for?

VARYA: [**Make something up.**] I packed it myself, and now I can't remember.

A pause. [VARYA: **I don't know what to say, is he going to say something?**] [LOPAHKIN: **I don't know what to say.**]

LOPAHKIN: [**I'll ask her where she's going.**] Where are you off to now, Miss Varvara?

VARYA: [**Why doesn't he get on with it?**] Me? I'm going to the Ragulins' . . . I've agreed to look after the house for them . . . [**Tell the truth.**] I'll be a sort of housekeeper.

LOPAHKIN: [**I should ask her to marry me now but I can't.**] And that's at Yashnevo? That'll be about fifty miles from here.

A pause. [LOPAHKIN: **I can't say it. I can't bring myself to ask.**]

So, life in this house is over now.

VARYA: [**I can't bear this.**] [*Examining the luggage.*] Where on earth is it . . . ? [**What is going on?**] Maybe I packed it away in the trunk . . . [**Perhaps he was leading up to it.**] Yes, life's finished in this house . . . there'll be nothing left . . .

LOPAHKIN: [**I can't say it!**] And I'm off to Kharkov now . . . by the same train. I've a lot of business on hand. I'm leaving Yepikhodov here to look after the place. I've taken him on.

VARYA: [**Why doesn't he ask!**] Not really!

LOPAHKIN: [**I just can't say it!**] This time last year we'd already had snow, if you remember, and now it's so mild and sunny. It's cold nonetheless . . . three degrees below.

VARYA: [**What is he going on about?**] I haven't looked.

A pause. [VARYA: **I don't know what to say.**]

[**This is ridiculous.**] Our thermometer's broken anyway.

A pause. [VARYA: **Say something, please ask me!**] [LOPAHKIN: **I can't say it, I can't.**]

Someone calls through the door from outside: 'Mr Lopakhin!'

LOPAHKIN: [As *if he had been waiting for this call.*] [**Thank God!**] Just coming! [*Hurriedly exits.*]

[VARYA: **That's it, it's all over, it's all over.**]

VARYA *is sitting on the floor, lays her head on a bundle of dresses, and begins quietly sobbing. The door opens, and* RANYEVSKAYA *tentatively enters.*

RANYEVSKAYA: Well?

A pause. [RANYEVSKAYA: **She's crying. He hasn't asked her. Poor Varya.**]

We have to go.[31]

What you choose as your thought bridge to get you across a thought jump will be personal to you. There is no one right thought. It will depend on the interpretation the director chooses, on what works best for the audience and on what will help you to own the lines, so they feel truthful. Also, you may find that the thoughts change as you go through rehearsal and learn more about the character and situation.

○ *Start by writing whatever thought or thoughts you imagine might come before you first speak in a speech and scene.*

○ *If working with a single speech, identify where in the speech there are thought jumps and write thoughts to join together the text either side of each jump.*

○ *As already mentioned, sometimes the thought will be a whole sentence or more; sometimes a conjunction word such as 'and' or 'but' is all that is needed.*

○ *If working with a scene, also write the thoughts that might occur whilst you are listening to what the other character or character says.*

○ *As already mentioned there is no right answer: you are simply finding the logic of a speech for yourself.*

○ *Once you have prepared the speech/scene as described, go through it, thinking the thoughts silently and saying the text aloud.*

How did you find that? Did you find the lines flowed more and felt more comfortable to say? This exercise helps you to chart the thought journey of a speech or scene and, as already mentioned, makes it much easier to remember since it is the thoughts that lead to the words. It is also excellent for preparing a script at short notice. I use it a great deal when helping actors prepare for film and TV castings.

Classical Texts

With classical texts, although there are thought shifts, which we will focus on in the next exercise, there are fewer thought jumps because more of what the character is thinking is spoken. However, the following steps are useful.

○ *Repeat the last line or half-line of the character that speaks before you and use this as the bridge into your own lines.*

Below is an extract from *Measure for Measure* with the repeated half-lines in bold. For the context of the scene see page 286:

CLAUDIO: Now, sister, what's the comfort?

ISABELLA: **What's the comfort?** Tomorrow you set on.

CLAUDIO: **Tomorrow you set on.** Is there no remedy?

ISABELLA: **Is there no remedy?** None, but such remedy as,
         to save a head,
     To cleave a heart in twain.

CLAUDIO: **To cleave a heart in twain.** But is there any?

ISABELLA: **But is there any?** Yes, brother, you may live;
     There is a devilish mercy in the judge,
     If you'll implore it, that will free your life,
     But fetter you till death.

CLAUDIO: **But fetter you till death.** Perpetual durance?

ISABELLA: **Perpetual durance?** Ay, just. Perpetual durance,
         a restraint,
     Though all the world's vastidity you had,
     To a determined scope.

CLAUDIO: **To a determined scope.** But in what nature?

ISABELLA: **But in what nature?** In such a one as, you
         consenting to't,
     Would bark your honour from that trunk you bear,
     And leave you naked.

CLAUDIO: **And leave you naked.** Let me know the point.

○ *Note where sentences start with words such as 'and', 'so', 'but', 'if', 'now', 'then', 'O', etc., as these often signal a shift of direction or a build.*

○ Also, note where successive sentences or phrases start in the same or similar way. For example, in Claudio's and Juliet's speeches where they constantly start with verbs.

Beat or Click Exercise

To mark your shifts of thought within a speech or scene

This exercise builds on the previous one and is best done once you know the text and have done quite a lot of work on it. I came across it when assisting Mike Alfreds in the 1980s, thought it was superb, and have used it ever since. As always I can only describe my version of it here.

It is fantastic for bringing precision and variety to your work. It is also a useful preventative measure if you tend to rush ahead. And it really tests whether you know your lines inside out or not. If you can only remember them when you rattle them off at speed it suggests they are rote-learnt and that the thoughts that link them are not clear.

In the exercise you mark the beginning of each new thought by saying the word '*beat*'. A new thought may be a whole sentence, a phrase, or even a single word, since we do sometimes stop mid-sentence to choose the next word or phrase. The shift may be to a completely new thought or may be an addition to, or a stepping up of, the thought you already have. The beat represents the injection of new energy that leads to whatever is said next.

The larger beats will tend to correspond to the thought shift you identified in the previous exercise. However, there are likely to be more, smaller beats identified for this exercise, where you might not be able to articulate what the thought shift is, but simply have a sense that there is a shift.

As an example, Electra's and Claudio's speeches have been marked up below. You will notice that sometimes there are double beats between the lines. This marks the fact that there is more than one thought shift. Of course, there is no right place for these smaller thought shifts, so the marking up of the speeches below is only one possible version.

ELECTRA: **beat** Sometimes she would let me stay while she undressed. **beat** Sometimes she would send the servants away **beat** and she would sit here while I brushed her hair. **beat beat** My mother. **beat** She would let me open jars and bottles, **beat** sniff and touch, **beat** she would let me uncover close things from drawers, **beat** treasures, **beat** and tell me where they came from.

beat Tell me stories of a life before. **beat beat** Sometimes she would hold out her hands for me and I would rub them with oil, **beat** taking the rings off, **beat** one by one, **beat** feeling the deep lines on her knuckles, **beat** shifting her skin, **beat** gently, **beat** over veins and bone. **beat beat** I wanted to climb back inside her, **beat** always, **beat** and settle down behind her heart.

*

CLAUDIO: **beat** Ay, **beat** but to die, **beat** and go
           we know not where,
       beat To lie in cold obstruction and to rot;
       beat This sensible warm motion to become
       A kneaded clod; **beat** and the delighted spirit
       To bathe in fiery floods, **beat** or to reside
       In thrilling region of thick-ribbèd ice,
       beat To be imprisoned in the viewless winds
       beat And blown with restless violence round about
       The pendent world; **beat** or to be worse than worst
       Of those that lawless and incertain thought
       Imagine howling, **beat** 'tis too horrible.
       beat The weariest and most loathèd worldly life
       That age, **beat** ache, **beat** penury, **beat** and imprisonment
       beat Can lay on nature is a paradise
       To what we fear of death.

○ *Try one of the speeches. Saying 'beat' out loud to mark each new thought.*

○ *Make sure that you say 'beat' just before the following word, phrase or sentence rather than tagging it onto the end of the previous one!*

○ *Once you have been through one of the speeches above a few times and have a sense of how the exercise works, try the exercise on a speech of your own choosing.*

How did you find that? Did you notice that because you had more time you were able to find the shifts? Did you also notice that, as a result, your voice changed more? Whenever you shift thought you will always get an accompanying voice change without any conscious effort on your part.

Note: If you find the beat difficult to work with, you can mark the shift by clicking your fingers or tapping the side of your thigh with your hand. If you want to continue working with the beat in rehearsals you can say it silently rather than aloud.

The more you work with this exercise, the more you will find that you be-come sensitive to thought changes in the text from the first time you pick it up.

Using the Beats When Listening

To mark the thought shifts when you are listening to other characters

This exercise is a fantastic way of making your listening alive and truthful, so that you neither blank nor overreact. It is especially useful if you have to listen to a long speech or exchange between other characters.

○ As you listen to the other character or characters say 'beat' silently in your head each time you feel there is a thought shift as a result of what is being said or done.

Not only will this help to keep your listening alive but it will also help you to find the stimulus for when you next speak.

Actions

So far we have looked at ways of exploring and identifying shifts in emotion and thought. Now I want to explore a method of charting the shifts in *action*. You may have come across this method and either love or hate it; you may know little or nothing about it. Whatever your experience, keep an open mind because understanding the idea behind this method is tremendously valuable whether you use it in this form or not.

It was Stanislavsky who came up with the idea of actions to encourage actors to be specific and active in a speech or scene rather than playing a single state. In life, consciously or unconsciously, we are always doing something to the other people around us – even if we are attempting to ignore them or block them. The emotions we experience are in response to how successful or not our actions are in achieving our objectives. So actions allow the actor to *do* rather than simply emote. This does not necessarily mean that they are doing something *physically* but that, as they speak or move or listen, they are *mentally* or *internally* doing something to the other person.

Actions are expressed in terms of transitive verbs. These are verbs describing what you can do to someone else, such as '*I challenge*', '*I tease*', '*I fascinate*', '*I terrify*', '*I implore*', '*I shun*'. Whereas intransitive verbs like

'*I cry*', '*I sit*', '*I sleep*', '*I think*', '*I say*', '*I enquire*', '*I moan*' describe things that cannot be done to someone else; they are what you yourself do.

Sometimes the action played will match with the external behaviour. For example someone might say, '*Come in, sit down, I'm so glad to see you*', and gesture the person to a chair with a smile while playing the action '*I welcome you*'. But sometimes the action will not match their words or gesture. Imagine someone saying the same phrase and gesturing in the same way but with the action '*I intimidate you*'. They are using the same words and gesture but their tone and manner will have changed and the effect on the other person will be very different.

You can also play actions when you are not speaking. For example, you could be playing the action '*I encourage you*' as you listen to someone, or you could be playing the action '*I unsettle you*'. Obviously, whichever action you play will affect the way in which you listen and it is these subtle shifts that we are looking for.

Getting to Grips with Actions

To understand how actions work

This first exercise gives you a chance to explore and understand actions and how they work.

Stage One – Playing the action directly

○ Choose an object in the room where you are working to represent a person, since you always need someone to perform the action to.

Obviously, if there is someone you can work with, even better.

○ Take the action '*I challenge*' and remember what it is like to challenge someone.

○ Then, focusing on the object/person, and thinking of challenging with your whole body and voice tone as well as your words, say: '*I challenge you*.'

Note: It is important to focus on challenging the object or person and not on demonstrating challenging behaviour. You are not showing a state, you are doing something to someone/something else.

○ Play the action a few times, each time fully committing to challenging with your body and voice.

○ Continue in the same way with the following actions: '*I tease you*', '*I comfort you*', '*I inspire you*', '*I terrify you*'.

How did you find that? Did you notice that the way you used your body and voice changed as you focused on doing something different to the person/object? Did you notice that you had more energy and purpose because you were doing something as you spoke?

Stage Two – Playing the action with covering text

Now we'll add some covering text, so that the words you say are not directly linked to the action you are playing. The line of text we are going to use is: '*It's raining today.*'

○ As before, focus on the object/person you are doing the action to.

○ Again, connect with the idea of challenging them.

○ Then, thinking '*I challenge you*' and committing fully, physically and vocally, to the action of challenging, say the line of text: '*It's raining today.*'

○ Repeat this line of text a few times. Each time ensuring that you are fully committing to playing the action of challenging.

○ Now work in the same way with the other actions you explored earlier: '*I tease you*', '*I comfort you*', '*I inspire you*', '*I terrify you*', each time playing these actions strongly whilst saying: '*It's raining today.*'

How was that? Again, did you notice how much you shifted physically and vocally? Did you notice how differently the line came out? Working with actions allows you to have endless variety and precision with your text.

Practising Actions

To gain flexibility, subtlety and confidence in playing actions

This will extend your repertoire of actions and your ability to shift between them, so giving greater flexibility to your work. It will also give you the confidence to work with actions in rehearsals and performance.

Marina Caldarone and Maggie Lloyd-Williams have compiled *Actions: The Actors' Thesaurus*,[32] which lists masses of transitive verbs and organises them into sense groups so that you can refine your choices of which actions to play.

○ Regularly take a line of text and practise playing different actions with the line.

Over the page is a list of actions to start you off, but feel free to add your own.

I amaze	I appal	I badger	I beg	I besiege
I bolster	I bully	I calm	I charm	I challenge
I cheer	I comfort	I dazzle	I defy	I delude
I dismiss	I enthral	I excite	I fascinate	I frighten
I gather	I grab	I horrify	I inspire	I insult
I lull	I mollify	I mystify	I nurture	I oppose
I pacify	I perplex	I quell	I reassure	I reject
I refuse	I rouse	I scare	I shock	I surprise
I tease	I terrify	I warn	I welcome	I worry

Working with Actions in Text

To understand how to use actions when rehearsing and performing

Now that you have a sense of how actions work, let's explore ways of using them in rehearsal. It is useful to have a thesaurus to hand to help you with ideas for actions if you run out of inspiration. I have suggested two ways of working; read through both and decide which you prefer.

Method One

○ Go through all your lines and for each section decide on the appropriate action.

As I mentioned earlier, a section may be a sentence, a phrase or a word. You need a new action every time you feel you are doing something different to the other character or characters.

○ Decide each action by asking yourself: 'What am I doing to the other character or characters here?' and noting the ideas that you have.

○ Test the actions you have come up with by playing each one as you say the particularly word, phrase or sentence and noticing whether it brings the text to life, making it easy and comfortable to say.

○ Write the action you feel is most helpful next to that word, phrase or sentence and then move on to the next.

It is best to work on one scene at a time and to work quite lightly, trusting that ideas will come. As always, it is the asking of the question that is important. Sometimes the first action you come up with will work for a while, then, in rehearsal, you will find an even better one.

○ *Once you have identified all your actions, take each scene and run through it, simply saying the actions and committing to them fully.*

○ *You can, as I have done in the example below, include descriptions of your actual physical actions such as entering, sitting, standing, crossing the room.*

> 'I enter' . . . 'I see you' . . . 'I greet you' . . . 'I walk over to you' . . . 'I flatter you' . . . 'I encourage you' . . . 'I get closer to you' . . . 'I press you' . . . 'I badger you' . . . 'I deny you' . . . 'I warn you' . . . 'I reject you', etc.

This can be a liberating exercise since it allows you to commit strongly. I first used it when I did a production of Euripides' *The Trojan Women*. Suddenly the whole play came to life. The actors had a sense of the immediacy of the piece and felt much more confident and less reverent and tentative.

○ *Once you have run through the scene saying only the actions, run through it again, this time saying the action, followed by the text to which it applies. As always, commit fully, physically and vocally.*

○ *Once you have performed the whole scene in this way, go back and do it again, simply saying the text while playing the actions.*

Method Two

Some actors find the above method too overwhelming or heavy-going. They find it difficult to find the actions, and the whole thing becomes a headache. If you find that happens to you, here is another way of working. It is important to trust your instincts at all stages of this exercise and go with what comes up, even if your conscious mind is less certain.

○ *Read through the scene you want to work on a few times.*

○ *Then, ask yourself: 'What actions do I think my character uses in this scene?' and jot down fairly quickly whatever comes to mind.*

○ *Take pieces of scrap paper and write a single action on each sheet, large enough to see it clearly from a distance.*

○ *Place the pieces of paper on the floor around the room so that you can see them. Also have some blank pieces of paper arranged on the floor amongst the rest.*

○ *Take up the scene again. Silently read the first word, phrase or sentence and then go and stand by the action that seems to fit it and say that section while playing that action strongly.*

○ *Continue in the same way, reading each word, phrase or section, choosing the action, standing by it and playing that action strongly as you speak the section.*

○ *If none of the actions seem to fit, go and stand by a blank piece of paper, asking yourself: 'What am I doing to the other character or characters here?' and wait for an idea to come up. Once it does, play that action strongly as you say the line.*

You should find that, because you are moving around and only having to think of one action at a time, the whole process becomes lighter and more playful.

Using Actions as First Aid

When you are lost and confused

If the second method still feels too arduous, then, instead of using the actions for the whole script, you can use them on the parts where you feel lost or confused about what is going on.

When dealing with repeated words or phrases

Actions are particularly helpful where you have to say the same word or phrase several times. For example: '*No, no . . . no.*' In real life there will be a shift between each repetition and you will naturally play different actions without thinking about it. In a play, however, such repetitions can often feel awkward. The answer is to explore what you are doing to the other person with each repetition. For example, with '*No, no . . . no*', your actions might be: '*I refuse you . . . I resist you . . . I deny you.*'

○ *Say 'No, no . . . no', playing these three actions, one on each 'no' and notice how that feels.*

The shifts may only be small but can you feel that the different actions give you a sense of variety and progression? Of course, you could choose a different set of actions that would take you in a completely different direction. For example: '*I pacify you . . . I comfort you . . . I charm you.*'

○ *Say 'No, no . . . no', playing these three new actions and notice how that feels.*

I am sure you can feel how that changes the way you play the three '*no*'s. Of course, the choice you make will depend on what is appropriate for the scene.

When the director wants you to play a line differently

The more flexible you are at shifting from action to action, the more confident you will be at exploring the many different ways to play a word, phrase or line. When a director asks you to play a section in a different way, ask yourself: '*What am I doing to the other character or characters now and what could I do instead that might give the director what he/she wants?'* If it is clear to you, simply play the new action. If not, experiment with different actions until you find one that causes the line to be said in the way the director wants.

All the exercises in this section help you to be more specific in charting the internal shifts of emotion, thought and action. This will make the journey of a speech or scene, and therefore of the whole play, much richer and more varied and, therefore, more interesting and enjoyable for you to play and the audience to watch.

IDENTIFYING TENSIONS AND SHIFTS BETWEEN CHARACTERS

If there are no tensions and shifts between characters, there is no reason for the audience to engage and the actors are left feeling awkward and uncomfortable. The following exercises offer different ways of exploring and marking the tensions and shifts between characters within a speech or scene. They all require you and your scene partners to make active choices and to be continually alive and shifting. Having done this, you will find that when you come to play the scene, even if you are physically still, you will retain a sense of inner movement that will keep the scene alive. All the exercises, by definition, need to be done with scene partners.

Towards, Away and Around

To mark shifts in how you are communicating with others in a speech or scene

This exercise explores the shifting relationships between you and the other characters, and each character's communicative impulse at any point in a speech or scene. In other words, whether your character is focusing on the character/s he/she is talking to [i.e. *towards*], or avoiding them [i.e. *away from*], or being more indirect [i.e. *around*].

You need to put aside any blocking you may have for a scene, since the movements you make will reflect *inner* shifts rather than outer ones.

○ *Each person chooses a starting place in the room, standing closer to or further away from each of the other characters, depending on their relationship with them at that point in the play.*

○ As you perform the scene you all move towards, away from or around the other characters as feels appropriate, both whilst you are speaking and whilst you are listening.

○ It is important that everyone in the scene keeps moving: at all times choosing one of the three directions very clearly.

Below is part of a scene from *The Caretaker* by Harold Pinter with *possible* shifts in direction marked in bold, simply to give you some idea of how the exercise works. I would never actually get the actors to decide in advance where the shifts were, they would do the scene and move according to what felt right at the time. In the scene, Mick and Davies meet for the first time. Mick's brother, Aston, had helped Davies the night before and offered him a place to stay.

MICK: ... [*Pause.*] [**around**] Did you sleep here last night?

DAVIES: [**around**] Yes.

MICK: [**around**] Sleep well?

DAVIES: [**away**] Yes!

MICK: [**around**] Did you have to get up in the night?

DAVIES: [**towards**] No!

   Pause.

MICK: [**around**] What's your name?

DAVIES: [*Shifting, about to rise.*] [**towards**] Now look here!

MICK: [**towards**] What?

DAVIES:! [**away**] Jenkins

MICK: [**away**] Jen ... kins.

   DAVIES *makes a sudden move to rise.* [**towards**]

   A violent bellow from MICK [**towards**] *sends him back.* [**away**]

   [*A shout.*] [**towards**] Sleep here last night?

DAVIES: [**away**] Yes ...

MICK: [*Continuing at great pace.*] [**towards**] How'd you sleep?

DAVIES: [**away**] I slept –

MICK: [**towards**] Slept well?

DAVIES: [**towards**] Now look –

MICK: [**towards**] What bed?

DAVIES: [**away**] That —

MICK: [**towards**] Not the other?

DAVIES: [**away**] No!

MICK: [**towards**] Choosy.

> *Pause.*

> [*Quietly.*] [**around**] Choosy.

> *Pause.*

> [*Again amiable.*] [**away**] What sort of sleep did you have in that bed?

DAVIES: [*Banging on the floor.*] [**towards**] All right!

MICK: [**around**] You weren't uncomfortable?

DAVIES: [*Groaning.*] [**away**] All right!

> MICK *stands, and moves to him.*

MICK: [**towards**] You a foreigner?

DAVIES: [**away**] No.

MICK: [**towards**] Born and bred in the British Isles?

DAVIES: [**away**] I was!

MICK: [**towards**] What did they teach you?

> *Pause.*

> [**away**] How did you like my bed?

> *Pause.*

> [**around**] That's my bed. [**around**] You want to mind you don't catch a draught.

DAVIES: [**around**] From the bed?

MICK: [**towards**] No, now, up your arse.

> DAVIES *stares warily at* MICK, *who turns.* DAVIES *scrambles to the clothes horse and seizes his trousers.* MICK *turns swiftly and grabs them.* DAVIES *lunges for them.* MICK *holds out a hand warningly.*

> [**away**] You intending to settle down here?

DAVIES: [**towards**] Give me my trousers then.

MICK: [**away**] You settling down for a long stay?

DAVIES: [**towards**] Give me my bloody trousers!

MICK: [**towards**] Why, where are you going?

DAVIES: [**towards**] Give me and I'm going, I'm going to Sidcup.

> MICK *flicks the trousers in* DAVIES' *face several times.*
>
> DAVIES *retreats.*
>
> *Pause.*[33]

As you will find, the whole scene becomes like a dance, alive with movement and one character may be moving towards another who is walking away from or around him/her, so you discover potential tensions as well as shifts. The shifts here, as with all the exercises in this section, give variety since you will find that lines will be said differently whether you are walking towards someone, away from them or around them. As always there is no one right choice and if you alter the directions you have chosen for the lines, you will alter the dynamics and therefore the meaning of the scene.

Tug of War

To explore the shifting power within a speech or scene

This exercise explores how the power shifts between characters in a scene and allows you to ensure that there is always a connecting tension between you and the other characters.

○ Take a towel: hold one end, whilst whoever you are playing the scene with holds the other end.

○ As you play the scene, keep the towel taut between you so your partner has to work at pulling you towards them and you have to work at pulling him/her towards you.

○ Whenever you feel the need to persuade or win over your partner more strongly pull the towel more firmly towards you, your partner does the same.

Where there are three characters in the scene, work in a triangle using three towels, so that each character is holding the end of two towels. When there are more than three characters, work with a single towel, with whoever is talking holding one end and whoever is listening *at that particular moment* holding the other end.

Exploring the Internal Dynamics of a Scene

Below is part of a three-person scene from *All My Sons* by Arthur Miller. It is marked up to show how the characters may pull for the duration of a whole phrase or sentence or on a particular word to emphasise it. The towel being pulled is the one *between* the person speaking and the person they are speaking to. However, all three towels should be kept taut throughout.

Again, this example simply gives you some idea of how the exercise might work. I would never ask the actors to plan in advance where the pulls occur, and there are likely to be far more small shifts back and forth when working on an actual scene than are shown in the example. Of course, there will be times when both characters are pulling strongly and this simply increases the level of tension.

In this scene, George has come to stop his sister, Ann, marrying Chris because George has discovered from his incarcerated father, that Chris's father lied in court and avoided punishment for a criminal decision he had made, leaving George's father, who was his business partner, to take the blame.

CHRIS: [**pulling strongly throughout the line**] What're you going to do, George?

GEORGE: [**pulling back**] He's too smart for me, I can't prove a phone call.

CHRIS: [**pulling throughout with an extra pull on 'dare'**] Then how dare you come in here with that rot?

ANN: [**pulling strongly**] George, the court –

GEORGE: [**pulling throughout with extra pull on 'know'**] The court didn't know your father! [**pulling throughout with extra pull on 'you'**] But you know him. [**pulling throughout**] You know in your heart Joe did it.

CHRIS: [*Whirling him around.*] [**pulling very strongly on 'lower' and continuing to pull throughout**] Lower your voice or I'll throw you out of here!

GEORGE: [**pulling strongly throughout**] She knows. She knows.

CHRIS: [*To ANN.*] [**pulling strongly throughout with extra pulls on both 'get's**] Get him out of here, Ann. Get him out of here.

ANN: [**pulling steadily throughout**] George, I know everything you've said. Dad told that whole thing in court, and they –

219

GEORGE: [*Almost a scream.*] [**yanking the towel back strongly throughout**] The court did not know him, Annie!

ANN: [**yanking the towel strongly**] Shhh! – [**pulling the towel steadily throughout**] But he'll say anything, George. You know how quick he can lie.

GEORGE: [*Turning to* CHRIS, *with deliberation.*] [**pulling steadily throughout**] I'll ask you something, and look me in the eye when you answer me.

CHRIS: [**pulling steadily throughout**] I'll look you in the eye.

GEORGE: [**pulling steadily throughout**] You know your father –

CHRIS: [**pulling steadily throughout**] I know him well.

GEORGE: [**pulling steadily throughout**] And he's the kind of boss to let a hundred and twenty-one cylinder heads be repaired and shipped out of his shop without even knowing about it?

CHRIS: [**pulling steadily throughout**] He's that kind of boss.

GEORGE: [**pulling steadily throughout**] And that's the same Joe Keller who never left his shop without first going around to see that all the lights were out.

CHRIS: [*With growing anger.*] [**pulling more strongly throughout**] The same Joe Keller.

GEORGE: [**pulling steadily throughout**] The same man who knows how many minutes a day his workers spend in the toilet.

CHRIS: [**pulling strongly throughout with extra pull on 'same'**] The same man.[34]

This exercise helps to raise the stakes since it forces you to physically commit. It is particularly useful in scenes in which there seems to be no conflict between characters, since by simply tugging, you begin to find what tension there might be even in the lightest, happiest or most loving situations. As with the *Spectrum* exercise it is a simple, broad-brushstroke exercise that I use fairly early on.

Exploring the Internal Dynamics of a Scene

Hands Wrestle

To explore the push and pull within a speech or scene

This exercise is the next stage on from the *Tug of War*. It allows you to explore the pushes as well as the pulls within a scene and also the degree of yielding or resistance to the pulls and pushes of the other character/s and so allows you to mark more subtle shifts.

○ *Sit or stand opposite the person you are working with and grasp hands, so your palms are touching and your fingers are interlocked.*

If there are more than two characters in the scene then switch to grasp each character's hands as you interact with them.

○ *As you play the scene, allow yourself to pull or push, resist or yield as feels right as you listen and speak.*

Below is the same extract from *All My Sons*, marked up to show how this exercise builds on the previous one. The pushes or pulls continue through the whole phrase or sentence that follows them. Again, this is only an example of choices the actors might make and is inevitably more simplistic than it would be if the actors were actually doing the exercise.

CHRIS: [**pull**] What're you going to do, George?

GEORGE: [**pull**] He's too smart for me, [**push**] I can't prove a phone call.

CHRIS: [**push**] Then how dare you come in here with that rot?

ANN: [**pull**] George, the court —

GEORGE: [**pull**] The court didn't know your father! [**push**] But you know him. [**push**] You know in your heart Joe did it.

CHRIS: [*Whirling him around.*] [**pull**] Lower your voice [**push**] or I'll throw you out of here!

GEORGE: [**pull**] She knows. [**pull**] She knows.

CHRIS: [*To ANN.*] [**push**] Get him out of here, Ann. [**push**] Get him out of here.

ANN: [**pull**] George, I know everything you've said. [**pull**] Dad told that whole thing in court, and they —

GEORGE: [*Almost a scream.*] [**push**] The court did not know him, Annie!

ANN: [**push**] Shhh! – [**pull**] But he'll say anything, George. [**pull**] You know how quick he can lie.

GEORGE: [*Turning to* CHRIS, *with deliberation.*] [**push**] I'll ask you something, and look me in the eye when you answer me.

CHRIS: [**push**] I'll look you in the eye.

GEORGE: [**push**] You know your father –

CHRIS: [**push**] I know him well.

GEORGE: [**push**] And he's the kind of boss to let a hundred and twenty-one cylinder heads be repaired and shipped out of his shop without even knowing about it?

CHRIS: [**push**] He's that kind of boss.

GEORGE: [**push**] And that's the same Joe Keller who never left his shop without first going around to see that all the lights were out.

CHRIS: [*With growing anger.*] [**push**] The same Joe Keller.

GEORGE: [**push**] The same man who knows how many minutes a day his workers spend in the toilet.

CHRIS: [**push**] The same man.

Both this exercise and the *Tug of War* give you the chance to connect strongly with the other actor/s in the scene and to explore and experience the dynamics between you.

Who's Driving?

To explore who is driving the scene at any point

One character is driving a scene at any point. In some cases the character that is driving constantly changes, in other cases a single character drives throughout. It is very important to identify who the scene driver is at any given moment, otherwise a scene can fall flat on the floor. The importance of this was brought home to me when working on the three-character scene from *The Comedy of Errors* that I mentioned earlier. The scene, which was potentially very funny, simply wasn't working: the two more experienced actors were filling the space with manic energy in an attempt to keep the scene afloat – but to no avail. As soon as we did this exercise, the problem, and the solution, became very clear. Before I go any further, let's look at the exercise.

○ Each person chooses where in the room he/she is when the scene starts. As in earlier exercises this has nothing to do with the scene blocking but, rather, is an expression of the internal relationship between the characters at this point in the play.

○ As you play the scene each person moves forward, whenever they feel they are driving the scene, as if they are pursuing the other characters around the room. If two characters end up driving at once, just go with that and see what happens. The important point is to avoid there being any time when no one is driving.

Note: There are some times when the playwright includes a moment where, through shock, surprise, confusion or suchlike, all the characters stop driving, but if this is the case it will become clear as you do this exercise, since the absence of anyone moving will make absolute sense and will only last for a moment before one or other character starts driving again.

Below is another short extract from *The Caretaker* by Harold Pinter, showing how the driver in a scene changes. As always, this is only an example and is likely to be far more simplistic than it would be if the actors were working through it in the moment.

[**ASTON drives**] ASTON *makes a slight move towards him.*
[**DAVIES drives**] DAVIES *takes his knife from his back pocket.*

DAVIES: Don't come nothing with me, mate. I got this here. I used it. I used it. Don't come it with me.

A pause. They stare at each other.

Mind what you do now.

Pause.

Don't you try anything with me.

Pause.

ASTON: I . . . I think it's about time you found somewhere else. I don't think we're hitting it off.

DAVIES: Find somewhere else?

ASTON: Yes.

DAVIES: Me? You are talking to me? Not me, man! You!

[**ASTON drives**]

ASTON: What?

223

[DAVIES drives]

DAVIES: You! You better find somewhere else!

[ASTON drives]

ASTON: I live here. You don't.

[DAVIES drives]

DAVIES: Don't I? Well, I live here. I been offered a job here.

ASTON: Yes . . . well, I don't think you're really suitable.

DAVIES: Not suitable? Well, I can tell you, there's someone here thinks I'm suitable. And I tell you. I'm staying on here as caretaker! Get it! Your brother, he's told me, see, he's told me the job is mine. Mine! So that's where I am. I'm going to be his caretaker.

ASTON: My brother?

DAVIES: He's staying, he's going to run this place, and I'm staying with him.

ASTON: Look. If I give you . . . a few bob you can get down to Sidcup.

DAVIES: You build your shed first! A few bob! When I can earn a steady wage here! You build your stinking shed first! That's what!

ASTON *stares at him.*

[ASTON drives]

ASTON: That's not a stinking shed.

Silence.

ASTON *moves to him.*

It's clean. It's all good wood. I'll get it up. No trouble.

DAVIES: Don't come too near!

ASTON: You've no reason to call that shed stinking.

DAVIES *points the knife.*

You stink.

DAVIES: What!

ASTON: You've been stinking the place out.

224

DAVIES: Christ, you say that to me!

ASTON: For days. That's one reason I can't sleep.

DAVIES: You call me that! You call me stinking!

ASTON: You better go.

[**DAVIES drives**]

DAVIES: I'LL STINK YOU!

He thrusts his arm out, the arm trembling, the knife pointing at ASTON's *stomach.*

[**they both drive**]

ASTON *does not move. Silence.* DAVIES' *arm moves no further. They stand.*

I'll stink you . . .

This exercise is excellent for helping you to take charge of a scene where it is appropriate. That was certainly what needed to happen in the scene from *The Comedy of Errors* that I described earlier.

There were three people in that scene: the two more experienced actors and one who was straight out of drama school. When we did the exercise, we realised that her character drove the whole scene. Yet because she was the most junior member of the cast she didn't feel it was her place to take charge of anything, especially when she wasn't speaking. Consequently, the other two actors were working in a vacuum, attempting to react to something that wasn't happening. It took a few runs through the exercise before she felt comfortable really pursuing the other actors around the room, but the more she did so the better the scene got for everyone concerned, and we were then able to take that understanding back into performance. It was a good lesson for us all.

My Corner or Yours?

To explore the struggle between the different characters' objectives within a speech or scene

This exercise follows the theme of all the earlier exercises in this section: that of physical commitment. It also allows you to chart the progress towards or away from your scene objective.

○ Each person identifies a part of the room that represents their scene objective.

○ Then, they stand in the middle of the room.

○ As they play the scene, each person attempts gently but firmly to pull whichever characters they wish/need to win over into their own space, whilst resisting being pulled into any of the other characters' spaces, unless their character wants to be won over.

There will be shifting struggles, and sometimes one person will be being pulled in two different directions whilst attempting to pull a third person in yet another direction.

Below is another extract from *All My Sons* by Arthur Miller. It's part of a scene where all four main characters are fighting hard for what they want. Chris and Ann share a corner of the room, since they have the shared objective of getting married. George and Mother have their own separate corners. Frank, at this point in the scene, does not need his own corner, since he is happy to oblige Chris's mother.

GEORGE: [*To* ANN.] [**pulling ANN into his corner**] Don't you understand what she's saying? She just told you to go. What are you waiting for now?

CHRIS: [**pulling ANN back into his corner**] Nobody can tell her to go. [*A car horn is heard.*]

MOTHER: [*To* FRANK.] [**pulling FRANK into her corner**] Thank you, darling, for your trouble. Will you tell him to wait, Frank?

FRANK: [*As he goes.*] [**allowing himself to be pulled**] Sure thing.

MOTHER: [*Calling out.*] [**pulling GEORGE and ANN into her corner**] They'll be right out, driver!

CHRIS: [**pulling ANN back into his corner**] She's not leaving. Mother.

GEORGE: [**pulling ANN into his corner**] You heard her say it, he's never been sick!

MOTHER: [**pulling CHRIS into her corner**] He misunderstood me, Chris! [CHRIS *looks at her, struck.*]

GEORGE: [*To* ANN.] [**pulling ANN into his corner**] He simply told your father to kill pilots, and covered himself in bed!

CHRIS: [**pulling ANN back into his corner**] You'd better answer him, Annie. Answer him.

MOTHER: [pulling **ANN** back into her corner] I packed your bag, darling.

CHRIS: [pulling **MOTHER** into his corner] What?

MOTHER: [pulling **ANN** further into her corner] I packed your bag. All you've got to do is close it.

ANN: [pulling **MOTHER** into her corner] I'm not closing anything. He asked me here and I'm staying till he tells me to go. [*To* GEORGE.] [pulling **GEORGE** into her corner] Till Chris tells me!

CHRIS: [pulling **GEORGE** into his corner] That's all! Now get out of here, George!

MOTHER: [*To* CHRIS.] [pulling **CHRIS** into her corner] But if that's how he feels —

CHRIS: [pulling **MOTHER** into his corner] That's all, nothing more till Christ comes, about the case or Larry as long as I'm here! [*To* GEORGE.] [pulling **GEORGE** into his corner] Now get out of here, George!

GEORGE: [*To* ANN.] [pulling **ANN** into his corner] You tell me. I want to hear you tell me.

ANN: [pulling **GEORGE** into his corner] Go, George!

This exercise can be great fun and bring a scene to life immediately. Obviously, it is important to work safely and to agree that everyone will stop immediately if someone calls out. It can also be a very emotionally charged exercise if you are working on a dark scene, so do stretch and shake out after you have done it. You will still retain what you have learnt.

Taking the Cushion

To explore the give and take within a scene

This exercise helps the pace of a scene and ensures there are no dead moments. It is great to do once everyone knows the lines and has a pretty good idea of the scene shape. It is also excellent as a warm-up before a performance.

○ *All the people in the scene stand close enough to each other to pass a cushion between them.*

○ *Place the cushion on the floor in the middle of the circle.*

○ The person who speaks first picks up the cushion and holds it while speaking.

○ As they finish speaking, the person who speaks next takes the cushion off them and says their lines.

○ Continue in the same way with each succeeding speaker taking the cushion from the preceding one

○ Ensure that the person taking the cushion does so immediately the previous speaker finishes speaking so that there are no gaps – unless there is an actual pause in the scene.

Note: Occasionally, it may be that the present speaker urges or forces the succeeding speaker to speak, in which case they can thrust the cushion into that person's hand rather than have it taken from them. The important point is that there are no dead moments.

Below is another extract from *The Caretaker* by Harold Pinter, which needs rapid picking up of cues. It's worth trying out with some friends to experience how the exercise works.

> DAVIES *crosses back with the bag.*
>
> MICK *rises and snatches it.*

MICK: What's this?

DAVIES: Give us it, that's my bag!

MICK: [*Warding him off.*] I've seen this bag before.

DAVIES: That's my bag!

MICK: [*Eluding him.*] This bag's very familiar.

DAVIES: What do you mean?

MICK: Where'd you get it?

ASTON: [*Rising, to them.*] Scrub it.

DAVIES: That's mine.

MICK: Whose?

DAVIES: It's mine! Tell him it's mine!

MICK: This is your bag?

DAVIES: Give it me!

ASTON: Give it to him.

MICK: What? Give him what?

DAVIES: That bloody bag!

MICK: [*Slipping it behind the gas stove.*] What bag? [*To* DAVIES.] What bag?

DAVIES: [*Moving.*] Look here!

MICK: [*Facing him.*] Where you going?

DAVIES: I'm going to get . . . my old . . .

MICK: Watch your step, sonny!

The exercises in this section all require that you commit thoroughly to them and, through committing, find the dynamic movement within a speech or scene. They help you to trust your instincts more strongly and react more spontaneously to others. They are also great fun to do and can really bring a scene to life.

EXPLORING THE SCENE JOURNEY SPATIALLY

Having connected with the situation, identified the shifts of emotion, thought and action within your character, and the tensions and shifts between characters, we are now going to explore the scene journey as a whole. This work is useful for bringing all the earlier work in this chapter together, but can also be done without the other work if you are short of time.

Exploring the Scene Journey

To identify the journey of the scene

The best way to describe this exercise is by showing how it works for a specific scene – in this case, Act 2 Scene 5, lines 75–121, from Shakespeare's *Twelfth Night*. Then, I will give you a process for working this way on your own speeches or scenes.

Background situation: Orsino is in love with Olivia, but she is not at all interested in him. Viola, who has been stranded far from home, has disguised herself, for protection, as a boy, calling herself Cesario. She has taken a job as one of Orsino's servants and ended up falling in love with him. Orsino, who has no idea that she is a woman, has sent her to woo Olivia, and Olivia, thinking Viola is a man, has fallen in love with her!

The scene itself: Orsino and Viola, disguised as Cesario, are alone. Orsino tells Viola to go again to woo Olivia on his behalf. Viola asks what she should do if Olivia won't be persuaded, but Orsino insists that Olivia must be. Viola then pretends to have a sister who was in love with a man rather like Orsino and tells how this sister never spoke of her love. Orsino becomes fascinated by Viola's story and for a short while is distracted from his obsession with Olivia. He asks what became of the sister, to which Viola can only answer, 'A blank, my lord', because she of course doesn't know what is going to become of her and her love for Orsino which she cannot express.

ORSINO: Let all the rest give place.

    CURIO *and* ATTENDANTS *retire.*

                    Once more, Cesario,
    Get thee to yond same sovereign cruelty.
    Tell her my love, more noble than the world,
    Prizes not quantity of dirty lands;
    The parts that fortune hath bestowed on her
    Tell her I hold as giddily as fortune;
    But 'tis that miracle and queen of gems
    That nature pranks her in attracts my soul.

VIOLA: But if she cannot love you, sir?

ORSINO: I cannot so be answered.

VIOLA: Sooth, but you must.
    Say that some lady, as perhaps there is,
    Hath for your love as great a pang of heart
    As you have for Olivia. You cannot love her.
    You tell her so. Must she not then be answered?

ORSINO: There is no woman's sides
    Can bide the beating of so strong a passion
    As love doth give my heart; no woman's heart
    So big, to hold so much. They lack retention.
    Alas, their love may be called appetite,
    No motion of the liver, but the palate
    That suffers surfeit, cloyment, and revolt,
    But mine is all as hungry as the sea,
    And can digest as much. Make no compare

Between that love a woman can bear me,
And that I owe Olivia.

VIOLA: Ay, but I know –

ORSINO: What dost thou know?

VIOLA: Too well what love women to men may owe.
In faith, they are as true of heart as we.
My father had a daughter loved a man
As it my be perhaps, were I a woman,
I should your lordship.

ORSINO: And what's her history?

VIOLA: A blank, my lord. She never told her love,
But let concealment like a worm i'th'bud
Feed on her damask cheek. She pined in thought,
And with a green and yellow melancholy
She sat like Patience on a monument,
Smiling at grief. Was not this love indeed?
We men may say more, swear more, but indeed
Our shows are more than will: for still we prove
Much in our vows, but little in our love.

ORSINO: But died thy sister of her love, my boy?

VIOLA: I am all the daughters of my father's house
And all the brothers, too – and yet I know not.
Sir, shall I to this lady?

ORSINO: Ay, that's the theme.
To her in haste; give her this jewel; say
My love can give no place, bide no denay.

○ *The first stage is to identify and summarise the situation in the scene from which
the scene journey will arise.*

Situation summary: **Orsino loves Olivia who doesn't love him. Viola knows
that Olivia not only doesn't love Orsino, but also has fallen in love with her.
Viola loves Orsino but in order to let him know that she loves him she would
have to drop her disguise, which is her only protection so far away from any
home or family.**

○ *Once you have identified the situation, set up the scene spatially.*

Setting up the scene spatially: On one occasion, when working on this scene, I was lucky enough to be in a space with wall bars, so I asked the actor playing Orsino to sit at the top of the wall bars and choose something on the ceiling beyond his reach to represent Olivia. I asked him to keep all his attention, throughout the scene, on that and not to turn to Viola unless something she said really claimed his attention. I asked the actor playing Viola to start the scene wherever she liked on the wall bars. I told her that she could move up and down as she chose but that the closer she got to the top and Orsino, the closer she was to revealing her love and the fact that she was a woman. We then played the scene, with fascinating results. The actor playing Orsino was able to mark when in the scene his attention was pulled away from thinking about Olivia. The actor playing Viola was able to mark how she moved up and down during the scene torn between her wish to reveal her love and the need to protect herself.

This way of working is such a release since it makes the situation extremely tangible and the shifts very clear. The more you are able to explore these shifts externally, the clearer the journey becomes for you and the more confidently you can play it.

If you don't happen to have wall bars, you could place Orsino at one end of room looking at an object just out of reach on the wall and ask Viola to start the scene wherever she chooses in the room and to move towards or away from Orsino as she feels appropriate. In other words, you could work horizontally instead of vertically. The benefit of the wall bars is that they increase the sense of Orsino being out of Viola's reach and of the risk she takes as she comes nearer to revealing herself.

Setting Up Your Own Scene Journey Exploration

To be confident about the process of exploring scene journeys spatially

So how do you apply this way of working to the scenes you are exploring? Below is the process you can use to help you come up with ideas for expressing the situation spatially. Sometimes the process is very quick and sometimes it takes a number of false starts, but it doesn't matter because you are learning more about the scene all the time.

○   *Read through the scene silently.*

○ Ask yourself: 'What is going on in this scene? What does each character want to achieve? What or who is each character focusing on? Are there any elements in the situation that might help or hinder one or more of the characters? How much is there at stake? How safe or dangerous is it for the characters to go for what they want? Can they openly go for what they want or do they need to hide their intentions?'

○ Then, ask yourself: 'How could I express this spatially? Are the characters close together or far apart? Are they on the same or a different level? Are they trying to get to each other or away from each other? Do there need to be barriers between them?' Trust whatever comes up and immediately try it out, since the best feedback comes from doing it.

○ If, as you start to try it out, it feels heavy and difficult, then stop and ask yourself: 'What could I change or add that might be more helpful?' Again, trust whatever comes up and try it out immediately.

○ Continue in this way, trying out the ideas you come up with and adapting them until you find whatever seems to help most.

You won't always come up with a perfect result, but because you have been asking yourself to think about the situation in more depth, this thought and exploration will continue subconsciously even after you have stopped working. The more you play around with this exercise, the easier you will find it and the more confident you will become.

The work in this section helps you to connect with the situation and journey of the scene and bring it to life in a rich and detailed way. This is invaluable for all texts but especially for classical texts where the situations can seem remote and unreal.

Summary

This chapter has explored the internal dynamics of speeches and scenes and the underlying shifts that bring a speech or scene to life. Working in this way allows your performance to be detailed and spontaneous and keeps the audience interested because the speech or scene never becomes static.

Below is a summary of the exercises in this chapter.

Bringing the Situation to Life
Connecting with the Situation

Identifying Shifts Within Your Character
Spectrum
Certain/Uncertain
Corners
Writing a Thought Script
Beat or Click Exercise
Using the Beats When Listening
Getting to Grips with Actions
Practising Actions
Working with Actions in Text
Using Actions as First Aid

Identifying Tensions and Shifts Between Characters
Towards, Away and Around
Tug of War
Hands Wrestle
Who's Driving?
My Corner or Yours?
Taking the Cushion

Exploring the Scene Journey Spatially
Exploring the Scene Journey
Setting Up Your Own Scene Journey Exploration

PART FOUR

Helpful Extras

How Do I Stop Sabotaging Myself?

DEALING WITH THE INNER CRITIC

When you are working, whether on your own, in rehearsal or even in performance, do you ever find that you are commenting negatively on what you're doing? This is your *inner critic* at work. Some people's inner critic turns up only very occasionally and even then is fairly mild, whilst others find that it is present most of the time and can be extremely destructive. Of course, the intention of the inner critic is to help you improve; but it rarely achieves this when in negative mode.

To get the best from your critic you need to learn how to shift it from debilitating judge to constructive coach, so that it becomes more bearable to listen to and you can benefit from the useful advice that lies beneath the criticism. It is also important to learn how to turn your critic off when you need to, to avoid self-consciousness and awkwardness.

TURNING THE CRITIC INTO A COACH

The exercises in this section are based on the work of Marshall B. Rosenberg.[35] As always, what I describe here is how I use it.

As Marshall Rosenberg points out, most of us have a tendency to use a language of judgements rather than a language of needs, both when communicating with ourselves and with others. Judgements refer to the past and describe *what has already happened*: '*That was a terrible performance*' or '*I couldn't connect with anything truthful.*' Our reaction to such judgements, at least in the short-term, tends to be either to accept them, and feel bad, or to reject them because they are too unbearable to face. Of course, sometimes, after having done either or both of these, we may then recover enough to ask: '*What can I do so that it's better next time?*' But if we feel too battered by our judgements, we don't have the energy or confidence to do this, and if the same thing happens a few more times we can begin to believe: '*That's the way it is*' and '*There's nothing I can do about it.*' So how do we get round this?

It is a question of translating *judgements* into *needs*. Whereas judgements refer to the past, to what has already happened, needs refer to the future, to what we want to happen. They give us a sense of where we want to go. By translating in this way you can transform a heap of dispiriting judgements into an accurate and detailed set of needs, which give you a clear and constructive sense of what to work on.

Turning Your Judgements Into Needs

To find out what positive needs lie behind your negative judgements

Stage One – Learning the process

○ *Jot down some of the judgements you make about your acting work.*

It is important at this stage that you work with judgements that *you* make about your acting. We will look later at dealing with judgements others make about your work.

○ *Choose one of the judgements to work on now.*

○ *Ask yourself: 'What, for me, is the positive need behind this negative judgement?'*

For example, if the negative judgement were, '*I never feel completely connected*' the positive need might literally be the opposite: '*I want to feel completely connected*' or, more specifically: '*I want to have a deeper connection with the situation the character is in.*'

Note: Sometimes, the positive need turns out not to be the literal opposite of your negative judgement. For example, 'I'd like to stop worrying about whether or not I'm connected, and trust that if I have done the work I will be.' *In such a case there is a discovery that the problem, and therefore the solution as well, lies in a different area.*

○ *Once you have a sense of what the positive need is, imagine someone doing this really well, in a way that you would like to do it.*

○ *Ask yourself: 'What do I imagine this person is doing and thinking?' Focus on specific behaviours.*

Note: You are not trying to guess what the person actually does. When you imagine what they do, you access your own wisdom about what is needed to achieve the result you want. And you are much more likely to take up ideas that you have come up with yourself. Imagining someone else is simply a device for skirting around your blocks in order to access the information you need. You can, later on, ask people whose work you admire about their process, since, once you have a clearer sense of what you need, you will be able to select from what they actually do the things that would also work for you.

Examples of specific behaviours for '*I want to have a deeper connection with the situation the character is in*' might be:

1. *Taking the time outside rehearsal to build up a sense of the situation.*

2. *Before each rehearsal, reconnecting with the situation.*

3. *During rehearsal and performance, focusing on what is being said and done by others in the scene and allowing yourself to react to that.*

○ Keep asking yourself: 'What else do I imagine they are doing?' In this way you make sure that you explore all possibilities.

○ Then, go through each behaviour asking: 'Can I break this down into even more specific behaviours?'

For example, '*Taking the time outside rehearsal to build up a sense of the situation*' might be broken down into:

1. *Gathering the facts of the situation.*

2. *Stimulating imagination by reading or looking at pictures, etc.*

3. *Taking time to imagine yourself as the character in that situation.*

○ Keep working through the behaviours you have identified until you have a list of specific and concrete actions that you can either work towards achieving yourself or find someone to help you with.

○ Then, ask yourself: 'Which of these actions do I think will make the most difference for me?'

Once you have identified these you can set about working on them. You can also try the following to notice the affect of shifting your thinking.

○ Recall your negative judgement and say it to yourself a few times, noticing how it makes you feel.

○ Then, say to yourself: 'I am in the process of learning how to . . .' followed by the list of actions you feel will make the most difference.

Note: It is important to use a phrase such as 'I am in the process of learning how to . . .' *rather than* 'I want to . . .' *because the brain is very specific, and if you say 'I want to . . . ' it will want whatever it is but it won't actually do anything about it!*[36] *Equally, it is important not to say 'I am . . . ' as if to suggest you are already behaving in the way you want, because this is untrue. You are working towards it but you are not there yet. If you were, the judgement would never have come up in the first place.*

○ As you say 'I am in the process of . . . ', followed by the list of actions, notice how that feels.

Did you find, when you focused on the list of actions rather than the negative judgement, that you had more energy and what you wanted seemed more achievable? The list of specific actions is not fluffy 'positive speak' but, rather, a much more accurate representation of the issue than the negative judgement. What's more, since our brains are very willing servants, they will do whatever we tell them. So, if you tell your brain, '*I'm no good at this*', then it will go ahead and be no good at it. If you tell it to '*find a way to learn how to be good at this*', it will do that too. This does not mean that you don't have to work at things; it simply means that you will have the confidence, focus and motivation to do the work, and in fact you will probably find that you want to work even harder because you feel so much better about the whole issue.

Stage Two – Using the process to clear up all your judgements

Once you have learnt the process, you can use it to clear up all the other judgements you have about your work and any new ones that may arise in the future.

○ Find a small notebook in which to write down any judgements you may make about yourself.

○ Carry it around with you and any time that you feel judgemental towards yourself, write down all the judgements you notice.

○ Then, when you are in a more positive mood, take one at a time and go through the process above.

This is excellent in two ways. Firstly, because you find out exactly what your inner critic is saying to you. Secondly, you usually find that your numerous judgements boil down to a few core needs and that what seem to be numerous issues or problems can be addressed by learning a few crucial behaviours.

Once you have had a good clear-out of your judgements, you can easily deal with any new ones that crop up, and you will find the whole process becomes much easier and quicker. Indeed, in the end, all you will have to ask if your internal critic pipes up is: '*What do you want me to do instead?*' Asking that simple question will instantly turn your critic into a coach and unleash a whole load of helpful advice so you not only feel better but also become far more effective.

Turning Others' Judgements Into Needs

To deal with others' judgements of you

In the same way that the judgements we make about ourselves can debilitate us, so can the judgements others make about us. You can use the *same* idea of searching for the need behind the judgement to lessen the negative effect of other people's criticisms and better understand what it is they want. This can be especially useful when dealing with a very critical director.

○ As the director criticises you ask yourself: 'What does he/she want? What is the need behind the criticism?'

In this way you will take the focus off yourself and, therefore, feel less attacked. You will also come across as open and interested rather than defensive and closed, and as a result you are likely to pick up a clearer sense of what is wanted.

Note: It is a good idea to centre yourself, as much as possible, while you are listening to any criticism, and keep asking: 'What do they want?' *This will make it easier for you to feel safe and stay open.*

TURNING OFF THE CRITIC

There is a golden rule about when to listen to your critic/coach: *Before and after but never during!* In other words, during rehearsal and performance you need to focus on connecting with the other actors rather than on what you are doing. This will allow you to be totally unself-conscious and to be present and responsive; whereas listening to your critic, even if it is saying positive things, will disconnect you from the situation and, therefore, from your instinctive responses.

Before you rehearse or perform you can say to yourself: '*What do I want to do well or better this time?*' Rather like *Turning Your Judgements Into Needs*, this focuses you positively and will help to direct your behaviour.

After you rehearse or perform you can ask yourself: '*What did I learn that will help me to do as well or better next time?*' Again, this will focus you forward and help you feel better if you have had a disastrous time, since it will allow you to concentrate on what you have learnt rather than what your think you did badly.

During rehearsal or performance, as I've already mentioned, your focus needs to be away from yourself, on the other actors and the situation. The next exercise explores how you can achieve this and how you can keep your focus outwards, even if your inner critic starts up, which it inevitably will from time to time.

Cameras Out

To focus your attention away from yourself

This exercise is described on page 18 in Part One. It allows you to move from self-consciousness to unself-consciousness at will. Turn back to the exercise either to refresh your memory or to try it out if you haven't already.

Summary

Turning your critic into a coach allows you to access effectively the wisdom the critic holds about how you can improve. Being able to turn your critic off in rehearsal and performance by focusing your attention outwards allows you to work unself-consciously even in difficult and pressurised situations. Learning how to translate others' judgements into needs also gives you the strength to deal with external criticism and so enable you to work creatively, whatever the situation.

Below is a summary of the exercises in this chapter.

Turning the Critic Into a Coach
Turning Your Judgements Into Needs
Turning Others' Judgements Into Needs

Turning Off the Critic
Cameras Out

How Do I Share the Work Truthfully?

TRANSFERRING FROM
REHEARSAL TO PERFORMANCE

The feeling of intimacy and spontaneity often found in the rehearsal room can be hard to carry over into the performance space. This chapter explores how you can preserve the intimacy and yet also ensure that the performance is fully shared with the audience. It also explores how you can retain the spontaneity of rehearsal within the necessarily set framework of performance.

INTIMACY

Many actors experience a tension between playing scenes with their fellow actors in a way which feels truthful, and sharing their work effectively with the audience, especially in large spaces. So how do you retain the intimacy between yourself and the other actors, whilst making your work accessible to the audience?

The crucial issue here is one of space: of being able to mentally extend your personal space to take in the whole area in which you are working. In this way you can both draw in the audience and retain a feeling of intimacy, since the whole stage and auditorium becomes your space. Your gestures and voice will also naturally extend to fill the space appropriately, without any sense of posturing or declaiming.

Expanding Your Space

To be able to shift the size of your space and so fill it

As with some of the earlier exercises, it's useful to practise what you don't want as well as what you do. This comparison will help you to understand the concept of space and how to play with it.

Small Space

○ *Stand and imagine that you are drawing your space in around you, so that it is very small. It can be helpful to imagine not wanting to draw attention to yourself, wanting to fade into the background.*

You may find that you bring your legs together, possibly slump a little and draw your arms into or across your body.

○ *Notice what it feels like to draw your personal space in like this. What happens to your breathing? Say some lines and notice how your voice feels and sounds.*

Did you feel smaller, less confident and less powerful? Did your find your breath was shallower or that you were holding it? Did your voice feel more constricted and sound weaker? Did you notice that it was as if you were standing on a small island of space and were separate from the rest of the room?

Pushing Out Space

○ *Stand and imagine you are expanding your personal space by making yourself seem as big as possible. It can be helpful to imagine that you are pretending to be strong and confident when you actually feel quite threatened.*

You may find that you spread your legs wider apart and cross your arms or put your hands on your hips or in some other way make yourself bigger. You may also find that your whole face tenses up, especially your eyes.

○ *Notice what it feels like to push your space out in this way. What happens to your breathing? Say some lines and notice how your voice feels and sounds.*

Although you may have felt much stronger, did you notice that there was also a lot of tension in your posture and breath? Similarly, although your voice may have felt more powerful, was there more tension in it? Did it sound harsher? Did you notice that although you had expanded your space, you were not really able to contact anything since it was all pushed away beyond you?

Open, Embracing Space

○ *Now stand and look around the room and take in the size of it. Imagine that your personal space is expanding to the edges of the room and that everything in the room is included and held within your space. It can be helpful to hold your arms out briefly, imagining that you are literally able to embrace the whole room.*

You may find that your posture is more open and relaxed and that you have a wider circle of vision.

○ *Notice how it feels to open your space out in this way. Say some lines and notice how your voice feels and sounds.*

Did you feel bigger but in a relaxed and easy way? Did you feel more connected within the room as if you could reach into every corner and hold the whole room, as it were, in the palm of your hand? Did your voice feel more open and free, and did it sound as if it were filling the space more and yet without effort?

This exercise will work in time even if it doesn't immediately. I use it when actors have to work in bigger spaces than they are used to, especially where they are moving from film to stage work. With film work, actors are used to embracing a smaller space, the camera comes to them, so to suddenly have to shift to a much bigger space feels incredibly unreal. However, once they have extended their space, the work can feel just as real: it is simply that it has a further reach.

Practising Expanding Your Space in General

Once you can expand your space to embrace the whole room then start to challenge yourself by practising in bigger spaces.

○ *In a station or a supermarket explore expanding your space until you have a sense of including everything within that building.*

○ *In a park or on the top of a hill expand your space as far as you can see.*

○ *Be aware how your body opens up as you expand.*

○ *Where possible, explore speaking and moving and notice what happens to your voice and gestures when you expand your space.*

Note: Being able to expand your space at will is not only useful for performing but also as you go about your life. It will give you greater presence and make others feel comfortable around you. Get used to shifting the size of your space depending on the dimensions of the space you are in and the number of people you want to engage and communicate with.

Practising Expanding Your Space in the Performance Space

It is very important that you spend time in the performance space with the house lights up so that you have a chance to properly take in the whole of the auditorium where the audience will be.

○ Begin by standing in the middle of the stage and gently expanding your space until you feel that you are including the whole of the stage and the whole of the auditorium. If you find it helpful, open your arms out as if you are holding the whole space. Then, relax them once you have a sense of your space having expanded fully.

Note: If you are working in the round, half-round or traverse, you will need to turn from time to time to take in each section of the audience until you have a sense of taking in the whole, including the part of the audience who are behind you.

○ Begin to move around the space, still keeping you space extended so that you continue to include the entire stage and auditorium.

○ As you become more and more comfortable, play with turning your back on the auditorium and still keeping your space extended.

○ Then, begin to speak some lines from the play.

○ It is also helpful to use the Backward Circle gesture as if your energy is going out to the whole audience to collect them and pull them towards you.

Once you have done this, it is vital to work with your scene partners, with half of you on the stage and the other half scattered around the auditorium.

○ First of all, each person takes the time to check that they have expanded their space to include the whole stage and the auditorium.

○ Then, you play scenes across the space, keeping the sense of openness and inclusiveness.

○ Halfway through, swap over, so that those in the auditorium come onto the stage and vice versa.

Speaking scenes across the auditorium allows you to *hear* the size of the space as well as see it.

Note: If you are working outdoors you extend your space to embrace the area where the audience are sitting. Again, it is very useful if you can work with the other actors so you can take it in turns to be on the stage and moving around the audience areas. Be aware that, because there are no walls for your voice to bounce off, you will not get the reassuring acoustic feedback you may be used to when working inside. This can lead you to push, so working with scene partners, who can check that they can hear you and then reassure you, is vital.

Adding Narrative

To help include the audience without losing your sense of truth

Plays are stories without the narrative: we have dialogue and action but no description. It can be very useful to put the narrative back in. It reminds you whom the play is for; it puts the audience back at the centre of the experience and makes it easy and natural for you to share your work with them.

○ *Rather than simply being your character, you are going to be the storyteller as well and add narration around your lines.*

For example: *Electra is in her dead mother's bedroom. She is sitting at the dressing table, wearing one of her mother's dresses over the top of her own clothes. Her brother Orestes is asleep on the bed. She says to herself:* 'Sometimes she would let me stay . . . '

The narrative description can be about what you are doing, thinking or feeling in between the lines; it does not have to be fixed.

○ *When you are doing the narration, focus on where the audience will be as if you are talking directly to them. When you are doing the actual lines, focus on the character/s you are talking to.*

The point of the narration is that it connects you with the audience and the fact that the story is for them, so that, when you turn back to the other actors to speak your lines, you still have a sense of the audience, almost as the third part of a triangular relationship.

This is a great exercise to practise during the rehearsal period since it keeps the audience in the picture. There is then less of a shock when you move from rehearsal into performance. Also, you will find that it sharpens your focus on the other characters rather than distracting you; and it often sheds a new light on the lines that can stop you from being self-indulgent and self-critical, since your attention is focused outward.

It is important to repeat these exercises every time you work in a new performance space, since even a small studio needs some expansion of your own space and some sense of audience inclusion. Many actors fail to truly connect with audiences in small spaces because they think they don't need to do anything. Equally, actors who are used to working in a bigger space need to adjust their sense of space or their performance may be too big. It is also important when changing from proscenium arch to round, half-round or traverse [or vice versa] to ensure that you have reshaped or redirected your space to take in all the audience. *This will not happen automatically.* The sooner you spend time ensuring that you are shifting your space to embrace that particular stage and auditorium, the sooner you will be able to be both intimate and engaging.

Note: If you are still finding it difficult to balance truthful intimacy with the need to take account of the audience, go and sit in the auditorium whilst two of your fellow actors do your scene at the volume you've been doing it. You will notice immediately how frustrating it is for an audience. You will notice that you feel excluded and don't care about the characters or what is happening to them. Stay in the auditorium and coach the actors on stage to increase their volume until it is at a comfortable level for you. You will notice that your response will shift: 'Now, I care!', 'Now, I feel engaged.' *Once a comfortable volume level for the audience has been established, go back on stage and stand next to your fellow actors whilst they play the scene at that volume. Then, play the scene yourself at this volume whilst one or more of your fellow actors sit in the auditorium. This never fails to work, and you will often find that you are playing with more confidence and energy and that your whole performance is far more effectively communicated to the audience.*

SPONTANEITY

In rehearsals you are discovering, finding out what your character would do in this or that situation, how he/she would react to this or that behaviour from another character or characters. As a result, wonderful moments of spontaneity occur which are engaging because they unfold unexpectedly in front of those watching. They happen in the here and now, they cannot be anticipated and those watching go through each step with the actors.

In performance, actors are often repeating earlier discoveries. They are moving at set times to set places; they are saying lines in a particular way; they may be required to reach a particular climax of emotion or thought at a particular point. How, then, can the spontaneity of rehearsals be maintained? Some directors achieve this by not setting the blocking and never giving line readings. This usually means that rehearsals have to be even more thorough in order that the actors have enough knowledge of their character and situation that whatever choices they make on stage they will keep the play on track. This is a great way of working but every actor has to be comfortable with it and be willing to work flexibly and sensitively with the other actors.

But if there is blocking and other shaping of the scene, how does the actor stick to this and yet still find spontaneity? In my experience there are three key factors: *Clear Motivation*, *Starting Points* and *Reacting* rather than acting. Many good actors do these instinctively. But everyone has times when their work does not flow, and if you are not conscious of what you do when you are working well, you will not be able to access spontaneity consciously on those occasions when it does not occur naturally.

Clear Motivation

To find the motivation behind everything you say and do

The first essential is to find a *motivation* for every move, line reading and any other direction you have been given, whether by the director or the playwright. If you move at a certain point or say a line in a certain way simply because the director told you to do it like that, it will never convince the audience and will probably feel less real and more uncomfortable for you. The director has described the *behaviour* he/she wants to see and/or hear on stage, but it is up to you to find a reason for doing it that way. Once you have done this, you will no longer have to *remember* to move or speak in that way because it will be natural to do so.

Starting Points

To establish the triggers that make a scene work

When a scene has gone well in rehearsal, and it is clear that the director would like it to be played that way in performance, it is important to ask yourself: '*What was my starting point for the scene?*' It may have been an objective; it may have been a thought; it may have been a sense of what had happened before. It is much more useful to ask yourself this than to ask what you actually did in the scene, because if you simply repeat the behaviour, without the motivations that arose from your starting point, whatever you do or say will seem hollow and unconvincing.

Reacting

To enable you to be responsive and spontaneous

Once you have your starting points for each scene and are clear about your motivations throughout, then it is time to focus entirely on what is happening around you: in other words, to focus on what the other characters are saying or doing. In this way, everything you do and say will be a natural response to their behaviour, and the audience will believe you because they see and hear that your behaviour is a response to the other characters rather than coming out of nowhere.

Cicely Berry always says that 'an actor must discover rather than know'. And this has been a guiding light for me. If the actor comes onto the stage knowing how they are going to act in each moment, then the audience only have a pale imitation of what was discovered in rehearsal. However, if an actor comes on with a sense of discovery, of not knowing exactly *how* they will make a move or say a line because tonight has never happened before, because those actors have never played to that audience before, have never had the experiences they had that day in quite the same way before, then the audience will join with the actor on a journey of discovery. Instead of a pale imitation of the original moment of discovery, there will be a freshness, a sense of everything happening for the first time, a pulsing heart at the centre of the performance.

This does not mean that the actor consciously changes his/her moves or the way they say their lines. These are the safety net and as long as the motivations are clear, they will occur naturally and will not have to be consciously remembered. The point is that the actor approaches each scene not knowing exactly how they will respond, so that they have to look and listen to the other actors *as if for the first time*. Only in this way will the audience experience a living play rather than a dead shell.

Summary

By learning how to expand your space you can have presence and a sense of intimacy, whatever the size of auditorium you are working in. By identifying the triggers that allow you to be as fresh and responsive as in rehearsals, you can learn to work with great spontaneity, however set your moves and lines may be.

Below is a summary of the exercises in this chapter.

Intimacy
 Expanding Your Space
 Adding Narrative

Spontaneity
 Clear Motivation
 Starting Points
 Reacting

How Do I Convince Them?

HANDLING AUDITIONS AND CASTINGS

CHOOSING PIECES

If you are picking pieces for general auditions, make sure that you choose ones that show you off. Auditions are not the time to stretch yourself. I get the actors I work with to read through a number of pieces and see which ones jump off the page straightaway. It is also important that the pieces stand alone: both in terms of the person auditioning not needing to know what happens in the rest of the play, and the speech having its own build rather than starting with all guns blazing. An emotional speech that works brilliantly in the context of a play where the audience has journeyed with you to that point may not work so well at 10.00 in the morning, completely out of context.

It is also important that each speech has a story or journey within it and that it has emotional changes. Only in this way can you show those auditioning you that you can hold an audience and shift thought and feeling. It is also important, if you are doing two pieces, that they contrast not just in tone – perhaps one being lighter and one more serious – but also in rhythm – one being more staccato and one more sustained, for example. Also, make sure that one is a stiller piece while the other has more movement.

Whether or not you know the people you are auditioning for, it is a good idea to put yourself in their shoes and imagine what they might be wanting. Ask yourself: '*If I were them what would I need to see and hear to be convinced that someone was the best person for the job?*' This will help you choose the pieces and decide on the best way to present them.

Keep the pieces short, no more than a minute each: you can always have an extra piece ready if they ask for more.

If you are auditioning for a specific play, do your research. Make sure you read the full play, and find out as much as possible about the people auditioning you. What have they directed before? Are there actors they work with regularly? If so, do these actors have anything in common? Again, put yourself in the shoes of those auditioning: imagine what they are looking for, what they need.

PREPARING PIECES

Once you have chosen the piece/s, use the exercises in Part Two to explore the rhythm and to connect with the words and the images behind them. Then, use the exercises in Part Three [on character, time and place, objectives, back story and internal dynamics] to explore the subtext. These will help you to work on the piece/s in a focused way; building it up layer by layer as you would in rehearsal, rather than simply repeating it with no specific goal in mind. If you are short of time then you can concentrate on *Walking the Sentences, Changing Direction, Changing Chairs, Three Times Through, Museum Visit, Writing a Thought Script*, and *Connecting with the Situation*. If it is a classical speech, also include *Moving the Metre* and *Walking the Verse*. You can do all these exercises in an hour or two, and you will find that you are learning the piece/s in the process.

Once you have worked on the piece/s it is important to create a strong starting point so that you know that you can connect right from the start. Use either *Connecting with the Situation* or *Keying In*.

Note: Once you are in the audition it is much better to start the scene silently, focusing on a particular spot where those auditioning can see your face and, most importantly, your eyes, and using a shortened version of one of the above two exercises. This engages those auditioning you, building their curiosity. Whereas if you start with your head down and your eyes shut, whilst it may focus you, it shuts them out and leaves them waiting, sometimes impatiently.

PREPARING YOURSELF

Before you go anywhere near any audition room you need to pass the audition with yourself. By this I mean that you have to convince yourself that you can do the job. Far too often, actors push any doubts they have to the back of their mind so they won't be distracted by them. The problem is these doubts return in the audition and they can both upset the actor and raise queries in the minds of those auditioning. So pay attention to any doubts you have and decide what you would need to do to remove them. It may be a question of finding someone to help you prepare who can give you some honest feedback.

Sort out what preparation you need to do physically, vocally and mentally to be ready for the audition. You may find *Centring*, *Backward Circle* and *360-Degree Vision* useful for settling any nerves. Alongside that, identify whether you need physical exercise to free you up – *stretching/rhythmic movement* – or sharpen your focus and wake you up – *walking fast but with ease* – or enable you to be more committed – *Walking with Purpose* – and experiment to find the best way of achieving whichever of these you need. Again, vocally identify whether you need to free your voice up – *humming and chewing, whilst rolling your shoulders up, back, down and forward; whilst dropping your chin onto your chest and rolling your head from shoulder to shoulder; whilst doing a few spine rolls* – or energise it – *making a car or motorbike revving sound with your lips* – or increase its expressiveness – *sliding easily up and down your range on 'ooee ooee ooee' with your lips rounded*. This work in itself should wake you up or free you up mentally as necessary.

The other vital exercise is *Cameras Out*. Shift your attention to those auditioning you. Instead of thinking of them as people who want to judge you or catch you out, think of them as people with a problem that needs to be solved. This is, after all, the truth. They need to find someone who is right for the role. So, if you can approach the audition with your focus on them and their need, that will help to lessen the pressure on you.

It is also a good idea to focus on making a good impression long-term, rather than attempting to get that specific job, since that is completely out of your control. If you are well prepared, your work is engaging and you seem relaxed and confident, they will remember you even if they can't give you this job and they may even recommend you to others.

SIGHT-READING

It may be that instead of, or as well as, doing an audition piece, you are asked to read from the script with little or no time to prepare. Many people find sight-reading difficult. This often relates to early experiences of reading aloud, as mentioned in the introduction to Part Two. Then, the focus was much less on connecting with what was being read and far more on fluency, on reading without any mistakes. Also, there was often a sense of pressure surrounding reading aloud – albeit unspoken. Most parents and teachers are anxious about their children's ability to read fluently and we tend to pick up their concern. But when it comes to auditions it is important to understand that what a director or casting person is looking for when you read is a sense of *connection* with what you are saying and the character you are saying it to. They are not worried if you stumble occasionally or mispronounce the odd word if they feel that you are connecting with the text and therefore bringing it to life. So, rather than worry too much about fluency, focus on connection.

The other big problem with sight-reading is that people tend to read far too fast. There seems to be a fear that the person listening will get bored and that pauses are fatal. Actually, the reverse is true: if you rattle the script off without connecting with it then it *will* be boring. But if you take the time to connect, those auditioning you will be drawn in and will actually get a chance to see that you can act!

It is very important to practise taking the time to connect with what you are saying and who you are saying it to. Start by practising the **Phrase by Phrase** exercise. This will slow you down and ensure that you connect both with the text and the person you're talking to. If you take a fresh piece of text each day and practise it in this way, you will find that any panic disappears and you become more comfortable going slowly. You will also establish the habit of connecting with the text first and then the person, rather than trying to connect with both simultaneously, which then means that you connect with nothing.

Once you are comfortable with this exercise, you can allow yourself to speed up slightly, but it is still important to give yourself the time to take in each phrase before you say it, rather than trying to say a phrase and read ahead at the same time. You will find that giving yourself slightly longer to look at each phrase will actually allow you to take each one in more quickly.

Note: It is worth asking someone else to do this exercise in front of you so that you can experience being in the listener's shoes. You will find that when they are pausing to take in the next phrase, you are absorbing what has just been said and often your curiosity level is being raised about what is coming next. Notice how different it is if the person reads faster: you will find that you have little or no time to take in what they are saying.

PREPARING SCRIPTS FOR
FILM AND TELEVISION CASTINGS

There are two main issues involved in preparing for a film or TV casting. Firstly, there is the time factor: actors are rarely given more than a couple of days and sometimes less than twenty-four hours to prepare anything from one to three scenes. Secondly, there is no way of knowing for sure what interpretation the director is looking for: he/she sometimes won't know themselves how exactly they want a scene or character played until they begin to audition.

So, how do you explore a scene or scenes deeply, even though you are having to work fast, and how do you give yourself a secure enough grounding from which to shift in any direction, according to what the director or casting director asks of you?

Establishing the Facts

To draw your attention to the known facts about your character and their situation

Start by reading through the character breakdown you been given.

○ Note all the facts about your character as you did in the chapter on building your character on page 155.

○ Read through the list, asking yourself: 'What if these were the facts of my life?' Sit quietly and allow your imagination to play with this question, trusting that useful information will come up consciously or unconsciously.

Then, read through each scene.

○ Note down the facts of each situation.

○ Again, ask yourself, 'What if these were the facts of the situation I found myself in?', and sit quietly, allowing your imagination to play with this question. Trust that useful information will come up.

You can also use the *Connecting with the Situation* exercise that we looked at in the chapter on internal dynamics [see page 195] to go more deeply into the situation of the scene.

This exploration of scene and character does not need to take long. You could spend five minutes gathering the facts for the character and five minutes allowing yourself to imagine *'What if . . . ?'*, and then take the same amount of time to explore the situation in each scene. So even if you had five scenes to work on, you could explore them all and the character in an hour, which is far more useful than simply reading through the scenes again and again.

Noticing What Occurs Between the Lines

To become equally aware of the non-spoken action

This is vital: actors often focus only on the words, yet, in a TV or film script, what happens between the lines is equally and sometimes more important.

O *Go through each scene noting any actions and reactions that are described.*

O *Read through the script, saying the lines out loud and reading the actions silently to yourself.*

O *Then, read through again, doing each action or reaction so it is marked as part of the rhythm of the scene.*

Even if you are not able to do the actions when you are reading in the casting, if you have explored them you will have a much better sense of the timing of the scene. Also, if they are filming you, as they often do at castings, they will want to see your non-verbal reactions, so you need to have explored these fully. You will also find you are better prepared to take direction.

Once you have done this exercise, use *Writing a Thought Script* and the *Beat or Click Exercise* to identify a clear thought journey through the scene or scenes. The more specific you are, the easier it will be to listen to direction and to exchange one thought for another if the director wants a different interpretation.

Unit-ing the Script

To identify the bigger shifts within a scene

This exercise helps you to identify and commit to the bigger shifts within a scene. It involves breaking the scene down into units, each of which represent a step within the journey of the scene.

O *Go through each scene and divide it into units by asking yourself: 'Which lines and non-verbal actions and reactions belong together as one step and when does a new step start?'*

This is a question of common sense, so trust yourself to come up with the answers and remember, as always, that it is the exploration itself that is useful. When you work through the scene again, you will very quickly notice whether a unit works or not.

○ *Give each unit a snappy title such as: 'I quickly take control of the situation', 'He tries to wriggle out of the argument', 'I refuse to let him off the hook'.*

○ *Then, read through each scene focusing on the title of each unit and committing to it as completely as possible.*

Again, this will help you to sharpen the journey of the scene and to shift energy and change tack rapidly, even though you have only had a short amount of preparation time. Along with the three previous exercises it will also help you to learn the lines, since it gives you a shape and a sense of logical progression through the scene.

Spectrum and *Corners* are excellent exercises for exploring the possible tensions and colours within the scenes. Again, they will allow you to be more responsive to the director, because you will have a deeper knowledge of and, therefore, security in the scenes. They will also help you to learn the scene since they give you a chance to explore it rather as you would in rehearsal.

Throughout all the exercises it is important as always to choose an object or objects to represent the other people you are talking to, so that you can ensure that you are really communicating and not simply working in a vacuum.

Note: The exercises described above are also very useful when working on a television or film script once you have been cast, since there is usually little or no rehearsal time. They give you the chance to explore and develop. When I have used the exercises to help both experienced and inexperienced actors prepare for films, the feedback from the directors has been excellent, especially because the actors have often been able to give the director what he/she wanted in fewer takes.

Finally, remember with castings and auditions that it is the *quality* of the preparation that you do which is important. Simply going over and over something will not necessarily help you connect more deeply or specifically with a speech or scene. You need to work on journey and shift and connection to the character and their situation.

Summary

Choosing Pieces
Tells a story
Builds
Works on its own
Shows shifts of thought and emotion

Preparing Pieces
Walking the Sentences
Changing Direction
Changing Chairs
Three Times Through
Museum Visit
Writing a Thought Script
Connecting with the Situation

Extra Exercises for Preparing Classical Pieces
All the exercises exploring verse, sound and language

For Creating Strong Starting Points
Connecting with the Situation
Keying In

Preparing Yourself
Centring
Backward Circle
360-Degree Vision
Freeing up physically
Sharpening up mentally
Walking with Purpose
Freeing up the voice
Energising the voice
Increasing expressiveness
Cameras Out

Sight-Reading
Phrase by Phrase

Preparing Scripts for Film and TV Castings
Establishing the Facts
Noticing What Occurs Between the Lines
Unit-ing the Script

What Do I Do When . . . ?

TROUBLESHOOTING

To locate the exercises referred to in this chapter simply look in the Exercise Finder on page 303 which will refer you to the relevant page.

STILLNESS AND EASE

I feel very self-conscious and lacking in confidence in rehearsals

We become self-conscious when we perceive a situation as being judgemental and stressful, our attention turns in as we begin to monitor ourselves and our inner critical voice starts up. If this happens you need to shift your perception and your attention. The best way of doing this is by working with the *Cameras Out* exercise. It is also useful to read the section on **Establishing a 'Creative Bubble'** and the chapter on **How Do I Stop Sabotaging Myself?**

I've suddenly started feeling extremely nervous before going on stage

The first step is to identify what could have triggered this nervousness. Did something happen in the last production you were doing or in earlier performances of this one that has knocked your confidence? Or did anything negative happen in rehearsals? Or do you feel less sure about the play or your character or the theatre you're performing in? Or is something going on in another area of your life that could have triggered the nervous feelings? Even if you are unable to come up with a clear trigger, asking yourself what might have caused it will stimulate your mind to continue to search unconsciously and may lead to useful information later.

The next step is to notice exactly what happens physically and mentally when you get nervous. Where in your body does it affect you most? What are the thoughts that you have? The clearer you are about these, the quicker you can find an effective way to deal with the nervousness.

The section on **Establishing a 'Creative Bubble'** contains several exercises which you can use once you have a clear idea of exactly what is going on. You may also find the chapter on **How Do I Stop Sabotaging Myself?** useful.

How can I feel more physically comfortably on stage?

If the cause of your discomfort is self-consciousness then it is a question of taking your attention off yourself and anchoring it on the other actors and on the situation your character is in. The *Cameras Out* exercise is the best way of doing this. You may also find it useful to read the section on **Establishing a 'Creative Bubble'**.

If you feel that you are generally tense, then you will need to work physically to release the tension and create a habit of greater ease and relaxation. You could choose Alexander Technique, Pilates, Feldenkrais, Tai Chi or Yoga [see page 310] depending on which you find you enjoy most. It is best to go to group classes or have individual sessions initially. Then, later you can develop your own twenty-minute sessions to do daily. If you feel that you need to be more fluid and flexible physically it may also be worth taking some dance classes. Choose something you enjoy which allows you to move freely and gain more confidence as you do so. You might also find it worthwhile reading the section on **Establishing a 'Creative Bubble'** since some of the exercises there can help you to relax.

How can I feel more physically free on stage?

As well as working as suggested in the section above, look at the exercises under **Identifying Shifts Within Your Character**. These help you to connect with the inner thought impulses in a script, letting them shift you physically.

How can I be more still on stage?

You need to look at how easy you find it to be still generally, both mentally and physically. If your mind is always busy, jumping from one thought to the next and you find it hard to sit still, then you are likely to find it hard to be still on stage. Having regular massages where you allow your mind to rest as well as your body can help, as can Yoga or Tai Chi. You may also find the exercises on *Centring* and the *Backward Circle* useful, as these will tend to anchor your energy in the centre of your body rather than it dissipating and causing your hands, feet and face to go into overdrive.

ENERGY

I know I'm trying too hard, how do I stop pushing and just let the work emerge?

The most effective way is to work physically: for example, by placing your hands on a wall and leaning against it with various degrees of effort until you fully understand the difference between trying too hard and fully committing with ease. Once you are able to lean with complete ease then run through your speech or scene whilst retaining that level of ease. In this way you will discover how you can commit fully without pushing. The *Purposeful Walk* exercise is also useful here.

You will also find that all the exercises for exploring text and subtext will be helpful, because each exercise gives you something physical to do, so that the work can simply emerge whilst you are busy focusing elsewhere.

I'm often told I lack energy

Lack of energy can be caused either by lack of confidence or by an habitual offstage style, which may be low-key. Working physically is the best way to find a good level of energy on stage without forcing it. The *Purposeful Walk* exercise will help you to gauge when you have appropriate energy. The exercises on **Structures and Rhythms** in the chapters on **Handling Modern and Classical Text**, and the exercises on **Identifying Shifts Within Your Character** in the chapter on internal dynamics, will help you to commit more, since they all involve physical movement.

I tend to trail away at the end of lines

There are several causes of trailing away. One is rushing ahead, which means that your attention moves on to the next line before you have finished saying the present one; another is losing confidence in what you're saying and so abandoning the line. Trailing away may also be the result of an habitual speech pattern or because you tend to run out of breath quickly.

If rushing is the cause, working with the *Backward Circle* will bring you into sync with yourself and stop you rushing ahead. You may need to work with the exercise regularly for quite some time to embed the change you need.

If lack of confidence, habitual trailing away, or running out of breath are the cause, then working physically will help you to develop the habit of following through and finding enough breath to support that where necessary.

Following Through

To develop the habit of following through to the end of lines, rather than letting them trail away

○ *Imagine that you have an object in your hand and that there is a shelf in front of you at eye level, and just out of reach.*

○ *As you say the line, stretch your hand out so that the imaginary object lands on the shelf as you say the last word of the line.*

○ *Then, relax your arm and repeat the same action for each line.*

You may also find it useful to work with *Walking the Sentences, Walking the Verse* and *Clicking the Final Word*.

How do I find more pace?

To find more pace you need to learn to think more quickly, without losing the detail of the shift of thought. Firstly, work on *Walking the Sentences* and *Changing Direction*, making sure that you always turn in a *new* direction and that there is a marked shift in thought and energy. Then, repeat the exercises, speeding up the turns without losing the degree of shift in thought and energy. After that, you can move on to the *Beat or Click*

Exercise, again starting by being precise about the degree of shift at the beat points and then speeding up the shifts without losing the precision. *Taking the Cushion* is a good exercise to work on with scene partners to speed up your reactions.

My performance feels stale

An effective way to renew your energy and refresh your performance is to do the scenes while physically stretching and moving in as many different directions as possible. The movement will shake you out of the habitual rut you may have fallen into. Doing the scenes whilst dancing, throwing or batting a ball against a wall or juggling will also have a dislodging effect allowing new discoveries and connections to be made.

It is also useful to look at what you are doing with the rest of your day and your preparation for the show. Have these fallen into a rut? Taking up a new activity or going to dance or singing classes or working on other texts or styles of theatre will input new energy and perspectives. Changing your warm-up will also help; so establish a different rhythm, either by changing the actual exercises you do or the order and way you do them.

EMOTION

My performance often seems cerebral and lacking in emotion

This is usually the result of excess planning and control, which tends to come from a lack of trust that your performance will evolve naturally if you spend time exploring all the layers of text and subtext. All the exercises in the book encourage you to discover, rather than know, and will build your trust. It is important that you commit to them physically and approach them playfully with a spirit of curiosity, rather than a desperate need to find an answer or 'the right way' to do it. Specific exercises that are good for getting you out of your head and helping you tap into emotion are *Changing Direction, Connecting with the Vowels* and *Museum Visit*.

You can also use distraction exercises to stop your brain from over controlling. Cicely Berry has some lovely exercises which can be used here. For example, asking an actor to draw what they can see out of the window whilst playing the scene, or to move and stack chairs or books. These exercises give the person's conscious controlling mind something to do, so that the scene takes care of itself.

It is important to experiment with what kind of warm-up helps you to find a playful, curious, open and trusting state. Certainly, it will need to be enjoyable and it may need to be varied: so sometimes you might free the body up with a massage and then follow that with some energising physical and vocal work, ending with some text you really enjoy; other times you might stretch the body out to some music you really like, before doing some voice work and ending with a song you like. There is no one right way to warm up. Each actor needs to experiment and find out what works best for them.

I'm often told I'm overemoting

All overemoting is the result of excess effort. The issue is: what is causing this excess? Is it habitual: in other words, you always try too hard? Or is it caused by lack of trust that the emotion will arise of its own accord if you focus on the situation the character is in? Or does it come from a concern that unless you demonstrate the emotion to the audience they won't 'get it'?

If the cause is habitual over effort, use the *Backward Circle* and *Purposeful Walk* exercises to learn how to ground your energy and fully commit with ease and without excess. Also, work with your back against a wall and the sense that the more you want your performance to go out, the more you need to lean back. You can use your arms freely; you simply keep your back and head resting against the wall. In this way you learn to release your performance rather than push it out.

If the cause is lack of trust that the emotion will arise of its own accord, use *Connecting with the Situation* and *Exploring the Scene Journey* to connect with the situation your character is in. Then, use *Spectrum*, *Corners* and *Beat or Click Exercise* to explore the inner shifts of your character. You can also use *Changing Directions* and *Connecting with the Vowels* to explore how the text enables the emotion to arise naturally.

If the cause comes from concern that unless you demonstrate the emotion the audience won't respond to it, you need first to clearly understand that the audience are expert at detecting emotions since they rely on this skill to navigate their way through life. As long as you have connected with the situation your character is in, and are responding to what the other characters are doing and saying, the audience *will* 'get it'. So, first focus on the exercises suggested here to make sure that you have a detailed connection with the situation and the potential inner shifts of your character. Then, use **Phrase by Phrase** and **Working with Actions in Text** to help you focus on the other characters and stay alive and responsive.

EXPRESSION

My work lacks colour and variety

External colour and variety come from inner shifts: of thought and emotion which are caused by what the other characters are doing and saying. The chapter on **Exploring the Internal Dynamics of a Scene** is useful here. If you are short of time, focus on **Spectrum**, **Corners** and **Beat or Click Exercise**. Colour and variety also come from a more specific connection with what you are saying, and the sounds that are used to say it. **Three Times Through** and **Physicalising the Words** are very useful for connecting with the images behind the words. **Connecting with the Vowels** will help you to explore the varying vowel lengths which will give you a greater variety of pace. It is also worth looking at the exercises in the section on rhythm in the chapter on **Building Your Character** since these offer a way of finding contrasting rhythms within a speech and scene.

How do I handle long speeches so that they have contrast and movement?

Firstly, you need to identify the overall journey of the speech: what is the character thinking and feeling at the beginning of it and how has this changed by the end? Was the character confused at the beginning and are they now clearer? Did they start with a problem and now have a solution? Were they doubtful about something which they are now sure about? There are endless possibilities, and, of course, a character may also be more confused, or worried or undecided by the end of a speech. The point is that there *has* to be a shift or there is absolutely no point in the audience watching and listening.

Once you have a sense of the journey use **Walking the Sentences**, **Changing Direction** and **Changing Chairs** to help you understand the structure and rhythm of the speech. Then, look for shift points in the scene. These are points where there seems to be a step up in argument and/or feeling, or a shift to a new line of argument and/or feeling. To find them you simply need to keep reading through the speech and asking yourself: '*Does this sentence flow on from the one before or is there a shift of focus, emphasis or argument?*'

Then, ask yourself what your character is trying to do to the character/s they are talking to. Use *Working with Actions in Text* to identify and play these intentions.

Finally, run through the speech asking your scene partner/s to attempt to interrupt you at the end of every sentence. This helps to heighten the energy and the communicative need of the speech because you have to fight to get through it, rather than knowing that everyone is going to shut up until you've finished.

When you are playing the speech in performance, focus on the other character/s and their reactions. Do they look as if they are thinking and feeling what you want them to or not? In this way the speech will stay alive since you will instinctively slightly shift the way you say each part to get the other characters thinking and feeling what you want them to.

TRUTHFULNESS AND CONNECTION

I'm always being told to slow down. How can I do that and still sound and feel natural?

If your mind is rushing ahead and you're gabbling the words, you need to use the *Backward Circle*. This will get you back into sync with yourself by anchoring your energy so there will be no need for you to pull back or restrain yourself and feel awkward. You will need to practise the exercise on a daily basis, but it will yield excellent results, especially since it also helps you to connect more deeply both vocally and emotionally.

In many cases it is not the speed of speaking that is the issue, it is the lack of breaks between each parcel of thought. This causes the text to come out in one long stream which is very hard for the audience, and indeed the other actors, to engage with. The following exercise helps you to break streams of text up into parcels or chunks, which not only helps the audience but also gives you the time to make a far deeper connection with what you're saying. As usual, the exercise works physically to externalise and make tangible what needs to happen mentally.

Chunking the Text

Separating the text into parcels so that both you and the audience have a chance to connect with what you are saying

You need a soft ball for this exercise. If you are working on your own, throw the ball against the wall and catch it again. If you are working with a scene partner you can throw it to them and they can throw it back.

Stage One

O *Say the first phrase then throw the ball at the wall or to your scene partner; make sure that you say the whole phrase before you throw, and avoid throwing whilst you are still speaking.*

O *Wait until you have the ball back in your hands before you say the next phrase, and again, throw it once you have finished speaking.*

O *Continue throughout the speech/scene you are working on, always throwing the ball between each phrase.*

Stage Two

If you are working on your own, use a plant, lamp or other object to represent whoever you are talking to, otherwise talk directly to your scene partner.

O *Say the first phrase to the object or your partner and then ask yourself: 'Have they got what I just said?'*

O *Say the next phrase and again mentally ask: 'Have they got that?'*

O *Continue through the whole speech or scene in the same way.*

When you are working with someone, focusing on them and asking yourself whether they have got what you have just said is a device which allows you to take your timing from them. In this way you will neither be too fast nor too slow since you will always be going at the speed which works for them. Obviously, once you are on stage you do not consciously need to be asking: 'Have you got that?', but it is good to keep your focus fully on the other actors so that you do not start speeding up.

You can also use *Changing Chairs* to help you parcel the text. This is especially helpful for giving you the time to connect with what you are saying. Both *Chunking the Text* and *Changing Chairs* need to be practised regularly to establish a slower pace that feels comfortable and natural.

I'm always being told I need to be louder. How can I do that and still feel truthful?

It is a question of practice and familiarisation. Firstly, you need to be sure that you can produce a louder voice that is easy, flexible and natural. For this you will need to do work on posture, physical ease, breath support and resonance. It's best to find a good voice teacher or voice book to help you do this. Resonance is particularly important for larger spaces and needs to be worked on regularly over time so that speaking with increased resonance feels and sounds natural. To be fully resonant your body needs to be toned and relaxed, with good posture; you need to increase the space in your mouth by opening a little wider between the back teeth – a finger's width is a good distance – and you need to take time over the vowels so the sound has a chance to resonate. Alternating between chanting and speaking your lines – feeling the sound rebound in your mouth and upper body as much when you speak as when you chant – will help you to create the habit of talking with greater resonance.

Also have a look at the chapter on **How Do I Share My Work Truthfully?** especially the exercise on *Expanding Your Space*.

My character is very different from me and I'm finding it hard to connect

It is much easier if you break the different elements of character down and work on these separately. Take time to consider the facts about your character and their situation; their overall motivation; their rhythm and the language they use: then you will be able to find a way in to playing them truthfully. The chapter on building a character, **Who Am I?**, covers all these elements and how to explore them.

I'm having difficulty connecting with the situations my character is in

This can happen particularly with classical texts. It is easy to be confused by the surface strangeness of the situation so it's important to take a step back and regard the situation in terms of basic human experience, encapsulating it in a single sentence if you can.

If you have time it is worth reading the chapters in Part Three on establishing time and place and fleshing out the back story; also, the exercise on *Connecting with the Situation* should prove useful. These will give you various ways of relating to the relevance of any situation. If you are short of time, go straight to *Connecting with the Situation*.

I have difficulty keying into the beginning of certain scenes

The chapters in Part Three on establishing time and place and fleshing out the back story will help, especially *Keying In*, as will *Starting Points* in the chapter on transferring from rehearsal to performance.

How can I connect more truthfully and deeply?

This takes time, trust and specific work. If you rush to find a way to play a character or scene you will end up manufacturing behaviour, which prevents deeper and more truthful connections. Equally, if you wait around for the work to emerge without doing any focused work, little of any depth is likely to occur. If you explore, layer by layer, the various elements of text and subtext, which the exercises in this book enable you to do, you will make deep connections with what your character says and with the underlying situations your character is in. If you do not have the time to read the whole book, decide whether you want to connect more with the text, your character or the underlying situations and dynamics and then read the relevant chapters. If you are in need of a few exercises that you can try out immediately, *Connecting with the Vowels* will help you to find the emotional heart of speeches and scenes, *Three Times Through* will help you to engage more with what you are saying, and *Connecting with the Situation* will help you to build up a strong sense of the situation your character is in.

How can I make it more believable and real?

The key here is to get your attention off yourself and onto the other actors: onto what you, as your character, are trying to do to their characters. The more you can focus on them, on listening when they are speaking, on noticing their reactions when you are speaking, the better, because then you will start behaving in a way that is more realistic and convincing for the audience. It is also likely to be more spontaneous and detailed, since you will be reacting moment by moment. Start by reading the section **Stop Acting, Start Talking** in the chapter on **Handling Modern Text**. Then, have a look at the following exercises: *Cameras Out*, *Using the Beat When Listening* and *Getting to Grips with Actions*. All of these will help you, in different ways, to shift your attention outwards.

TEXT

I'm finding the text difficult to connect with

This happens not only with classical text, but also with modern texts that are written in a style which we find alien. What is needed is trust and patience: trust that if you explore each element of the text, you can connect with it; and patience to take the time to do so.

All the exercises in the text chapters are designed to explore the various elements of the text: they allow you to make the text your own and feel confident and comfortable with it. The exercises in the section on **Exploring Structure and Rhythm** examine how the punctuation gives you clues to the thought rhythms of your character, their emotional to and fro, and the logic of what they are saying. The exercises in the sections on **Discovering Emotional Flow** and **Balancing Sound and Sense** help you engage with the sounds in the text so you can connect emotionally and commit to what your character says with energy, ease and conviction. The exercises in the sections on **Connecting with the Words and Images** and **Internal Geography** help you to own the words your character says and use them with confidence and vitality.

I'm frightened of classical text

You are not alone in this: many actors are daunted by classical text, by the complexity of the language and the remoteness of the situations. You need to take it gently, exploring text and subtext layer by layer, so they become less daunting. As you do this you will realise that you can connect with what is said and the way it is said and that the situations *do* have parallels with your own experience.

Work through the exercises in the chapter on **Handling Classical Text**, either using the speeches given there or ones you have chosen for yourself. Take your time, doing each exercise at least twice, and noticing what you personally learn from it. If you're not sure about a particular exercise, you can then go back to it again later to explore it further. Work with an attitude of playful curiosity and confidence; trust that you will be learning subconsciously even if you are not sure what you are discovering on a conscious level.

Once you have finished the classical text exercises move on to the chapter exploring the internal dynamics of a scene. This will help you to identify the situations your character is in and to mark the underlying shifts of thought and emotion that occur. In this way you will be able to embed the text in a reality that makes it much easier and more convincing to say.

I find it difficult to honour the shape of text and to be truthful

So often, honouring the text and being truthful are set at odds with each other and the actor is left feeling that it is impossible to do justice to both at the same time. It is certainly true that in performance it is difficult to focus on the shape and structure of the text, because all your attention needs to be on the situation your character is in, on what he/she wants, and on listening and responding to the other characters. This means that work on the text needs to be done during the rehearsal period. The exercises in the chapters on **Handling Modern and Classical Text** enable you to explore the various structures and also the sounds and language used. Working through your text using these exercises will make you aware of the way it is shaped and as long as you take the time to embed the shape thoroughly, by repeating each exercise a number of times, you will find that, when you are on stage, you naturally honour the shape of the text without having to think about it consciously.

I'm told that I focus too much on the text and not enough on the subtext, especially when I'm working on classical plays

It is good to focus on the text; the crucial question is one of timing. During the rehearsal period it is important to focus on the structure of the text and sounds and language used; then, in performance, the attention needs to shift to the situation your character is in, to listening and responding to the other characters and to achieving your character's intention. The exercises in the chapters on **Handling Modern and Classical Text** will enable you to focus appropriately on the shape of the text, whilst the chapters in Part Three on character, time and place, objectives, back story and internal dynamics will help you explore the subtext so that it is easier for you to key into this once on stage.

DEALING WITH DIRECTORS

General Note

Of course, it is wonderful when you are able to work with a director who really fires and stretches you, but the reality is that this will not happen on every production. So, it is a waste of time getting annoyed, frustrated or upset when a director does not work in a way that suits you. Getting annoyed will not help you to create work you can be proud of. It is much more useful to treat the situation as a learning opportunity and work out how you can get what you need from that director. In this way you will be in control of the quality of work you produce. The whole of this book is designed to make you more independent so that you can fill in any gaps in the rehearsal process for yourself. The **Exercise Finder** and the **Index** will guide you to relevant exercises. You may also find it useful to look at the section on **Establishing a 'Creative Bubble'** which gives you ways of staying calm, confident and in control, whatever is happening around you. In addition, when the director is giving notes, listen with the thought in your mind: '*What is it he/she wants?*' This will stop you from taking things too personally, since it will keep your attention on how you can achieve what is needed rather than on what the director thinks of you. It is also useful to learn to ask questions in a way that draws out more information from the director. If you ask in a calm, curious and interested manner, the director will not feel that you are unable to cope nor will he/she feel that you are challenging him/her. It is important to remember that directors can lose confidence too and that they can be as lost as you at times – only they are not supposed to show it!

How do I cope when the director is giving me lots of line readings?

Firstly, calm yourself so you can attend to what the director is saying. The exercises in the section on **Establishing a 'Creative Bubble'** will help you do this. When directors give line readings it is because that is the only way they feel they have of communicating to you what they want. In order that you do not feel hemmed in or forced to do an imitation of them it is important, for each line, to ask yourself: '*What would my character need to be thinking or wanting to achieve to say the line in that way?*' In other words you have to work backward to find the motivation behind the lines. Then you will feel comfortable and truthful saying them in the way the director has indicated.

How do I deal with a move/line reading I don't believe in and feel awkward doing?

You need to find a reason for doing that move or saying that line in a particular way. In other words, what is the character's motivation; what are they trying to do to the other character/s? Once you have established this, the move or line will flow naturally and seem truthful. If you are really stuck, have a look at the section on **Actions**.

How do I work out what the director wants from me?

The more you commit and give the director something to react to, the better. This does not mean that you need to give a finished performance right from the start or that you have to come up with endless weird and wonderful ways of playing a scene. What it does mean is that you need to play each scene fully, using what you know at that point, rather than being tentative. Directors are refining their ideas all the time, selecting, from what you give them, the elements they think will work best and the more you give, the easier it is for them to respond.

The director doesn't like me

This can be a common feeling, which may or may not reflect how the director actually feels about you. Of course, it is not a pleasant situation to be in, especially if the director makes his/her dislike clear. Firstly, you need to recognise and accept that it is not going to be enjoyable and that it is very unlikely to change. Then, you need to focus on how you can protect yourself so that you are able to access your best work. Using *Cameras Out* and the exercises in the section on **Establishing a 'Creative Bubble'** will help you do this. As will *Turning Others' Judgements into Needs*. Then, simply behave in a professional and respectful way and keep reminding yourself that their dislike of you is their problem and not yours. Of course, if they are behaving in a really unacceptable way, you can discuss it with your agent and, if necessary, Equity.

I don't like the director

This is your problem and not the director's. Put your dislike to one side and get on with your job. Avoid winding yourself up by moaning to friends about him/her. Rehearsal periods are not that long and you need not work with that director again. If you feel that you have to accept another job with the same director, then you also need to accept that that is the decision *you* have made.

On a more positive note, it might be worth considering why you dislike the director. Most dislike arises when the other person has a different value system from us. We tend in this case simply to label the person as 'wrong'. If you can turn off your judgement and start to be curious about what motivates him/her to behave in the way he/she does, you may find that you gain some understanding about what is important to that person which at least allows you to tolerate them, even if you can't like them. *Turning Your Judgements into Needs* can help with this.

Summary

This chapter has looked at some of the problems actors can encounter. If you could not find an answer to any of your issues here, go to the Index which gives a comprehensive list of the areas covered in the book.

Conclusion

To a large extent we are often not aware of the minutiae of how we think, feel or behave. This poses a problem for actors when attempting to recreate 'real' thinking, feeling and behaviour in performance. All kinds of weird and not so wonderful results ensue. The solution is to accept that you cannot directly and consciously recreate what you do in 'real life'. What you can do, however, is recreate the *stimuli* that lead to 'real' thinking, feeling and behaviour. These stimuli can be recreated by exploring the clues the text gives you about your character and situation, and by building the details of the subtext that the text implies. The exercises in this book are designed to help you do that. By establishing the details of character and situation – the personal and situation rules I referred to in the opening chapter – you feed yourself with the same information as you are fed in 'real life' situations and your reactions will be correspondingly 'realistic'. Once you get the stimuli right it is simply a question of being present and responding.

In *An Actor Prepares*, Stanislavsky tells a story that sums the point up beautifully. An actress is asked by her teacher to imagine that she is looking for a pin she has lost. The actress moves about the stage, with dramatic gestures, pretending to look for a pin. Nothing she does in any way resembles what someone might do if they were really searching. After a while the teacher stops her. He tells her that there is a pin hidden somewhere on stage and that she needs to find it. This time she really looks and, of course, what she does is far more interesting and unique than the clichéd looking she had displayed the first time. Of course, there was no pin actually hidden, but believing that there was had given her the stimuli to respond authentically.

The more you build the detailed stimuli you need and the more you trust that, with that stimuli in place, responses will come from you which are both truthful and interesting for the audience, the more original and authentic your work will be.

Appendices

And What About . . . ?

EXTRA NOTES ON CLASSICAL TEXT

IRREGULAR IAMBIC PENTAMETER LINES

What makes lines irregular? How do you deal with them and what clues do they give you?

Irregular lines are ones that have more *or* less than ten syllables. Below are examples of various types, how you can recognise them and what they tell you.

Note: See page 75 for a description of regular iambic pentameter lines and how to deal with them.

Extra Syllables

If the extra syllables occur on weak beats in the line this does not upset the rhythm. They just slot themselves in between the strong beats without taking up any more time. However, it's worth exploring them here since they can catch you out at first, and they do affect the way the line feels to say.

Extra weak syllables at the beginning or in the middle of lines

The extra weak beat in the examples below means that there are *two weak beats* instead of one at some point in the line. The italics mark these.

> '*Towards* **Phoe**bus' **lodg**ing. **Such** a **wag**goner'
>   [*Romeo and Juliet*]

> 'So **he** dis**solved** and **show**ers *of* **oaths** did **melt**'
>   [*A Midsummer Night's Dream*]

> 'Will **be** my **knell**. Go **play**, boy, **play**. *There have* **been**,'
>   [*The Winter's Tale*]

281

The weak beats will simply slot themselves in if you mark each strong beat firmly.

The extra weak beats tend to give a sense of compression, as if the character is trying to squeeze more into the line. The reasons why the character may be doing this and the emotions they are feeling can, of course, be very different. The point is that if you notice what the line is doing, you can be much more aware of the clues and support that Shakespeare is giving you.

Extra weak syllables at the ends of lines

> 'O **cow**ard **con**science, **how** dost **thou** af**flict** me!'
> [*Richard III*]

> 'And **why**, I **pray** you? **Who** might **be** your **mother**,'
> [*As You Like It*]

> 'I **left** no **ring** with **her**; what **means** this **la**dy?'
> [*Twelfth Night*]

Lines that end in this way are said to have *feminine endings*. These lines are easy enough to work out since they are regular until the final weak beat, but they may confuse you as you go into the next line, which is why it's a good idea to have a silent beat between each line when you're focusing on the metric rhythm.

The weak beat at the end of the line does make the line feel different to say from a line that ends on a strong beat. Try the following experiment.

○ *First of all mark the rhythm of a couple of ordinary lines by marching strongly on the spot. Notice how it feels to end on a strong beat.*

> ti-**tum** ti-**tum** ti-**tum** ti-**tum** ti-**tum**
> ti-**tum** ti-**tum** ti-**tum** ti-**tum** ti-**tum**

There is usually a sense of certainty or finality.

○ *Now mark the rhythm of a couple of feminine-ending lines, again marching strongly on the spot. Notice how it feels to end on a weak beat.*

> ti-**tum** ti-**tum** ti-**tum** ti-**tum** ti-**tum** *ti*
> ti-**tum** ti-**tum** ti-**tum** ti-**tum** ti-**tum** *ti*

The *feminine ending* can give the line a sense of uncertainty, of questioning or searching. It feels less finished, less final and more expectant. It can also give a sense of exclamation or surprise or a sense of playfulness. As always, it is important to notice whether a line ends on a strong or weak beat and then decide what clues that gives you about your character's intention and feeling at that point.

Of course it is possible to find lines which have extra weak beats both in the line and at the end:

> 'And **take** my **milk** for **gall**, you **murder**ing min**is**ters,'
> [*Macbeth*]

> '*I am* **barred**, like **one** infec**tious. My** third com**fort**,'
> [*The Winter's Tale*]

Note: In this last example, when you return to the sense stress, the stress on 'My' is likely to shift forward to 'third' throwing extra emphasis onto this word.

Extra Strong Beats

> '**Un**less I **spake**, or **looked**, or **touched**, or **carved**
> to **thee**' [*The Comedy of Errors*]

> 'As **my** young **mis**tress' **dog**. Now **my** sick **fool** Roderigo'
> [*Othello*]

Note: When you return to the sense stress, the stress on the second 'my' is likely to spread backward to include 'Now', and forward to include 'sick', throwing extra emphasis on the whole phrase.

These lines have an extra strong beat as well as an extra weak beat. This *does* make a difference to the rhythm. There is the same sense of wanting to cram more into the line, but because of the extra strong stress the line often comes across as more emphatic. Where a new sentence starts in the middle of the line, whether spoken by the same character or by another, there is often a sense of the second half of the line overlapping or interrupting the first.

Missing Syllables

> 'That me**thought** her **eyes** had **lost** her **tongue**'
> [*Twelfth Night*]

> 'Got **'tween** asleep and **wake**? Well **then**' [*King Lear*]

> 'A **bro**ther's **mur**der. Pray **can** I **not**' [*Hamlet*]

> 'For **He**cuba' [*Hamlet*]

The above lines have missing beats. Below I have replaced the missing beats with 'ti' or **'tum'** as appropriate. This is the best way to work when you are *Moving the Metre*.

'That [**tum**] me**though**t her **eyes** had **lost** her **tongue**'
[*Twelfth Night*]

'Got '**tween** a**sleep** and **wake**? [ti-**tum**] Well **then**'
[*King Lear*]

'A **bro**ther's **mur**der. [**tum**] Pray **can** I **not**' [*Hamlet*]

'For **Hec**uba [ti-**tum** ti-**tum** ti-**tum**]' [*Hamlet*]

Once you return to speaking the text normally you may discover that the missing syllables suggest a pause or an action or movement, or that the line spreads itself out. It's a question of what feels right as you work on the character and the scene.

Sometimes there is no syllable missing but, rather, a word is spread out, by which I mean it is given more syllables than it would be given at other times or than we would give it in normal speech.

E.g. 'cru-el':
'Be**cause** I **would** not **see** thy **cru**el **nails**' [*King Lear*]

Also, sometimes 'ed' at the end of words is given its own beat.

E.g. 'gall-ed':
'As **fear**fully as **doth** a **gall**èd **rock**' [*Henry V*]

In both cases the word is given extra weight and time. You do not have to necessarily pronounce the separate beats strongly when you actually speak the text, but you do need to give the word a little extra time; spread it out over the two or three beats.

Note: Different editions of Shakespeare's text mark the final 'ed' in words, and whether it has its own beat or not, differently. So some editions will replace the 'e' with an apostrophe, 'loath'd', when 'ed' does not have its own beat. Some editions will put an accent over the 'e', 'loathèd', when 'ed' does have its own beat.

Identifying Irregular Lines

To work out quickly and easily whether a line is irregular and, if so, in what way

○ Step or march the speech or scene you are working on strongly in rhythm as described on page 77.

○ As you go through it, mark any lines that don't seem to fit into the rhythm and then go back and look through them as suggested below.

○ Count the number of syllables.

○ If there are ten, then the sense stress is probably different from the metric stress. In that case, mark the strong stresses, i.e. every second syllable, and then beat out the line completely ignoring the sense.

○ If there are fewer than ten syllables, firstly, check that these could not be gained by giving any of the words in the line an extra syllable – as in the examples of 'gallèd' or 'cruel' above. If no syllables can be gained in this way, work out where in the line you think the missing syllable/s is/are and replace it/them with a 'ti' or **'tum'** or 'ti-**tum**', depending on where the missing syllable occurs.

○ If there are more than ten syllables, firstly, look at whether the line has a feminine ending. If it hasn't, or if there are more than eleven syllables, look within the line to see if there are any extra weak syllables between the strong ones.

○ If you still have extra beats then look at whether these are strong ones – though this occurs less often.

○ Once you have sorted the lines, go though the whole speech again, physically marking the rhythm strongly.

Being able to work through lines in this way will give you a much greater appreciation of how the text works and how much time to give particular words or phrases. It will also mean that irregular lines are much less likely to trip you up and that instead you will be able to use their irregularity to inform your acting choices.

SHARED LINES

In scenes, characters often share verse lines, so what effect does this have? If the shared lines are kept intact then the character speaking the second part of the line will pick up his/her cue very quickly and this can add pace and tension.

Have a look at the following exchange from *Measure for Measure*. Claudio is in prison, awaiting execution for having got his girlfriend pregnant. He has asked his sister, Isabella, to go to Angelo, who has sentenced him, and plead for a pardon. This, Isabella has done and Angelo has fallen in love with her. He offers to pardon Claudio if she will sleep with him. Isabella is horrified, especially since she is about to become a nun and she believes sleeping with Angelo would endanger her soul. She returns to Claudio to tell him to prepare for death, fearing that when she tells him of Angelo's offer, he may want her to accept it.

ISABELLA: Tomorrow you set on.

CLAUDIO: Is there no remedy?

ISABELLA: None, but such remedy as, to save a head,
      To cleave a heart in twain.

CLAUDIO: But is there any?

ISABELLA: Yes, brother, you may live;
      There is a devilish mercy in the judge,
      If you'll implore it, that will free your life,
      But fetter you till death.

CLAUDIO: Perpetual durance?

ISABELLA: Ay, just. Perpetual durance, a restraint,
      Though all the world's vastidity you had,
      To a determined scope.

CLAUDIO: But in what nature?

ISABELLA: In such a one as, you consenting to't,
      Would bark your honour from that trunk you bear,
      And leave you naked.

CLAUDIO: Let me know the point.

○ *Read through the lines with a friend, in two different ways.*

○ *Firstly, pausing each time before Claudio replies to Isabella.*

○ *Secondly, speaking immediately Isabella stops speaking.*

Do you notice that when Claudio responds immediately the scene is much tighter? Now there are times when mid-line pauses can be effective, but these need to be chosen, rather than the result of slow reactions on the part of the actor speaking the second half of the line. So it is always worth keeping shared lines intact to start with, to discover how this affects a scene and then only adding pauses if they make the scene more truthful and engaging for the audience.

Practising Shared Lines

To be able to keep the rhythm of shared lines and pick up cues quickly

○ Take a scene where there are plenty of shared lines.

○ Mark the rhythm physically as before, you doing your lines and your partner/s doing theirs.

○ Keep the shared lines intact so they flow on as if being spoken by one person.

The example from *Measure for Measure* is marked up for you to practise on. Remember that you are beating out the metric stress *not* the sense stress. The notes following the example show where the stress would shift when you return to the sense and how this would throw greater emphasis onto certain words or phrases. The reason for beating out the metric stress and ignoring the sense stress at this point is to establish the underlying beat supplied by the iambic pentameter, so that you better appreciate the tension and shaping of the text that is created when the metric and sense stress differ.

ISABELLA: Tomorrow **you** set **on**.[a]

CLAUDIO: Is **there** no **remedy**?[b]

ISABELLA: None, **but** such **remedy** as, to **save** a **head**,[c]
            To **cleave** a **heart** in **twain**.

CLAUDIO: But **is** there **any**?

ISABELLA: [ti-**tum** ti-**tum**] Yes, **brother**, **you** may **live**;[d]
            There **is** a **devilish mercy** in the **judge**,
            If **you'll** implore it, **that** will **free** your **life**,
            But **fetter you** till **death**.

CLAUDIO: Perpetual **durance**?

ISABELLA: Ay, **just**. Per**petual durance**, a re**straint**,[e]

Though **all** the **world's** vas**tid**ity you **had**,
To **a** de**ter**mined **scope**.

CLAUDIO: But **in** what **na**ture?[f]

ISABELLA: In **such** a **one** as, **you** con**sen**ting **to't**,
          Would **bark** your **honour from** that **trunk** you **bear**,
          And **leave** you **na**ked.

CLAUDIO: **Let** me **know** the **point**.

When you return to the sense stress:

Note a: The stress on 'you' *and* 'on', *in the first half of the first line, is likely to spread to include* 'set' *so giving the whole phrase more emphasis, since this is the conclusion of her speech: tomorrow he will be executed.*

Note b: The stress on 'remedy', *in the second half of the first line, is likely to be spread over* 'no' *as well, so giving this greater emphasis. Claudio wants to find out if there is any way he can avoid execution.*

Note c: The stress on 'but', *in the second line, is likely to shift back onto* 'none', *emphasising the point that, as far as Isabella is concerned, there is no acceptable way for him to avoid execution.*

Note d: The line 'Yes, brother, you may live' *only has six syllables. So either there may be a pause before she says the line or there may be pauses within the line with stress being thrown onto the following words:* 'Yes, brother, [pause] you may live.'

Note e: The stress on 'just', *in the eighth line, is likely to spread to include* 'Ay', *as Isabella picks up on Claudio's phrase* 'Perpetual durance?' *He is thinking of life imprisonment but she is thinking of the imprisonment of his soul if she had to sin to save him.*

Note f: The stress on 'in', *in the tenth line, is likely to spread to* 'what' *as Claudio presses Isabella to spell out exactly how he may be saved.*

NAME–SHIFTS BETWEEN FORMAL AND INFORMAL

The following scene from *As You Like It* [Act 1 Scene 3] is an excellent examples of name–shifts. At the beginning of the scene Duke Frederick bursts in, accompanied by his lords, and banishes his niece Rosalind from the court. Rosalind had stayed in the court with her cousin, Celia, when her own father had been banished by the present Duke, her uncle. In the following extract, the names they *call* each other appear in bold, and the names by which they *refer* to each other are in italics. Read through it and notice the changes in how the Duke, Rosalind and Celia address and refer to each other and how these show the shifts in relationship during the scene.

Enter DUKE, *with* LORDS.

DUKE: **Mistress**, dispatch you with your safest haste
      And get you from our court.

ROSALIND: Me, **uncle**?

DUKE: You, **cousin**.
      Within these ten days if that thou beest found
      So near our public court as twenty miles,
      Thou diest for it.

ROSALIND: I do beseech **your grace**,
      Let me the knowledge of my fault bear with me.
      If with myself I hold intelligence
      Or have acquaintance with mine own desires,
      If that I do not dream or be not frantic –
      As I do trust I am not – then, **dear uncle**,
      Never so much as in a thought unborn
      Did I offend **your highness**.

DUKE: Thus do all *traitors*:
      If their purgation did consist in words,
      They are as innocent as grace itself.
      Let it suffice thee that I trust thee not.

ROSALIND: Yet your mistrust cannot make me a *traitor*.
      Tell me whereon the likelihoods depends.

DUKE: Thou art *thy father's daughter*, there's enough.

ROSALIND: So was I when **your highness** took his dukedom,
      So was I when **your highness** banished him.
      Treason is not inherited, **my lord**,
      Or, if we did derive it from our friends,
      What's that to me? My father was no *traitor*,

Then **good my liege**, mistake me not so much
To think my poverty is treacherous.

CELIA: **Dear sovereign**, hear me speak.

DUKE: Ay, **Celia**, we stayed her for your sake,
Else had she with her father ranged along.

CELIA: I did not then entreat to have her stay;
It was your pleasure and your own remorse.
I was too young that time to value her,
But now I know her. If she be a *traitor*,
Why so am I: we still have slept together,
Rose at an instant, learned, played, eat together,
And wheresoe'er we went, like Juno's swans
Still we went coupled and inseparable.

DUKE: She is too subtle for thee, and her smoothness,
Her very silence, and her patience
Speak to the people, and they pity her.
Thou art *a fool*; she robs thee of thy name,
And thou wilt show more bright and seem more virtuous
When she is gone. Then open not thy lips:
Firm and irrevocable is my doom
Which I have passed upon her; she is banished.

CELIA: Pronounce that sentence then on me, **my liege**,
I cannot live out of her company.

DUKE: You are *a fool*. – You, **niece**, provide yourself.
If you outstay the time, upon mine honour
And in the greatness of my word, you die.

Exit DUKE, with LORDS.

Do you notice the changes? Can you begin to make some guesses as to the shifts these changes suggest? Obviously, much will depend on the interpretation of the director, but what is important is to observe the use of names in a text and how these changes give you clues to the journey of the scene and the shifting relationships between the characters.

The Duke first addresses Rosalind formerly as 'mistress'. Then, when Rosalind addresses him as 'uncle', he responds with 'cousin', acknowledging perhaps the family connection. He does not address her directly again until the end of the scene, when he calls her 'niece', perhaps indicating that even though he acknowledges their family relationship he's banishing her as he did his brother, her father, so there is no use her appealing to family ties.

He refers to Rosalind twice. The first: 'Thus do all traitors' comes in response to her plea of innocence, which has perhaps been so strong and heartfelt that he feels the need to counter it by suggesting that all traitors protest their innocence in this way. After all, this scene is taking place in public. The lords of the court are present and the last thing the Duke wants is for Rosalind to start winning them over. The second reference, 'thy father's daughter', is the only proof he comes up with when Rosalind demands what reason he has to call her a traitor.

Let's now look at what Rosalind calls the Duke and how that changes. She starts by appealing to him as her relation: 'uncle'. When this doesn't soften him she addresses him formally as 'your grace'. As she attempts to convince him of her innocence she again appeals to the family ties, 'dear uncle', but then returns to the address of a humble subject: 'your highness'. She twice uses the same title a couple of speeches later in the scene, but here she is challenging him so it would be necessary to ask: *'Is she still being respectful in the midst of her challenge or has her use of the title become more ironic?'* In the same speech she addresses the Duke as 'my lord' and then 'good my liege'. 'My lord' comes in the midst of another challenge and the same question might be asked: *'Is it part of the challenge or an attempt to stay respectful within it?'* I like the idea of her having to remain respectful even while perhaps furious with him – he does, after all, have huge power over her and she only has the power of her argument. 'Good my liege' seems to be part of a final attempt to persuade him that she is not a traitor. By calling him 'my liege' she is acknowledging that she owes him her allegiance, her loyalty. After this she does not speak again until the Duke has left; the rest of the scene is between the Duke and his daughter, Celia.

So what happens in this second part of the scene? The Duke starts by addressing his daughter by her name, acknowledging their closeness even in a public setting. However, when she continues to plead for Rosalind his tone changes and he tells her, 'Thou art a fool' and then 'You are a fool'. He has moved from being a fond to dismissive father, from intimate to formal address.

Note: Duke and Rosalind use 'you' and 'your' to each other throughout.

What about from Celia's point of view? She starts by addressing him formally as a subject who had come to plea for someone's life might: 'Dear sovereign'. She does not address him directly again until her last speech to him, in which she addresses him as 'my liege'.

Obviously, there is more than one way of interpreting name-shifts. What is crucial is that you notice them, and the journey they might imply, and that you commit fully to using the names.

COMPLEX LISTS AND SENTENCES

Working through the complex list and sentence below will give you a great deal of experience and confidence in terms of handling complex structures in Shakespeare's text.

Handling Lists

To get to grips with more complex lists and how they build

The list comes from a speech of Henry's in *Henry V* [Act 4 Scene 1], which we looked at earlier. In the speech Henry is talking about ceremony. He addresses ceremony directly, as if it were a person, listing all the rituals that go with being a king; and pointing out that none of these helps the king to sleep as soundly as a poor man who has to work hard.

> HENRY: I am a king that find thee; and I know
> 'Tis not the balm, the sceptre and the ball,
> The sword, the mace, the crown imperial,
> The intertissued robe of gold and pearl,
> The farcèd title running 'fore the king,
> The throne he sits on, nor the tide of pomp,
> That beats upon the high shore of this world,
> No, not all these, thrice-gorgeous ceremony,
> Not all these, laid in a bed majestical,
> Can sleep so soundly as the wretched slave.

Firstly, take the main thrust of the phrase on its own first. I have added a phrase in brackets that summarises the list. The sense of the phrase is: 'I am a king, so I know all about you, ceremony; I know that none of the trappings of ceremony surrounding a king will allow him to sleep as soundly as the poor man who has to slave all his life.'

○ *Say the main thrust through several times including the part in brackets.*

> I am the king that find thee; and I know
> 'Tis not . . . [any of the trappings of ceremony]
> Can sleep so soundly as the wretched slave.

○ *Now add each item on the list separately.*

Note: Here is an explanation of the meaning of each item on the list, if you should need it: 'Balm' is the oil used to anoint the king at his coronation. The 'sceptre', the 'ball', the 'sword' and the 'mace' are all symbols of authority carried by the king on ceremonial occasions. The adjective 'imperial', used to describe the crown, means 'authoritative'. The adjective 'intertissued' means 'interwoven' and so describes the robe being worn by the king as being interwoven with gold and pearls. 'The farcèd title running before the king' refers to the numerous fancy titles by which the king is addressed. 'Farcèd' literally means 'stuffed'. The 'tide of pomp,/ That beats upon the high shore of the world' probably refers to the pageant and ceremony which surrounds the king. A metaphor is used here so the pomp becomes a tidal sea, maybe suggestion the shifting nature of kingly authority in an age when kings could be and were overthrown.

> I am a king that find thee; and I know
> 'Tis not **the balm,**
> Can sleep so soundly as the wretched slave.

> I am a king that find thee; and I know
> 'Tis not *the balm,* **the sceptre**
> Can sleep so soundly as the wretched slave.

> I am a king that find thee; and I know
> 'Tis not *the balm, the sceptre* **and the ball,**
> Can sleep so soundly as the wretched slave.

> I am a king that find thee; and I know
> 'Tis not *the balm, the sceptre and the ball,*
> **The sword,** . . . .
> Can sleep so soundly as the wretched slave.

> I am a king that find thee; and I know
> 'Tis not *the balm, the sceptre and the ball,*
> *The sword,* **the mace,** . . . .
> Can sleep so soundly as the wretched slave.

I am a king that find thee; and I know
'Tis not *the balm, the sceptre and the ball,*
The sword, the mace, **the crown imperial**,
Can sleep so soundly as the wretched slave.

I am a king that find thee; and I know
'Tis not *the balm, the sceptre and the ball,*
The sword, the mace, the crown imperial,
The intertissued robe of gold and pearl,
Can sleep so soundly as the wretched slave.

I am a king that find thee; and I know
'Tis not *the balm, the sceptre and the ball,*
The sword, the mace, the crown imperial,
The intertissued robe of gold and pearl,
The farcèd title running 'fore the king,
Can sleep so soundly as the wretched slave.

I am a king that find thee; and I know
'Tis not *the balm, the sceptre and the ball,*
The sword, the mace, the crown imperial,
The intertissued robe of gold and pearl,
The farcèd title running 'fore the king,
The throne he sits on,........,
Can sleep so soundly as the wretched slave.

I am a king that find thee; and I know
'Tis not *the balm, the sceptre and the ball,*
The sword, the mace, the crown imperial,
The intertissued robe of gold and pearl,
The farcèd title running 'fore the king,
The throne he sits on, **nor the tide of pomp,**
That beats upon the high shore of this world,
Can sleep so soundly as the wretched slave.

I am a king that find thee; and I know
'Tis not *the balm, the sceptre and the ball,*
The sword, the mace, the crown imperial,
The intertissued robe of gold and pearl,
The farcèd title running 'fore the king,
The throne he sits on, nor the tide of pomp,

> *That beats upon the high shore of this world,*
> **No, not all these, thrice-gorgeous ceremony,**
> **Not all these,** . . . .
> Can sleep so soundly as the wretched slave.

> I am a king that find thee; and I know
> *'Tis not the balm, the sceptre and the ball,*
> *The sword, the mace, the crown imperial,*
> *The intertissued robe of gold and pearl,*
> *The farcèd title running 'fore the king,*
> *The throne he sits on, nor the tide of pomp,*
> *That beats upon the high shore of this world,*
> *No, not all these, thrice-gorgeous ceremony,*
> *Not all these,* **laid in a bed majestical,**
> Can sleep so soundly as the wretched slave.

How did you find that? Could you feel that you were much more in control and that you could handle the list, however long and complicated because *you* had put it together?

I promise you that if you take any list apart in this way and build it up piece by piece you will be able to handle it from then on, and it will cease to feel like a complicated beast that can escape you and leave you stranded and helpless.

Handling Complex Sentences

To get to grips with more complex sentences and how they are constructed

Below is a twenty-three-line sentence from the same speech we have been looking at. It is enough to freak anyone on a first reading. Since we have already worked through the list contained within the sentence it probably won't be quite as daunting for you. Even if it is, read it through so that you can compare how you feel about it now with how you feel about it after we have taken it apart.

> No, thou proud dream,
> That play'st so subly with a king's repose;
> I am a king that find thee; and I know
> 'Tis not the balm, the sceptre and the ball,
> The sword, the mace, the crown imperial,

> The intertissued robe of gold and pearl,
> The farcèd title running 'fore the king,
> The throne he sits on, nor the tide of pomp
> That beats upon the high shore of this world,
> No, not all these, thrice-gorgeous ceremony,
> Not all of these, laid in a bed majestical,
> Can sleep so soundly as the wretched slave,
> Who with a body fill'd and vacant mind
> Gets him to rest, cramm'd with distressful bread;
> Never sees horrid night, the child of hell,
> But, like a lackey, from rise to set
> Sweats in the eye of Phoebus, and all night
> Sleeps in Elysium: next day after dawn,
> Doth rise and help Hyperion to his horse,
> And follows so the ever-running year
> With profitable labour to his grave:
> And, but for ceremony, such a wretch,
> Winding up days with toil and nights with sleep,
> Had the fore-hand and vantage of a king.

So let's sort it out. Firstly, we need to go through and identify which are the subordinate clauses – those that can be removed without affecting the main thrust of the sentence.

'No,' begins the main sentence, but 'thou proud dream' can be temporarily removed because it does not affect the sense. It is simply Henry addressing ceremony, to whom he is talking at this point. The next line, 'That play'st so subly with a king's repose', is a description of 'proud dream' and so it too can be removed for the moment.

'I am a king that find thee; and I know/ 'Tis not' therefore continues the main sentence which is followed by the list we looked at earlier and which we are going to summarise for the moment.

The second 'No' is a repetition of the idea which is contained in ''Tis not' so it too can be removed for now without altering the sense. 'Not all these' refers to the list of the trappings of ceremony and is another repetition which can be removed for now. 'Thrice-gorgeous ceremony' is another name for ceremony so it can be removed temporarily without affecting the sense and main thrust.

'Not all of these' is a repetition of the idea expressed in the earlier phrase 'not all these', so it too can be lifted out for the moment without affecting the overall sense. As can 'laid in a bed majestical', which describes what all the trappings of ceremony are doing. So the sentence continues with 'Can sleep so soundly as the wretched slave'.

The following nine lines, which comprise of three subordinate clauses, describe the 'wretched slave' and so can be lifted out for now without any loss to the main thrust of the sentence. The main sentence continues with 'And, but for ceremony such a wretch'.

The following line, 'Winding up his days with toil and nights with sleep', describes the wretch and so can be removed for now. Which leaves us with the last line, 'Had the fore-hand and vantage of a king', to complete the sentence.

So the main sentence, with the list summarised, goes like this:

> No, ...
> I am a king that find thee; and I know . . .
> 'Tis not [any of the trappings of ceremony] . . .
> Can sleep so soundly as the wretched slave . . .
> And, but for ceremony, such a wretch,
> Had the fore-hand and vantage of a king.

Does this already feel a lot easier? Just to clarify the sense. Henry is talking to ceremony, as if it were a person, and he says that as a king he knows the truth about ceremony. He has found ceremony out, if you like, and he knows that none of the trappings of ceremony enable him to sleep as soundly as a poor man who has to slave all his life. Without ceremony, such a poor man is better off than the king.

○ *Speak the simplified sentence above a few times so that you feel on top of it and are clear about its meaning.*

It is important that the meaning is clear because as you start to add each clause you need to hold on to that strongly, keeping the forward motion as you use the subordinate clauses to describe or repeat.

○ *Now let's add in the subclauses one by one. As you do so, think of the main sentence as the part that moves forward and the additions as tangents that are there to describe or, in the case of the repetitions, to add emphasis.*

The first addition, 'thou proud dream,/ That play'st so subly with a king's repose', is addressed to ceremony and describes how Henry experiences ceremony.

> No, **thou proud dream,**
> **That play'st so subly with a king's repose**
> I am a king that find thee; and I know . . .
> 'Tis not [any of the trappings of ceremony] . . .
> Can sleep so soundly as the wretched slave . . .
> And, but for ceremony, such a wretch,
> Had the fore-hand and vantage of a king.

The second addition is the list, but we are going to leave it out for now and add it in later.

The third addition, 'No, not all these, thrice-gorgeous ceremony,/ Not all of these, laid in a bed majestical' picks up the idea of ''Tis not [all the trappings of ceremony]', repeating it three times: 'No' – 'not all these' – 'not all of these.' So as you add this section be aware of the repetitions and how they build. Also, in this section Henry calls ceremony by a second name: 'thrice-gorgeous ceremony'. Remember earlier he called ceremony a 'proud dream', so be aware of calling ceremony by this second name. Finally, Henry describes all the trappings of ceremony as being laid out in a royal bed. In fact of course it is the king who is in the bed, but Henry uses this idea to suggest that all the trappings of ceremony are laid in the bed with the king.

> No, *thou proud dream,*
> *That play'st so subly with a king's repose*
> I am a king that find thee; and I know . . .
> 'Tis not [any of the trappings of ceremony] . . .
> **No, not all these, thrice-gorgeous ceremony,**
> **Not all of these, laid in a bed majestical,**
> Can sleep so soundly as the wretched slave . . .
> And, but for ceremony, such a wretch,
> Had the fore-hand and vantage of a king.

The fourth addition, 'Who with a body fill'd and vacant mind/ Gets him to rest, cramm'd with distressful bread', describes the wretched slave who goes to bed with a full belly and a empty mind; his belly crammed with the bread he has earned through the stress of hard work.

No, *thou proud dream,*
That play'st so subly with a king's repose
I am a king that find thee; and I know . . .
'Tis not [any of the trappings of ceremony] . . .
No, not all these, thrice-gorgeous ceremony,
Not all of these, laid in a bed majestical,
Can sleep so soundly as the wretched slave,
Who with a body fill'd and vacant mind
Gets him to rest, cramm'd with distressful bread;
And, but for ceremony, such a wretch,
Had the fore-hand and vantage of a king.

The fifth addition, 'Never sees horrid night, the child of hell,/ But like a lackey, from rise to set/ Sweats in the eye of Phoebus, and all night/ Sleeps in Elysium', is a further description of the 'wretched slave', who never has bad dreams which themselves are the horrid side of night and the product – 'the child' – of hell. Rather, he works like a lackey from sunrise to sunset, sweating in the sun – 'the eye of Phoebus' – and then sleeps in heaven – 'Elysium' – all night, meaning that he sleeps blissfully because he's physically exhausted.

No, *thou proud dream,*
That play'st so subly with a king's repose
I am a king that find thee; and I know . . .
'Tis not [any of the trappings of ceremony] . . .
No, not all these, thrice-gorgeous ceremony,
Not all of these, laid in a bed majestical,
Can sleep so soundly as the wretched slave,
Who with a body fill'd and vacant mind
Gets him to rest, cramm'd with distressful bread;
Never sees horrid night, the child of hell,
But like a lackey, from rise to set
Sweats in the eye of Phoebus, and all night
Sleeps in Elysium . . . .
And, but for ceremony, such a wretch,
Had the fore-hand and vantage of a king.

The sixth addition, 'next day after dawn,/ Doth rise and help Hyperion to his horse,/ And follows so the ever-running year/ With profitable labour to his grave', continues to describe the 'wretched slave' **who after a good** night's sleep gets up so early that it is as if he is helping the sun to rise – in ancient myth it was believed that the sun-god rode across the sky in a chariot, and the image here is of the wretch helping the sun-god onto his horse. And in this way – getting up early and working all day – the slave spends his life working hard and yielding rewards that he can see until he dies.

No, *thou proud dream,*
That play'st so subly with a king's repose
I am a king that find thee; and I know . . .
'Tis not [any of the trappings of ceremony] . . .
No, not all these, thrice-gorgeous ceremony,
Not all of these, laid in a bed majestical,
Can sleep so soundly as the wretched slave,
Who with a body fill'd and vacant mind
Gets him to rest, cramm'd with distressful bread;
Never sees horrid night, the child of hell,
But like a lackey, from rise to set
Sweats in the eye of Phoebus, and all night
Sleeps in Elysium: **next day after dawn,**
Doth rise and help Hyperion to his horse,
And follows so the ever-running year
With profitable labour to his grave:
And, but for ceremony, such a wretch . . .
Had the fore-hand and vantage of a king.

The seventh addition, 'Winding up days with toil and his nights with sleep', describes 'such a wretch' who spends his life working all day and sleeping all night. Literally this is expressed as 'winding up days' because in ancient mythology there was a belief that each person had a thread of life which was wound in and cut off by fate when the time to die was reached.

No, *thou proud dream,*
That play'st so subly with a king's repose
I am a king that find thee; and I know . . .
'Tis not [any of the trappings of ceremony] . . .
No, not all these, thrice-gorgeous ceremony,
Not all of these, laid in a bed majestical,
Can sleep so soundly as the wretched slave,

Who with a body fill'd and vacant mind
Gets him to rest, cramm'd with distressful bread;
Never sees horrid night, the child of hell,
But like a lackey, from rise to set
Sweats in the eye of Phoebus, and all night
Sleeps in Elysium: next day after dawn,
Doth rise and help Hyperion to his horse,
And follows so the ever-running year
With profitable labour to his grave:
And, but for ceremony, such a wretch,
Winding up days with toil and nights with sleep,
Had the fore-hand and vantage of a king.

Finally add the list back in and speak the whole sentence.

No, *thou proud dream,*
That play'st so subly with a king's repose
I am a king that find thee; and I know ...
'Tis not the balm, the sceptre and the ball,
The sword, the mace, the crown imperial,
The intertissued robe of gold and pearl,
The farcèd title running 'fore the king,
The throne he sits on, nor the tide of pomp
That beats upon the high shore of this world,
No, not all these, thrice-gorgeous ceremony,
Not all of these, laid in a bed majestical,
Can sleep so soundly as the wretched slave,
Who with a body fill'd and vacant mind
Gets him to rest, cramm'd with distressful bread;
Never sees horrid night, the child of hell,
But like a lackey, from rise to set
Sweats in the eye of Phoebus, and all night
Sleeps in Elysium: next day after dawn,
Doth rise and help Hyperion to his horse,
And follows so the ever-running year
With profitable labour to his grave:
And, but for ceremony, such a wretch,
Winding up days with toil and nights with sleep,
Had the fore-hand and vantage of a king.

How is the sentence now that you have worked through it in this way? I know it takes a while but you will end up making sense of the text and learning it at the same time. Then, you can be free to concern yourself with how you want to play it, which is of course always the point to reach as soon as possible.

It is worth taking the time to break down complex sentences in the way I have suggested, because with practice it becomes quicker and easier and therefore much more pleasant to do, and along the way you'll gain a great deal of confidence.

Summary

Learning how to deal with irregular and shared lines, complex lists and sentences will allow you to feel much more confident when approaching any classical text.

Below is a summary of the areas and exercises covered in this appendix.

Irregular Iambic Pentameter Lines
Identifying Irregular Lines

Shared Lines
Practising Shared Lines

Name-shifts Between Formal and Informal

Complex Lists and Sentences
Handling Lists
Handling Complex Sentences

And Where Will I Find That?

THE EXERCISE FINDER

WHERE DO I START?
The Basics

WHO AM I?
Building Your Character

WHAT'S BEEN GOING ON BEFORE?
Fleshing Out the Back Story

WHAT'S GOING ON NOW?
Exploring the Internal Dynamics of a Scene

Bringing the Situation to Life

Identifying the Shifts Within Your Character

Identifying Tensions and Shifts Between Characters

Exploring the Scene Journey Spatially

HOW DO I STOP SABOTAGING MYSELF?
Dealing with the Inner Critic

HOW DO I SHARE THE WORK TRUTHFULLY?
Transferring from Rehearsal to Performance

HOW DO I CONVINCE THEM?
Handling auditions and castings

WHAT DO I DO WHEN . . . ?
Troubleshooting

AND WHAT ABOUT . . . ?
Extra Notes on Classical Text

Endnotes

1. For more information about Sonia Moriceau's work, visit www.soniamoriceau.org.

2. For more information about Marshall B. Rosenberg's work, visit www.cnvc.org.

3. The origins of this model are not clear – some claim the source could go as far back as Confucius or Socrates! More recently, it has been attributed to many, including Abraham Maslow. What seems to be agreed upon is that the initial model was developed by Gordon Training International. For more information, I would advise you to search online for 'Four Stages of Learning'.

4. Pilates classes can be found in most reputable health clubs and gyms. For information visit www.bodycontrol.co.uk or www.pilatesfoundation.com. A comprehensive book on Pilates is *Official Body Control Pilates Manual*, by Lynne Robinson, Helge Fisher, Jacqueline Knox and Graham Thomson [Macmillan].

5. For information about Yoga and Yoga classes, visit www.yoga.co.uk or www.bwy.org.uk. A practical and informative book on Yoga is *Yoga for You*, by Tara Fraser [Duncan Baird Publishers].

6. Callanetics classes are harder to find in the UK, but information can be found online at www.callanetics.com. There are a wide range of easy-to-follow DVDs available to buy. There are a wide range of exercises in the book *Complete Callanetics*, by Callan Pinckney [Leopard Books].

7. For more information about the Alexander Technique and classes, visit www.alexandertechnique.com or www.stat.org.uk. A good book on the Alexander Technique is *The Alexander Technique Manual*, by Richard Brennan [Connections Book Publishing].

   For more information about the Feldenkrais Technique, visit www.feldenkrais.co.uk. A comprehensive and informative book is *Awareness Through Movement*, by Moshe Feldenkrais [HarperCollins].

   Always ensure that you are taught by a teacher who is fully qualified. Only work directly from books or DVDs if you have a good level of movement experience already. Always consult a doctor if you are in any doubt as to whether a particular method is safe for you.

8. *The Way Home*, by Chloë Moss [Nick Hern Books]

9. *Orestes: Blood and Light*, by Helen Edmundson [Nick Hern Books]

10. *Notes on Falling Leaves*, by Ayub Khan-Din [Nick Hern Books]

11. *Shimmer*, by Linda McLean [Nick Hern Books]

12. *Mojo*, by Jez Butterworth [Nick Hern Books]

13. *A Mouthful of Birds*, by Caryl Churchill and David Lan, in *Churchill: Plays Three* [Nick Hern Books]

14. *As You Like It*, edited by H.J. Oliver [Penguin Books]

15. *Twelfth Night*, edited by Elizabeth Story Donno [Cambridge University Press]

16. *Measure for Measure*, edited by J.M. Nosworthy [Penguin Books]

17. The names refer to how many times the paper, on which the plays were printed, was folded. The Folio pages were folded fewer times and were therefore larger. The Quartos were folded more times and were therefore smaller. The Quarto size, slightly larger than this book, was used for individual plays whereas the Folio, slightly larger than A4, was used for a collection of the plays. 'Good' and 'Bad' Quartos refer to accuracy of the Quartos in reproducing Shakespeare's original.

18. *Eats, Shoots & Leaves*, by Lynne Truss [Profile]

19. *Understanding Poetry*, by James Reeves [Heinemann Education]

20. Ibid.

21. *Reunion*, by David Mamet, in *Mamet Plays: Two* [Methuen]

22. *A Midsummer Night's Dream*, edited by R.A. Foakes [Cambridge University Press]

23. *Romeo and Juliet*, edited by Brian Gibbons [Arden Shakespeare]

24. Henry calls them 'Yeomen' which literally meant men who owned property but were not of noble birth.

25. *Henry V*, edited by J.H. Walter [Arden Shakespeare]

26. For more information, see *Shakespeare's Words*, by David Crystal and Ben Crystal [Penguin Books].

27. *King Lear*, edited by R.A. Foakes [Arden Shakespeare]

28. *Restoration Comedy in Performance*, by J.L. Styan [Cambridge University Press]

29. *The Beaux Strategem*, by George Farquhar, in an edition edited by Simon Trussler [Nick Hern Books]

30. For more information, see *Laban for All*, by Jean Newlove and John Dalby [Nick Hern Books].

31. *The Cherry Orchard*, by Anton Chekhov, translated by Stephen Mulrine [Nick Hern Books]

32. For more information, see *Actions: An Actor's Thesaurus*, by Marina Caldarone and Maggie Lloyd-Williams [Nick Hern Books]

33. *The Caretaker*, by Harold Pinter [Faber and Faber]

34. *All My Sons*, by Arthur Miller [Penguin Books]

35. For more information, see *Nonviolent Communication*, by Marshall B. Rosenberg [Puddledancer Press], or visit www.cnvc.org.

36. Thanks to Tony Buzan for this insight.

Index

Exercises appear in bold italics